THE
TRADITIONAL
SWEATER
BOOK

THE
TRADITIONAL
SWEATER
BOOK

Madeline Weston

DORLING KINDERSLEY LONDON

CONTENTS

Editor Melanie Miller
Art Editor Michele Walker
Designer Ann Cannings
Editorial Director Amy Carroll

First published in Great Britain in 1986
by Dorling Kindersley Publishers Limited,
9 Henrietta Street, London WC2E 8PS

Copyright © 1986
Dorling Kindersley Limited, London

British Library Cataloguing in Publication Data
Weston, Madeline
  The traditional sweater book.
  1. Knitting – Great Britain – Patterns
  I. Title
  746.43′2041′0941   TT819.G7

ISBN 0-86318-179-1

Printed and bound in Italy

INTRODUCTION

When I opened The Scottish Merchant in 1970, in partnership with my husband David Tomlinson, I had no idea that I would become interested in traditional knitting, or the slightest bit knowledgeable on the subject. The shop was intended as a showplace for the best of Scottish craft – glass, jewellery, pottery, textiles, all of a high standard of design and quality.

During the first year, we were introduced to Margaret Stuart, who had sent us a parcel of beautiful knitwear from the Shetland Isles. I can still recall the excitement when we opened the box, which contained pale, delicately-knitted lace shawls and scarves, and vibrantly-coloured Fair Isle hats and sweaters. We had never seen anything like it before.

After sending a tentative order for a few more pieces, and displaying the knitwear in the shop, it was obvious from the reaction that our customers were also amazed by this beautiful knitting. The Fair Isle knitwear that was available from other sources at this time used small, mean patterns, and pastel colours; in particular sweaters with round "Fair Isle" yokes in a Norwegian star pattern were being mass produced, for export to France.

The difference between these and the patterns that Margaret showed us were enormous, and we discovered that she was determined that the knitting heritage of the Shetland Isles would not disappear. She encouraged the knitters to go back to the older patterns, with their strong bands and traditional colours which were originally obtained from vegetable dyes. Margaret had a collection of old pieces of Fair Isle knitting from around 1910 and 1920 which had belonged to her grandmother Margaret Stout, and her mother Margaret Dennis, and she used these as samples for her knitters to copy. Sometimes garments or old photographs in the local museum were used, and an old scarf found in a jumble sale provided yet more inspiration. Because one of the most important colours formerly used, the red that was produced from madder dye, was now unobtainable, Margaret had the Shetland Wool Brokers dye it up for her specially. Over the years of working together The Scottish Merchant has become one of Margaret's most important outlets, and Margaret's knitwear has become one of the shop's trade marks.

Also in the first year or so of trading, we came across a small group of handknitters on the remote Hebridean island of Eriskay. Their parish priest wrote to us asking if we might possibly sell their traditional jersey or "gansey", and explained that the production would be very limited as there were only about a dozen knitters, and each jersey took several weeks to knit. The sample that accompanied this letter was a masterpiece of patterning and construction; it was knitted entirely in one piece, without seams, in a fine, tightly-spun worsted wool. It was covered with textured stitch patterns with enchanting names like Horse-shoe, Marriage Lines, Harbour Steps, Tree of Life. Once again, we had never seen anything like it before. Neither had the staff on *Queen* magazine who immediately featured it. I remember that we sold these sweaters for about £20.00 each, a sum which would now just about cover the cost of the yarn alone.

From these beginnings, and in response to the demand of customers, knitwear became more and more a part of the shop's stock, until by 1973 when the premises were enlarged, it was virtually a knitwear shop.

The seventies were also the time when interest in knitting revived generally, when young designers began to work with colour and pattern in a fresh way. The practical but boring image of knitting, seen largely during the Second World War, and in the economically stringent period afterwards, gave way to a more exciting approach. Suddenly knitting was influenced by such diverse items as oriental rugs, patchwork and embroidery, as well as the more traditonal patterns. Many of the now famous and established knitwear designers were then exploring different approaches to knitting, and one journalist has rightly called this the time of "the knitwear revolution".

So there are two strands to the contents of this book – the "traditional" and the "designer", and the lines weave in and out of each other. It is easy to see when a "designer" has taken a motif from an old jersey, perhaps an Aran in a museum, and used it in a different way, or switched from wool to silk or cotton. What is less easy to see is where the "traditional" knitters have been influenced by the patterns that came their way from other sources. The Fair Isle knitters in Shetland have, in the past, copied motifs from curtain material or wallpaper and incorporated them in their work. Any craft is a living thing, with cross fertilisation from old to new, and from one medium to another. The purpose of this book is to set down some of these old patterns alongside designers' interpretations of them.

The sweaters fall naturally into four sections according to their origins, thus we have multi-coloured knitting from Fair Isle, lace knitting from the Shetland Isles, textured fishermen's ganseys from Cornwall and the east coast of England and Scotland, and chunky Arans from the Isle of Aran, off the west coast of Ireland. At the start of each of the four main sections is an introduction giving a little of the historical and geographical background to the area and its knitting, to set the section in perspective.

All the garments in *The Traditional Sweater Book* are classic and timeless, and the patterns, which might otherwise not have been recorded, are simply and clearly presented. Now you can knit for yourself some of the beautiful garments that are traditional to the knitters of the British Isles, and enjoy wearing garments that are part of the heritage of one of our oldest crafts.

Madeline Weston

USEFUL INFORMATION

YARN

Because this is a book of traditional knitting, and the designs rely on colour or stitch pattern for their effect, the sweaters are made from standard, readily available yarns (4 ply, double knitting, etc). Specific information as to the brand names of the yarns used has not been included on the individual patterns, since generally speaking, any standard yarn of the equivalent thickness may be used. However, if you do wish to use *exactly* the same yarn as shown, details of the actual yarns used, plus information on where they may be obtained, is given on page 143.

Yarn quantities

Although it is now fifteen years since Britain went metric, some yarn manufacturers still supply yarn in ounces rather than in grams. Rather than round yarn quantities up or down to the nearest metric equivalent, the yarn quantities given in the patterns are consistent with the manufacturers' labelling. Consequently some patterns specify grams and some specify ounces. If you find the yarn you purchase is sold by the ounce when we have specified grams, or vice versa, turn to page 142 for a list of equivalent weights.

Yarn is usually sold in 25 gram balls, 50 gram balls, 100 gram balls or hanks, 1 ounce balls or hanks, or 2 ounce hanks. We have specified the yarn according to how it was originally purchased.

All the yarn quantities stated in the book are based on average requirements, and are, therefore, approximate.

Substituting yarn

As already mentioned, you may substitute any yarn of a similar thickness for the yarn specified in the pattern, as long as you can produce a tension square with the same number of stitches and rows to the centimetre as specified in the pattern.

When substituting different *types* of yarns (ie cotton for wool, or vice versa), you may need more, or less, than the weight of yarn stated in the pattern since different fibres vary in weight. Cotton is heavier than wool, for example, so it takes a greater weight of cotton to knit a garment than to knit the same garment in wool. The length of the thread is also affected by the spin – weight for weight, tightly spun yarn will not go as far as more loosely spun yarn. So you will need a greater weight of tightly spun yarn to complete a garment than if the garment is made in more loosely spun yarn.

When substituting yarns it is always safer to buy more yarn than you think you may need, rather than less, since you can often return unused balls to the place of purchase.

Yarn thickness

The term ply is sometimes misleading as it describes both the technical make-up of the yarn and the thickness of the yarn as commonly sold in the shops. For instance Shetland jumper-weight wool is, technically a 2 fold (ply) yarn, however it is the same thickness as a standard 4 ply.

4 ply is the standard, most common weight yarn on which other yarn weights are based.

Double knitting is equivalent to 2 strands of 4 ply.

Aran is equivalent to 3 strands of 4 ply.

Chunky is equivalent to 4 strands of 4 ply (or 2 strands of double knitting) and is sometimes known as double double knitting.

2 ply is equivalent to half the thickness of 4 ply.

5 ply guernsey wool is the only less common yarn used in these patterns. This is the same yarn as was originally used to make fisher ganseys. It is a 5 ply worsted, very tightly spun. In thickness it falls between a standard 4 ply and a double knitting but because it is more tightly spun, it produces a harder fabric.

Using several colours of yarn

Where more than one colour of yarn is used in a pattern – this mainly occurs in the Fair Isle sweaters – the yarns are coded A, B, C etc. These codes are then used throughout the pattern instructions. If many colours are used in a pattern, you may find it helpful to mark your balls of wool with the relevant code.

Dye lot

When buying yarn make sure it all comes from the same dye lot – this is indicated by a code on the label.

MEASUREMENTS

Measurements that occur within the pattern instructions are given in centimetres. However since most people still think of their body measurements in terms of inches, both metric and imperial measurements are given in the garment sizings. Conversion charts are provided on page 142.

For most of the patterns a range of sizes is given, making many of the sweaters suitable for both women and men. The sizes given at the beginning of the measurements section are "to fit", and this "to fit" measurement includes an allowance for ease of movement. The *actual* measurements of the sweaters are also given, directly underneath the "to fit" measurements, so you can see exactly what allowance has been made for ease, and, if you wish, knit your garment a size larger or smaller.

TENSION

It is very important that you check your tension before embarking on a pattern, otherwise your finished garment may not be the correct size. Information about checking tension is given on page 134.

NEEDLES

At the beginning of every pattern is a list of the needles needed to knit the sweater. This list specifies the thickness ($2\frac{1}{2}$mm, $3\frac{1}{2}$mm etc), and the type (circular, double-pointed etc). The size of the needles is given only as a guide, since the actual size you need to obtain the given tension may well be different from the needle size listed. If you are using needles which are sized by the old, imperial method, a conversion chart is provided on page 142.

BASIC TECHNIQUES
For novices, or those whose skills are rusty, all the basic techniques needed for knitting the sweaters are explained in full on pages 130-141. This section also contains information about special techniques needed, such as Fair Isle knitting and knitting in the round.

FAIR ISLE KNITTING
The multi-coloured, patterned designs from Fair Isle may look difficult to knit, but don't be put off, once you have embarked on a garment you will find it is not as difficult as it appears.

In spite of the complex multi-coloured appearance, there are never more than two colours of yarn in a row, and if you work in the round, which is the traditional way,

you will find it easy to follow the pattern charts since the right side is always facing you. For more information about Fair Isle knitting and working from pattern charts see page 139.

KNITTING IN THE ROUND
Traditionally knitting has been worked in the round, on a set of double-pointed needles, rather than back and forth on two needles. This was done for practical reasons – the sleeves, knitted down from the shoulder, could easily be unravelled from the cuff, making it easy to carry out any necessary repairs to the cuffs and elbow. Also, by knitting the garment in one piece the need for seams was eliminated, thus producing a stronger garment.

Where applicable, pattern instructions for the traditional Fair Isles and ganseys have been given for working in the round, using either a set of double-pointed needles, or a circular needle. More information about knitting in the round is given on page 138.

ABBREVIATIONS

alt	alternate(ly)
beg	begin(ning)
bind 1(2)(3)	yfwd, knit 1(2)(3), pass yfwd over knit 1(2)(3)
cm	centimetre(s)
cont	continu(e)(ing)(ity)
dc	double crochet
dec	decreas(e)(ing)
foll	following
g	gram(s)
g st	garter stitch (every row k)
in	inch(es)
inc	increas(e)(ing)
k	knit
k2 tog	knit two stitches together
k-wise	knitwise
mm	millimetre(s)
oz	ounce(s)
patt	pattern
p	purl
p2 tog	purl two stitches together
p-wise	purlwise
psso	pass slipped stitch over
rem	remaining
rep	repeat
rep from *	repeat all the instructions that follow asterisk
skpo	slip 1, k1, pass slipped stitch over
sl	slip
st(s)	stitch(es)
st st	stocking stitch (1 row k, 1 row p) or (every round k)
tbl	through back loop(s)
tog	together
yb	yarn back
yfwd	yarn forward
yrn	yarn round needle

CABLES AND BOBBLES

c4f	sl next 2 sts on to cable needle and leave at front of work, k2 from left-hand needle, k2 from cable needle
c4b	sl next 2 sts on to cable needle and leave at back of work, k2 from left-hand needle, k2 from cable needle
c6f	sl next 3 sts on to cable needle and leave at front of work, k3 from left-hand needle, k3 from cable needle
c6b	sl next 3 sts on to cable needle and leave at back of work, k3 from left-hand needle, k3 from cable needle
cr3r	sl next st on to cable needle and leave at back of work, k2 from left-hand needle, p1 from cable needle
cr3l	sl next 2 sts on to cable needle and leave at front of work, p1 from left-hand needle, k2 from cable needle
cr5	sl next 3 sts on to cable needle and leave at back of work, k2 from left-hand needle then p1, k2 from cable needle
mlb	make large bobble thus: (k1, yfwd, k1, yfwd, k1) all in next st, turn, p5, turn, k5, turn, p2 tog, p1, p2 tog, turn, sl 1, k2 tog, psso
msb	make small bobble thus: (k1, yfwd, k1) all in next st, turn, p3, turn, k3, turn, p3, turn, sl 1, k2 tog, psso

WORKING NOTES

Square brackets [ ]
Figures in square brackets refer to larger sizes, where there is only one set of figures it applies to all sizes.

Round brackets ( )
Repeat all the instructions between brackets as many times as indicated.

When a number of stitches are given in italics at the end of a row or round, this denotes the number of stitches you should have on your needles at this point in the pattern.

GANSEY

Fisher ganseys were originally worn
as everyday workwear by fishermen
in all areas of Britain.
They feature a wide variety of patterns,
which are formed by the simple use
of purl stitches on a stocking stitch ground.

Traditional ganseys have been produced in the fishing communities of the coastal villages of Britain for about 150 years, and this production reached its peak in the middle of the nineteenth century. To find the origins of gansey knitting, we have to look back to the sixteenth and seventeenth centuries. In Elizabethan times an enormous amount of knitted garments were exported from the Channel Islands. Although it is tempting to say that because "gansey" is a derivation of the word Guernsey, then the garments fishermen wore must be derived from the Channel Islands style of garment, there are very marked differences between the two. The Guernsey sweater from the Channel Islands was almost unpatterned compared with ganseys from other areas, and although knitted in the round, the sleeves were sewn into place, whereas the fisher gansey is free of any seams.

There are, however, some remarkable similarities between the fisher gansey and earlier Italian garments. In the seventeenth century, fine silk knitwear was imported from Italy, and there is a silk shirt from Venice supposed to have been worn by King Charles I at his execution that is a perfect example. It has brocade-like patterns formed by purl stitches against a plain ground. It is knitted in the round, has straight armholes and shoulder seams, the yoke area has a different pattern from the lower part, and is divided from the main body by a band of purl stitches. All these features are common to both these early Italian silk shirts or vests, and the later, heavier fishermen's sweaters.

Although the basic gansey is similar throughout Britain in that it is knitted without seams, from hard 4 or 5 ply worsted wool, usually in navy blue, there are marked variations in the patterns. The patterns were never written down but were passed from mother to daughter or from neighbour to neighbour, and would be constantly added to. Patterns travelled as the fishermen and the workforce of "lassies" who gutted the fish travelled with the herring fleet each season. Men and women from the north-east coast of Scotland would work their way south during the

herring fishing season, and might visit many ports in Northumberland, Yorkshire, and travel as far south as Norfolk. Old photographs taken around the middle of the nineteenth century show fishermen proudly wearing their ganseys, and the women knitting as they walk to and from their work.

There are, however, a lot of features common to the fisher ganseys of different areas, and it is interesting to look at some of them. The basic gansey design is the same as the 17th century Italian silk shirts, but because the gansey was made as a workman's garment, there is usually additional width beneath the armholes formed by gussets, which makes movement easier and the garment longer-lasting. The cast on of the rib and first few rows might be worked double to make a very strong, hard-wearing, edge. The gansey was sometimes very long and would often be worn folded up at the lower edge, though the sleeves could be quite short and finish well above the wrist. This was so that when the fishermen were at sea the wet cuff ends would not chafe.

Another distinctive feature of ganseys is the way the shoulder seams are joined – this is done by knitting the two together and casting off at the same time. This forms an attractive ridge at the top of the shoulder; sometimes a small panel of contrasting pattern is knitted on one side, and the grafting is done on the inside; this makes a band called the "shoulder strap" across the shoulder and the styles of patterns on these vary from place to place.

The heavier patterning that often appears on the chest part of the gansey is intended to give maximum warmth where it is needed, but the sleeves were often totally or partially plain. They were unravelled and re-knitted when they were worn out, and so it was much easier to have only plain knitting to rework. Since the sleeves were worked by picking up the stitches at the sides of the armholes and working downwards, this was a simple task.

Above the ribbing, at either side of the plain knitting, two purl stitches were often worked to mark each side of the garment. These were called "seam stitches", although there were, of course, no seams. These helped the knitter work out the positions of the patterns, and they provided a point of reference when working the gussets. The seam stitches often continued down the sleeves.

Everything about the construction of the gansey is practical – the shape provides freedom of movement and comfort, and the closeness of the knitting makes a virtually waterproof and windproof garment. The yarn used was tightly spun worsted wool which would "turn water", and the dark navy dye was not adversely affected by salt water.

The actual motifs of the patterns are a reflection of the life of the fishing communities, but whether the names were invented to describe the patterns, or the patterns were knitted to represent the names is impossible to say. Some of the names are obviously descriptive of items of everyday importance in the fishermen's life: Anchor, Harbour steps, Cable, Fish net, while others are more emotive or even religious: Wave, Starfish, Marriage lines, Tree of life, Heart in home, and Star.

Whatever the exact origins of the fisher gansey, we

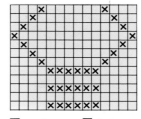

Stitch pattern charts

☒ purl   ☐ knit

Patterns that contain only knit and purl stitches may be represented in chart form. In these charts one symbol represents a knit stitch and another a purl stitch. Whereas the pattern charts for the Fair Isle designs form an integral part of the pattern instructions, the stitch pattern charts for the ganseys on the following pages are given in addition to full written pattern instructions. Stitch pattern charts for particular sweaters often vary depending on the size of the garment. The charts shown in this section are for the actual garment shown. For more information about stitch pattern charts see p. 138.

find that before the Industrial Revolution there was a vast body of hand-knitters in this country who knitted for a living. This industry was run in the form of contract knitting, and was very important in Scotland and Cornwall and places that were remote from big cities. This home industry was organized by merchants and wholesalers who supplied the fleece, and later spun yarn, to the women in their homes. It survived in Cornwall until the turn of this century, when a gansey which took two weeks to make might earn the knitter about three shillings and sixpence. After the Industrial Revolution, when knitting frames largely replaced the hand-knitters, only the more remote areas continued to produce and market their hand-knitted garments, selling them at fairs or markets or through agents. For these more remote coastal communities knitting was an essential supplement to their income from fishing.

If women and even young girls knitted for the agents because they needed the money, then the ganseys they knitted for their men folk were labours of love, and they could indulge their pride in their craft and produce an enormous variety of patterns from just two simple stitches: knit and purl. Some knitters would work the wearer's initials into the garment above the welt – sometimes the name in full, or even the name of the boat. The men all had their Sunday best ganseys which they would wear to Chapel, and in Cornwall the young bride would knit her future husband an elaborate patterned gansey called a "bridal shirt".

As is the case with most crafts, the coming of industrialization caused a decline in the knitting of fishermen's ganseys, and a rise in popularity of machine-made sweaters, which were so much cheaper. By the 1930s the skills and patterns were fast disappearing and it would only be a little while before interested researchers would begin collecting patterns and old photographs and garments in order to prevent this art from dying out altogether. Perhaps the knitters of Eriskay in the Outer Hebrides represent one of the last groups of women whose traditional patterned ganseys still have the same importance in the economic and social life of the community as they did in many different towns and villages around the coast one hundred years ago.

Left: Staithes, a typical Yorkshire fishing village

FLAMBOROUGH

GANSEY

This all-over patterned gansey is knitted in the traditional way, in one piece on double-pointed needles, so there's no sewing together to be done at the end. It's based on an old gansey that belonged to Mr George Mainprize (born 1875), and features a Moss stitch diamond pattern, and a Ladder stitch. Pattern instructions for the child's version are on p. 18.

MATERIALS

Yarn

Standard 5 ply Guernsey wool

7 [8, 9, 10, 11] × 100g balls, grey

Needles

1 circular needle size 3mm, 80cm long

1 set of four double-pointed needles size 3mm

Notions

2 stitch holders

Traditional design by Rae Compton

MEASUREMENTS

To fit chest 91 [97, 102, 107, 112]cm	
36 [38, 40, 42, 44]in	
1 Actual chest size 100 [105, 109, 113, 118]cm	
39¼ [41¼, 43, 44½, 46½]in	
2 Length to back neck 61 [62, 65, 66, 68]cm	
24 [24¼, 25½, 26, 26¾]in	
3 Sleeve seam 46 [47, 49, 50, 52]cm	
18 [18½, 19¼, 19¾, 20½]in	

Tension

28 sts and 38 rows measure 10cm over stocking stitch on 3mm needles (or size needed to obtain given tension)

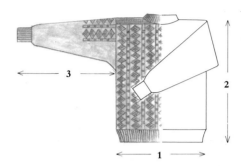

BACK and FRONT

This garment is knitted in one piece to the armholes. Using circular needle size 3mm, cast on 264 [272, 288, 296, 312] sts. Work in rounds as follows:
Round 1 (P1, k2, p1) to end.
Rep last round until rib measures 8 [8, 9, 9, 10]cm.
Next round **P1, k13 [12, 11, 8, 9], *inc in next st, k12 [10, 14, 12, 16]; rep from * 7 [9, 7, 9, 7] times more, inc in next st, k12 [11, 10, 7, 8], p1; rep from ** once more. *282 [294, 306, 318, 330] sts.*
Next round *P1, k139 [145, 151, 157, 163], p1; rep from * once more.
Rep last round 10 times more. Commence patt.
Round 1 **P1, k13, *p8 [9, 10, 11, 12], k13; rep from * 5 times more, p1; rep from ** once more.
Round 2 **(P1, k6) twice, *p2, k4 [5, 6, 7, 8], p2, k6, p1, k6; rep from * 5 times more, p1; rep from ** once more.
Round 3 **P1, k5, p1, k1, p1, k5, *p2, k4 [5, 6, 7, 8], p2, k5, p1, k1, p1, k5; rep from * 5 times more, p1; rep from ** once more.
Round 4 **P1, k4, (p1, k1) twice, p1, k4, *p2, k4 [5, 6, 7, 8], p2, k4, (p1, k1) twice, p1, k4; rep from * 5 times more, p1; rep from ** once more.
Round 5 **P1, k3, (p1, k1) 3 times, p1, k3, *p2, k4 [5, 6, 7, 8], p2, k3, (p1, k1) 3 times, p1, k3; rep from * 5 times more, p1; rep from ** once more.
Round 6 **P1, k2, (p1, k1) 4 times, p1, k2, *p2, k4 [5, 6, 7, 8], p2, k2, (p1, k1) 4 times, p1, k2; rep from * 5 times more, p1; rep from ** once more.
Round 7 **(P1, k1) 7 times, *p2, k4 [5, 6, 7,

8], p2, k1, (p1, k1) 6 times; rep from * 5 times more, p1; rep from ** once more.
Round 8 As round 6.
Round 9 As round 5.
Round 10 As round 4.
Round 11 As round 3.
Round 12 As round 2.
These 12 rounds form patt. Cont in patt until work measures 36 [36, 37, 37, 38]cm from beg, ending with round 12.

Moss stitch diamond and ladder pattern
Size 1

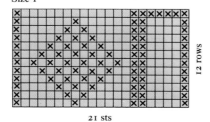

12 ROWS

21 sts

Shape for gusset
Next round *P1, patt 139 [145, 151, 157, 163], p1, pick up loop lying between sts and k tbl – referred to as m1; rep from * once more.
Next round *P1, patt 139 [145, 151, 157, 163], p1, k1; rep from * once more.
Next round *P1, patt 139 [145, 151, 157, 163], p1, m1, k1, m1; rep from * once more.
Next round *P1, patt 139 [145, 151, 157, 163], p1, k3; rep from * once more. Cont in this way, inc 1 st at each end of each gusset on next round and every foll alt round until the round "*p1, patt 139 [145, 151, 157, 163], p1, k21; rep from * once more" has been worked. Work a further 2 rounds.
Divide for front
Next round P1, m1, patt 139 [145, 151, 157, 163], m1 and turn; leave rem sts on needle. Work backwards and forwards.
Next round (K1, p6) twice, *k2, p4 [5, 6, 7, 8], k2, p6, k1, p6; rep from * 5 times more, k1 and turn; leave rem sts on needle.
***Cont in patt as follows:
Row 1 K6, p1, k1, p1, k5, *p2, k4 [5, 6, 7, 8], p2, k5, p1, k1, p1, k5; rep from * 5 times

15

more, k1.

Row 2 K1, p4, (k1, p1) twice, k1, p4, *k2, p4 [5, 6, 7, 8], k2, p4, (k1, p1) twice, k1, p4; rep from * 5 times more, k1.

Row 3 K4, (p1, k1) 3 times, p1, k3, *p2, k4 [5, 6, 7, 8], p2, k3, (p1, k1) 3 times, p1, k3; rep from * 5 times more, k1.

Row 4 K1, p2, (k1, p1) 4 times, k1, p2, *k2, p4 [5, 6, 7, 8], k2, p2, (k1, p1) 4 times, k1, p2; rep from * 5 times more, k1.

Row 5 K2, (p1, k1) 6 times, *p2, k4 [5, 6, 7, 8], p2, k1, (p1, k1) 6 times; rep from * 5 times more, k1.

Row 6 As row 4.

Row 7 As row 3.

Row 8 As row 2.

Row 9 As row 1.

Row 10 (K1, p6) twice, *k2, p4 [5, 6, 7, 8], k2, p6, k1, p6; rep from * 5 times more, k1.

Row 11 K14, *p8 [9, 10, 11, 12], k13; rep from * 5 times more, k1.

Row 12 As row 10.

These 12 rows form patt. Cont in patt until armholes measure 19 [20, 22, 23, 24]cm, ending with a wrong side row. P 1 row***.

Shape neck

Next row P47 [49, 51, 53, 55] sts and turn; leave rem sts on needle.

Complete right front neck first.

Row 1 P1, (k1, p1) to end.

Rows 2 to 4 Purl.

Rep last 4 rows 4 times more then rows 1 and 2 once. Leave these sts on spare needle. With wrong side of front facing, sl centre 47 [49, 51, 53, 55] sts on to stitch holder, rejoin yarn to rem sts and p to end. Complete to match right front neck.

With right side of back facing, sl first 23 sts on to safety pin, rejoin yarn, m1, patt 139 [145, 151, 157, 163], m1 and sl last 23 sts onto safety pin. Work backwards and forwards.

Next row (K1, p6) twice, *k2, p4 [5, 6, 7, 8], k2, p6, k1, p6; rep from * 5 times more, k1. Work as given for front from *** to ***.

Graft shoulders

With right sides of back and front together, cast off 47 [49, 51, 53, 55] sts, taking 1 st from each needle and working them tog. Sl next 47 [49, 51, 53, 55] centre back sts on to stitch holder, rejoin yarn to rem sts and complete to match first shoulder.

NECKBAND

With right side facing and using set of four double-pointed needles size 3mm, pick up and k 17 sts down left front neck, k across 47 [49, 51, 53, 55] centre front sts, pick up and k 17 sts up right front neck, k across 47 [49, 51, 53, 55] centre back sts. *128 [132, 136, 140, 144] sts.* Work 11 rounds in k2, p2 rib. Cast off in rib.

SLEEVES

With right side facing and using set of four double-pointed needles size 3mm, pick up and k 121 [127, 133, 139, 145] sts evenly around armhole edge then p1, k21, p1 sts from safety pin. *144 [150, 156, 162, 168] sts.* Work in rounds as follows:

Next round P to last 22 sts, k21, p1. Commence patt.

Round 1 K25 [26, 27, 28, 29], p2, k4 [5, 6, 7, 8], p2, *k6, p1, k6, p2, k4 [5, 6, 7, 8], p2; rep from * twice more, k25 [26, 27, 28, 29], p1, yb, skpo, k17, k2 tog, p1.

Round 2 K25 [26, 27, 28, 29], p2, k4 [5, 6, 7, 8], p2, *k5, p1, k1, p1, k5, p2, k4 [5, 6, 7, 8], p2; rep from * twice more, k25 [26, 27, 28, 29], p1, k19, p1.

Round 3 K25 [26, 27, 28, 29], p2, k4 [5, 6, 7, 8], p2, *k4, (p1, k1) twice, p1, k4, p2, k4 [5, 6, 7, 8], p2; rep from * twice more, k25 [26, 27, 28, 29], p1, yb, skpo, k15, k2 tog, p1.

Round 4 K25 [26, 27, 28, 29], p2, k4 [5, 6, 7, 8], p2, *k3, (p1, k1) 3 times, p1, k3, p2, k4 [5, 6, 7, 8], p2; rep from * twice more, k25 [26, 27, 28, 29], p1, k17, p1.

The sleeves of the child's gansey feature a different pattern from that on the adult's.

Round 5 K25 [26, 27, 28, 29], p2, k4 [5, 6, 7, 8], p2, *k2, (p1, k1) 4 times, p1, k2, p2, k4 [5, 6, 7, 8], p2; rep from * twice more, k25 [26, 27, 28, 29], p1, yb, skpo, k13, k2 tog, p1.

Round 6 K25 [26, 27, 28, 29], p2, k4 [5, 6, 7, 8], p2, *k1, (p1, k1) 6 times, p2, k4 [5, 6, 7, 8], p2; rep from * twice more, k25 [26, 27, 28, 29], p1, k15, p1.

Round 7 K25 [26, 27, 28, 29], p2, k4 [5, 6, 7, 8], p2, *k2, (p1, k1) 4 times, p1, k2, p2, k4 [5, 6, 7, 8], p2; rep from * twice more, k25 [26, 27, 28, 29], p1, yb, skpo, k11, k2 tog, p1.

Round 8 K25 [26, 27, 28, 29], p2, k4 [5, 6, 7,

8], p2, *k3, (p1, k1) 3 times, p1, k3, p2, k4 [5, 6, 7, 8], p2; rep from * twice more, k25 [26, 27, 28, 29], p1, k13, p1.
Round 9 K25 [26, 27, 28, 29], p2, k4 [5, 6, 7, 8], p2, *k4, (p1, k1) twice, p1, k4, p2, k4 [5, 6, 7, 8], p2; rep from * twice more, k25 [26, 27, 28, 29], p1, yb, skpo, k9, k2 tog, p1.
Round 10 K25 [26, 27, 28, 29], p2, k4 [5, 6, 7, 8], p2, *k5, p1, k1, p1, k5, p2, k4 [5, 6, 7, 8], p2; rep from * twice more, k25 [26, 27, 28, 29], p1, k11, p1.
Round 11 K25 [26, 27, 28, 29], p2, k4 [5, 6, 7, 8], p2, *k6, p1, k6, p2, k4 [5, 6, 7, 8], p2; rep from * twice more, k25 [26, 27, 28, 29], p1, yb, skpo, k7, k2 tog, p1.
Round 12 K25 [26, 27, 28, 29], p8 [9, 10, 11, 12], *k13, p8 [9, 10, 11, 12]; rep from * twice more, p1, k9, p1.
These 12 rounds establish patt. Cont in patt as set, dec 1 st at each end of gusset on next round and 2 foll alt rounds. Work 1 round straight.
Next round Patt 121 [127, 133, 139, 145], p1, yb, sl 1, k2 tog, psso, p1.
Next round Patt 121 [127, 133, 139, 145], p1, k1, p1.
Next round Patt 121 [127, 133, 139, 145], p2 tog, p1.
Next round Patt 121 [127, 133, 139, 145], p2. Rep last round twice.
Next round Skpo, patt to last 4 sts, k2 tog, p2.

Rep last 4 rounds 8 times. Work 3 rounds straight.
Next round Skpo, k to last 4 sts, k2 tog, p2.
Next 3 rounds K to last 2 sts, p2.
Rep last 4 rounds until 69 [73, 77, 85, 89] sts rem. Cont straight until sleeve measures 38 [39, 40, 41, 42]cm.
Next round K7, *k2 tog, k11 [12, 13, 15, 16]; rep from * to last 10 sts, k2 tog, k6, p2. *64 [68, 72, 80, 84] sts.*
Work 8 [8, 9, 9, 10]cm in rounds of k2, p2 rib. Cast off in rib.

FINISHING

Block as given on p. 140.

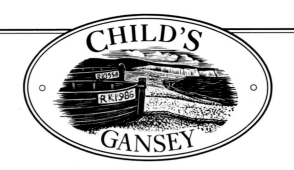

CHILD'S GANSEY

A small-size version of the Flamborough gansey on p. 14, this all-over patterned sweater is made from traditional 5 ply worsted guernsey wool, and knitted in the round.

MATERIALS

Yarn

Standard 5 ply Guernsey wool

4 [5, 6, 7] × 100g balls, cream

Needles

1 circular needle size 2¾mm, 60cm long

1 set of double-pointed needles size 2¾mm

Notions

3 stitch holders

MEASUREMENTS

To fit chest 61 [66, 71, 76]cm

24 [26, 28, 30]in

1 Actual chest size 66 [72, 76, 81]cm

26 [28, 30, 32]in

2 Length to back neck 45 [48, 50, 53]cm

17¾ [19, 19½, 21]in

3 Sleeve seam 31 [34, 37, 40]cm

12¼ [13¼, 14½, 15¾]in

Tension

28 sts and 38 rows measure 10cm over stocking stitch on 2¾mm needles (or size needed to obtain given tension)

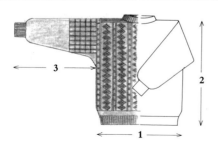

BACK and FRONT

This is knitted in one piece up to the armholes. Using 2¾mm circular needle, cast on 168 [176, 192, 200] sts. Work in rounds as follows:

Round 1 (P1, k2, p1) to end.

Rep round 1 until rib measures 4 [5, 6, 7]cm.

Next round **P1, k7 [6, 7, 8], *inc in next st, k10 [8, 12, 9]; rep from * 5 [7, 5, 7] times more, inc in next st, k8 [7, 8, 9], p1**; rep from ** to ** once more. *182 [194, 206, 218] sts.*

Next round *P1, k89 [95, 101, 107], p1; rep from * once more.

Rep last round 7 [11, 11, 15] times. Commence patt.

Round 1 **P6 [7, 8, 9], *k5, p1, k5, p6 [7, 8, 9]; rep from * 4 times more**; rep from ** to ** once more.

Round 2 **K6 [7, 8, 9], *k4, p1, k1, p1, k10 [11, 12, 13]; rep from * 4 times more**; rep from ** to ** once more.

Round 3 **P2, k2 [3, 4, 5], p2, *k3, (p1, k1) twice, p1, k3, p2, k2 [3, 4, 5], p2; rep from * 4 times more**; rep from ** to ** once more.

Round 4 **K6 [7, 8, 9], *k2, (p1, k1) 3 times, p1, k8 [9, 10, 11]; rep from * 4 times more**; rep from ** to ** once more.

Round 5 **P2, k2 [3, 4, 5], p2, *k1, (p1, k1) 5 times, p2, k2 [3, 4, 5], p2; rep from * 4 times more**; rep from ** to ** once more.

Round 6 As round 4.

Round 7 As round 3.

Round 8 As round 2.

Round 9 **P2, k2 [3, 4, 5], p2, *k5, p1, k5, p2, k2 [3, 4, 5], p2; rep from * 4 times more**; rep from ** to ** once more.

Round 10 Knit.

These 10 rounds form patt. Cont in patt until work measures 26 [28, 29, 31]cm from beg, ending with round 10.

Shape for gusset

Next round *Patt 91 [97, 103, 109], pick up loop lying between sts and k tbl – referred to as m1; rep from * once more.

Next round *Patt 91 [97, 103, 109], k1; rep from * once more.

Rep last round twice.

Next round *Patt 91 [97, 103, 109], m1, k1, m1; rep from * once more.

Next round *Patt 91 [97, 103, 109], k3; rep from * once more.

Rep last round twice.

Next round *Patt 91 [97, 103, 109], m1, k3, m1; rep from * once more.

Next round *Patt 91 [97, 103, 109], k5; rep from * once more.

Rep last round twice.

Cont in this way inc 1 st at each side of each gusset on next round and 2 foll 4th rounds. Work 3 rounds.

Divide for back and front

Next round Patt 91 [97, 103, 109] sts and

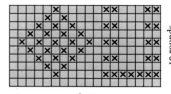

Moss stitch diamond and ladder pattern

10 rounds

18 sts

turn; leave rem sts on a spare needle. Complete front first.

***Work backwards and forwards as follows:

Row 1 (Wrong side) P6 [7, 8, 9], *p2, (k1, p1) 3 times, k1, p8 [9, 10, 11]; rep from * to end.

Row 2 P2, k2 [3, 4, 5], p2, *k3, (p1, k1) twice, p1, k3, k2 [3, 4, 5], p2; rep from * to end.

Row 3 P6 [7, 8, 9], *p4, k1, p1, k1, p10 [11, 12, 13]; rep from * to end.

Row 4 P2, k2 [3, 4, 5], p2, *k5, p1, k5, p2, k2 [3, 4, 5], p2; rep from * to end.

Row 5 Purl.

Row 6 P6 [7, 8, 9], *k5, p1, k5, p6 [7, 8, 9]; rep from * to end.

Row 7 As row 3.

Row 8 As row 2.

Row 9 As row 1.

Row 10 P2, k2 [3, 4, 5], p2, *(k1, p1) 5 times, k1, p2, k2 [3, 4, 5], p2; rep from * to end.

These 10 rows form patt. Cont in patt until armholes measure 13 [14, 15, 16]cm, ending with a wrong side row. P 1 row***.

Shape neck

Next row P29 [31, 33, 35] sts and turn; leave rem sts on a spare needle. Complete right side of neck first.

Row 1 P1, (k1, p1) to end.

Rows 2 to 4 Purl.

Rep the last 4 rows 3 times more then rows 1 and 2 again. Leave these sts on a stitch holder. With wrong side of front facing, sl centre 33 [35, 37, 39] sts on to a stitch holder, rejoin yarn to rem sts, p to end. Complete as given for right side of neck. With right side of back facing, sl first 11 sts on to a safety pin, rejoin yarn to rem sts, patt 91 [97, 103, 109] and turn, sl last 11 sts on to a safety pin. Work as given for front from *** to ***.

Graft left shoulder With back and front right sides together, cast off 29 [31, 33, 35] sts, taking 1 st from each needle and working into them tog. Sl next 33 [35, 37, 39] sts on back on to a stitch holder, rejoin yarn to rem sts and graft right shoulder as given for left shoulder.

NECKBAND

With right side facing and using set of double-pointed needles size 2¾mm, pick up and k 15 sts down left side neck, k across 33 [35, 37, 39]

centre front sts, pick up and k 15 sts up right side neck, k across 33 [35, 37, 39] centre back sts. *96 [100, 104, 108] sts.* Work 8 rounds in k2, p2 rib. Cast off in rib.

SLEEVES

With right side facing and using set of double-pointed needles size 2¾mm, pick up and k 86 [92, 98, 107] sts evenly around armhole edge then k 11 sts from safety pin. Work in rounds as follows:
Round 1 P86 [92, 98, 107], k11.
Round 2 Knit.
Round 3 P2, *k2 [3, 4, 5], p2; rep from * to last 11 sts, skpo, k7, k2 tog.
Round 4 Knit.
Round 5 P2, *k2 [3, 4, 5], p2; rep from * to last 9 sts, k9.
Round 6 Knit.
Round 7 P2, *k2 [3, 4, 5], p2; rep from * to last 9 sts, skpo, k5, p2 tog.
Round 8 Knit.
Round 9 P2, *k2 [3, 4, 5], p2; rep from * to last 7 sts, k7.
Round 10 Knit.
These 10 rounds establish patt. Cont in patt as set and working dec at each side of gusset on next round and foll 4th round. Work 3 rounds straight.
Next round Patt to last 3 sts, sl 1, k2 tog, psso.
Next round Patt to last st, k1.
Rep last round 4 times.
Next round Work 2 tog, patt to last 3 sts, work 2 tog, k1.
Rep last 6 rounds 4 times. Work 2 rounds straight.
Next round K to last st, p1.
Rep last round once.
Next round Skpo, k to last 3 sts, k2 tog, p1.
Next round K to last st, p1.
Rep last round 3 times.
Rep last 5 rounds until 59 [61, 65, 68] sts rem. Cont straight until sleeve measures 25 [28, 31, 34]cm from beg.
Next round K4 [6, 4, 6], *k2 tog, k3 [4, 5, 3]; rep from * to last 5 [7, 5, 7] sts, k2 tog, k2 [4, 2, 4], p1. *48 [52, 56, 56] sts.*
Work 20 rounds in k2, p2 rib. Cast off in rib.
Work other sleeve in same way.

FINISHING

Block as given on p. 140.

Traditional design by Rae Compton

WOVEN CHECKS
GANSEY

This pretty collared sweater is knitted in 4 ply weight wool. The Moss stitch and Woven checks pattern featured on it is a variation of a basket weave pattern.

MATERIALS

Yarn

Standard 4 ply wool

9 [10] × 50g balls, pink

Needles

1 pair size 2¾mm

1 pair size 3¼mm

Crochet hook

Notions

3 buttons, 1.5cm in diameter

MEASUREMENTS

To fit chest 81-86 [91-97]cm

32-34 [36-38]in

1 Actual chest size 100 [110]cm

39½ [43¼]in

2 Length to back neck 59 [61]cm

23¼ [24]in

3 Sleeve seam 49cm, 19¼in

Tension

28 sts and 40 rows measure 10cm over pattern on 3¼mm needles (or size needed to obtain given tension)

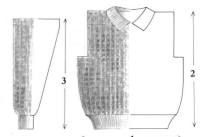

Designed by Debbie Scott

BACK

Using 2¾mm needles, cast on 112 [126] sts.
Work 8cm in k1, p1 rib.
Next row Rib 12 [4], *inc in next st, rib 2 [3];
rep from * to last 10 [2] sts, rib to end. *142
[156] sts.*
Change to 3¼mm needles. Commence patt.
Row 1 (Right side) Knit.
Row 2 P2, *(k1, p1) twice, k1, p2; rep from *
to end.
Row 3 K2, *(k1, p1) twice, k3; rep from * to
end.
Rows 4 to 7 Rep row 2 and row 3 twice.
Row 8 P2, (k12, p2) to end.
Row 9 K2, (p12, k2) to end.
Row 10 Purl.
Row 11 K2, *(p1, k1) twice, p1, k2; rep from
* to end.
Row 12 P2, *(p1, k1) twice, p3; rep from *
end.
Rows 13 to 16 Rep rows 11 and 12 twice.
Row 17 P7, (k2, p12) to last 9 sts, k2, p7.
Row 18 K7, (p2, k12) to last 9 sts, p2, k7.
These 18 rows form patt. Cont in patt until
work measures 36 [38]cm from beg, ending
with a wrong side row.
Shape armholes Cast off 14 sts at beg of next
2 rows. *114 [128] sts.* Cont straight until
armholes measure 17cm, ending with a wrong
side row**.
Divide for back neck opening
Next row Patt 57 [64] sts and turn; leave rem
sts on a spare needle.
Complete right side and back first. Cont
straight until armhole measures 22cm, ending
at armhole edge.
Shape shoulder Cast off 17 [19] sts at beg of
next row and foll alt row. Work 1 row. Cast off
rem 23 [26] sts. With right side facing, rejoin
yarn to rem sts and patt to end. Complete as
given for first side of back.

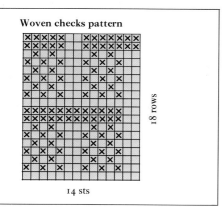

Woven checks pattern

18 rows

14 sts

FRONT

Work as given for back to **.
Shape neck
Next row Patt 47 [51] sts and turn; leave rem
sts on a spare needle.
Complete left side of neck first. Cast off 3 sts
at beg of next row and foll alt row and then 2
sts on foll 2 alt rows. Dec 1 st at neck edge on
foll 3 right side rows. *34 [38] sts.* Cont straight
until front matches back to shoulder, ending
at armhole edge.
Shape shoulder Cast off 17 [19] sts at beg of

next row. Work 1 row. Cast off rem 17 [19] sts.
With right side facing, rejoin yarn to rem sts,
cast off 20 [26] sts, patt to end. Patt 1 row.
Complete as given for first side of neck.

SLEEVES

Using 2¾mm needles, cast on 52 sts. Work
8cm in k1, p1 rib.
Next row Rib 6, (inc in next st, rib 1) to last
6 sts, rib to end. *72 sts.*
Change to 3¼mm needles. Cont in patt as
given for back, inc 1 st at each end of every
foll 5th row until there are 128 sts. Cont
straight until sleeve measures approximately
54cm from beg, ending with row 7 of patt.
Cast off.

COLLAR

Using 2¾mm needles, cast on 78 [86] sts.
Work 7cm in k1, p1 rib. Cast off in rib.
Make another piece to match.

FINISHING

Block each piece as given on p. 140. Join
shoulder seams. Sew cast off edge of collar
pieces from centre back to centre front. Using
crochet hook, make 3 buttonhole loops on
right side of back opening. Sew on buttons.
Mark each side of sleeve 5cm down from cast
off edge. Sew in sleeves, sewing rows above
markers to cast off stitches at armholes. Join
side and sleeve seams.

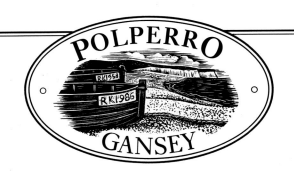

POLPERRO GANSEY

This warm Shetland wool jacket is beautifully patterned with Chevron and Moss stitch panels. The pattern is taken from a gansey worn in Polperro, Cornwall, around 1840. The dropped shoulder provides an easy and comfortable fit, suitable for men or women.

MATERIALS

Yarn

This garment is knitted in Shetland 2 ply soft spun wool, which is a thick, loosely twisted wool, equivalent in thickness to two strands of Shetland 2 ply jumper weight wool. The yarn is used double throughout (ie equivalent to four strands of 2 ply jumper weight wool).

20 [22] × 2oz hanks, light grey

Needles

1 pair size 6½mm

1 pair size 7½mm

Notions

8 buttons, 3cm in diameter

2 buttons, 2.5cm in diameter

MEASUREMENTS

To fit chest 91-102 [107-116]cm

36-40 [42-46]in

1 Actual chest size 117 [133]cm

46 [52¼]in

2 Length to back neck 65 [69]cm

25½ [27]in

3 Sleeve seam 45 [49]cm

17¾ [19¼]in

Tension

12 sts and 18 rows measure 10cm over pattern on 7½mm needles (or size needed to obtain given tension) using 2 strands of yarn together

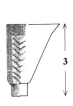
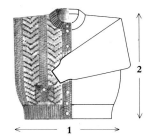

Special note

Instructions are given for both a woman's front fastening and a man's front fastening.

POCKET LININGS

Using 7½mm needles and 2 strands of yarn together, cast on 13 [17] sts. Beg k row, work 12 rows in st st. Leave these sts on a spare needle. Make another pocket lining to match.

RIGHT FRONT

Woman's jacket

Using 6½mm needles and 2 strands of yarn together, cast on 35 [41] sts.

Row 1 (Right side) K1, (p1, k1) to end.

Row 2 (P1, k1) to last 7 [9] sts, k1, (p1, k1) to end.

These 2 rows form moss st and rib patt.

Row 3 Patt 3 [4], cast off 1, patt to end.

Row 4 Patt to end, casting on 1 st over the 1 st cast off in previous row.

Rows 5 to 14 Rep rows 1 and 2, 5 times.

Row 15 As row 3.

Row 16 Patt 3, *inc in next st, patt 4 [5]; rep from * 3 times more, inc in next st, patt 7 [8], cast on 1, patt to end. *40 [46] sts.*

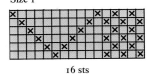

Chevron and moss stitch pattern
Size 1

16 sts

6 rows

Chevron and moss stitch pattern
Size 2

18 sts

6 rows

Change to 7½mm needles. Commence main patt.

Row 1 K1, (p1, k1) 3 [4] times, *(k5, p1) twice, (k1, p1) 2 [3] times; rep from * once more, k1.

Row 2 K1, *(p1, k1) 2 [3] times, p5, k1, p1, k1, p4; rep from * once more, k1, (p1, k1) 3 [4] times.

Row 3 K1, (p1, k1) 3 [4] times, *(k3, p1) 3 times, (k1, p1) 2 [3] times; rep from * once more, k1.

Row 4 K1, *(p1, k1) 2 [3] times, p3, k1, p5, k1, p2; rep from * once more, k1, (p1, k1) 3 [4] times.

Row 5 K1, (p1, k1) 3 [4] times, *k1, p1, k7, p1, (k1, p1) 3 [4] times; rep from * once more, k1.

Row 6 K1, *(p1, k1) 3 [4] times, p9, k1; rep from * once more, k1, (p1, k1) 3]4[times.

These 6 rows form main patt. Patt 4 [10] rows.

Next row Patt 3 [4], cast off 1, patt to end.

Next row Patt to end, casting on 1 st over the 1 st cast off in previous row.

Patt 6 [0] rows.

Place pocket

Next row Patt 14 [16], sl next 13 [17] sts on to stitch holder, patt across 13 [17] sts of pocket lining, patt to end. Cont in patt making buttonholes as before on foll 10th and 11th [16th and 17th] rows and 3 foll 17th and 18th rows.

Shape neck

Next row Patt 7 [9] and sl these sts on to safety pin, patt to end.

Patt 1 row. Cast off 3 [4] sts at beg of next row. Dec 1 st at neck edge on next 2 rows then on 2 [3] foll alt rows. *26 [28] sts.* Patt 9 [7] rows straight. Cast off.

Man's jacket

Work as given for right front of woman's jacket omitting buttonholes.

LEFT FRONT

Woman's jacket

**Using 6½mm needles and 2 strands of yarn together, cast on 35 [41] sts.
Row 1 (Right side) K1, (p1, k1) to end.
Row 2 K1, (p1, k1) 3 [4] times, (k1, p1) to end.
These 2 rows form moss st and rib patt******.
Patt 13 rows.
Next row Patt 11 [13], *inc in next st, patt 4 [5]; rep from * to last 4 sts, inc in next st, patt to end. *40 [46] sts.*
***Change to 7½mm needles. Commence main patt.

Designed by Rae Compton

23

Row 1 K1, *(p1, k1) 2 [3] times, (p1, k5) twice; rep from * once more, k1, (p1, k1) 3 [4] times.
Row 2 K1, (p1, k1) 3 [4] times, *p4, k1, p1, k1, p5, (k1, p1) 2 [3] times; rep from * once more, k1.
Row 3 K1, *(p1, k1) 2 [3] times, (p1, k3) 3 times; rep from * once more, k1, (p1, k1) 3 [4] times.
Row 4 K1, (p1, k1) 3 [4] times, *p2, k1, p5, k1, p3, (k1, p1) 2 [3] times; rep from * once more, k1.
Row 5 K1, *(p1, k1) 2 [3] times, p1, k7, p1, k1; rep from * once more, k1, (p1, k1) 3 [4] times.
Row 6 K1, (p1, k1) 3 [4] times, *k1, p9, (k1, p1) 3 [4] times; rep from * once more, k1.
These 6 rows form main patt***. Patt 12 rows.

Place pocket
Next row Patt 13, sl next 13 [17] sts on to stitch holder, patt across 13 [17] sts of pocket lining, patt to end. Patt 64 [70] rows.

Shape neck
Next row Patt 7 [9] and sl these sts on to safety pin, patt to end.
Patt 1 row. Cast off 3 [4] sts at beg of next row. Dec 1 st at neck edge on next 2 rows then on 2 [3] foll alt rows. 26 [28] sts. Patt 10 [8] rows straight. Cast off.

Man's jacket
Work as given for left front of woman's jacket from ** to **.
Row 3 Patt to last 4 [5] sts, cast off 1, patt to end.
Row 4 Patt to end, casting on 1 st over the 1 st cast off in previous row.
Rows 5 to 14 Rep row 1 and 2, 5 times.
Row 15 As row 3.
Row 16 Patt 3 [4], cast on 1, patt 7 [8], *inc in next st, patt 4 [5]; rep from * 3 times more, inc in next st, patt 3. 40 [46] sts.
Work as given for left front of woman's jacket from *** to ***. Patt 4 [10] rows.
Next row Patt to last 4 sts, cast off 1, patt to end.
Next row Patt to end casting on 1 st over the 1 st cast off in previous row. Patt 6 [0] rows.

Place pocket
Next row Patt 13, sl next 13 [17] sts on to stitch holder, patt across 13 [17] sts of pocket lining, patt to end.
Cont in patt making buttonholes as before on foll 10th and 11th [16th and 17th] rows and 2 foll 17th and 18th rows. Patt 16 rows straight then work 1 buttonhole row.

Shape neck
Next row Patt 3 [4], cast on 1, patt 3 [4] and sl these 7 [9] sts on to safety pin, patt to end.
Complete as given for left front of woman's jacket.

BACK

Using 6½mm needles and 2 strands of yarn together, cast on 60 [70] sts. Work 15 rows in k1, p1 rib.
Next row Rib 5 [4], *inc in next st, rib 4 [5]; rep from * to end. 71 [81] sts.
Change to 7½mm needles. Commence main patt.
Row 1 (Right side) (K1, p1) 3 [4] times, *(k5, p1) twice, (k1, p1) 2 [3] times; rep from * to last st, k1.
Row 2 (K1, p1) 3 [4] times, *p4, k1, p1, k1, p5, (k1, p1) 2 [3] times; rep from * to last st, k1.
Row 3 (K1, p1) 3 [4] times, *(k3, p1) 3 times, (k1, p1) 2 [3] times; rep from * to last st, k1.

Row 4 (K1, p1) 3 [4] times, *p2, k1, p5, k1, p3, (k1, p1) 2 [3] times; rep from * to last st, k1.
Row 5 (K1, p1) 3 [4] times, *k1, p1, k7, (p1, k1) 3 [4] times, p1; rep from * to last st, k1.
Row 6 (K1, p1) 3 [4] times, *k1, p9, (k1, p1) 3 [4] times; rep from * to last st, k1.
These 6 rows form main patt. Rep these 6 rows 16 [17] times more. Cast off.

SLEEVES

Using 6½mm needles and 2 strands together, cast on 32 [38] sts. Work 15 rows in k1, p1 rib.
Next row Rib 4 [3], *inc in next st, rib 3 [4]; rep from * to end. 39 [45] sts.
Change to 7½mm needles. Work 6 rows in patt as given for back. Cont in patt, inc 1 st at each end of next row and every foll 4th row until there are 63 [69] sts, working extra sts into st st. Work 3 [9] rows straight in patt.
Next row Inc in first st, (p1, k1) to last 2 sts, p1, inc in last st.
Next row P1, (k1, p1) to end.
Next row Inc in first st, (k1, p1) to last 2 sts, k1, inc in last st.
Next row K1, (p1, k1) to end.
Rep last 4 rows twice more. 75 [81] sts. Cast off.

NECKBAND

Join shoulder seams. With right side facing, sl 7 [9] sts on right front safety pin on to 6½mm needle, using 2 strands of yarn together, pick up and k 18 sts up right front neck, 21 [23] sts across back neck, 18 sts down left front neck and k1, (p1, k1) 3 [4] times from left front safety pin. 71 [77] sts.
Row 1 (Wrong side) K1, (p1, k1) 3 [4] times, k1, (p1, k1) to last 7 [9] sts, k1, (p1, k1) 3 [4] times.
Row 2 K1, (p1, k1) to end.
These 2 rows form moss st and rib patt.
Patt 1 row.
Next row Patt 3 [4], cast off 1, patt to end.
Next row Patt to end, casting on 1 st over the 1 st cast off in previous row.
Patt 2 rows. Cast off in patt.

POCKET EDGINGS

With right side facing and using 7½mm needles and 2 strands of yarn together, rejoin yarn to the 13 [17] sts on holder (k1, p1) 3 [4] times, cast off 1, p1 (st used in casting off), (k1, p1) 2 [3] times.
Next row (K1, p1) 3 [4] times, cast on 1, (p1, k1) 3 [4] times.
Next row K1, (p1, k1) to end.
Rep last row once. Cast off.

FINISHING

Block as given on p. 140. Mark position of armholes 30 [33]cm down from shoulders on back and fronts. Sew in sleeves. Join side and sleeve seams. Catch down pocket linings and sides of pocket edgings. Sew on buttons as shown in photograph.

NEWBIGGIN GANSEY

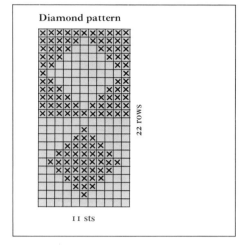

Vertical panels of diamonds in plain and purl decorate this generously sized pullover. The pattern originates from the village of Newbiggin on the Northumberland coast, and is made up here in a heavy-weight, soft Shetland yarn.

MATERIALS

Yarn

This garment is knitted in Shetland 2 ply soft spun wool, which is a thick, loosely twisted wool, equivalent in thickness to two strands of Shetland 2 ply jumper weight wool.

14 × 2oz hanks, grey

Needles

1 pair size 3¾mm

1 pair size 4½mm

MEASUREMENTS

To fit chest 107-117cm, 42-46in

1 Actual chest size 126cm, 49½in

2 Length to back neck 68cm, 26¾in

3 Sleeve seam 50cm, 19¾in

Tension

17 sts and 23 rows measure 10cm over pattern on 4½mm needles (or size needed to obtain given tension)

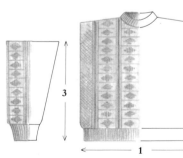

Pattern panel

Repeat of 38 sts.

Row 1 (Right side) (P2, k into front of 2nd st then k first st, sl both sts off needle tog – referred to as tw2) twice, k11, tw2, p2, tw2, p11, tw2.

Row 2 P2, k5, p1, k5, p2, k2, p7, k1, p5, (p2, k2) twice.

Row 3 (P2, tw2) twice, k4, p3, k4, tw2, p2, tw2, p4, k3, p4, tw2.

Row 4 P2, k3, p5, k3, p2, k2, p5, k5, p3, (p2, k2) twice.

Row 5 (P2, tw2) twice, k2, p7, k2, (tw2, p2) twice, k7, p2, tw2.

Row 6 P2, k1, p9, k1, p2, k2, p3, k9, p1, (p2, k2) twice.

Row 7 As row 5.

Row 8 As row 4.

Row 9 As row 3.

Row 10 As row 2.

Row 11 As row 1.

Row 12 P15, k2, p2, k11, (p2, k2) twice.

Row 13 (P2, tw2) twice, p5, k1, p5, tw2, p2, tw2, k5, p1, k5, tw2.

Row 14 P6, k3, p6, k2, p2, k4, p3, k4, (p2, k2) twice.

Row 15 (P2, tw2) twice, p3, k5, p3, tw2, p2, tw2, k3, p5, k3, tw2.

Row 16 P4, k7, p4, k2, p2, k2, p7, k2, (p2, k2) twice.

Row 17 (P2, tw2) twice, p1, k9, p1, tw2, p2, tw2, k1, p9, k1, tw2.

Row 18 As row 16.

Row 19 As row 15.

Row 20 As row 14.

Row 21 As row 13.

Row 22 As row 12.

These 22 rows form panel pattern.

BACK

Using 3¾mm needles, cast on 96 sts. Work 7cm in k1, p1 rib.

Next row Rib 9, (inc in next st, rib 5) to last 3 sts, rib 3. *110 sts.*

Change to 4½mm needles. Commence patt.

Row 1 (Right side) (K2, p2) 3 times, tw2, rep row 1 of panel patt twice, (p2, tw2) twice, (p2, k2) 3 times.

Row 2 (P2, k2) 5 times, rep row 2 of panel patt twice, p2, (k2, p2) 3 times.

Row 3 (P2, k2) 3 times, tw2, rep row 3 of panel patt twice, (p2, tw2) twice, (k2, p2) 3 times.

Row 4 (K2, p2) 3 times, (p2, k2) twice, rep row 4 of panel patt twice, p2, (p2, k2) 3 times. These 4 rows establish patt. Cont in patt as set, working appropriate rows of panel patt until work measures 65cm from beg, ending with row 2 of panel patt.

Shape shoulders Cast off 10 sts at beg of next 8 rows. Leave rem sts on spare needle.

FRONT

Work as given for back until front measures 61cm from beg, ending with row 14 of panel patt.

Shape neck

Next row Patt 49 and turn; leave rem sts on a spare needle. Complete left side of neck first. Dec 1 st at neck edge on next 9 rows.

Shape shoulder Cast off 10 sts at beg of next row and 2 foll alt rows. Work 1 row. Cast off rem sts.

With right side facing, sl centre 12 sts on to a safety pin, rejoin yarn to rem sts, patt to end. Complete as given for left side neck.

SLEEVES

Using 3¾mm needles, cast on 50 sts. Work 7cm in k1, p1 rib.

Next row Rib 2, (inc in next st, rib 3) to end. *62 sts.*

Change to 4½mm needles. Commence patt.

Row 1 (Right side) K9, tw2, p2, tw2, p11, tw2, (p2, tw2) twice, k11, tw2, p2, tw2, p9.

Row 2 K3, p1, k5, p2, k2, p7, k1, p5, (p2, k2) twice, p2, k5, p1, k5, p2, k2, p7, k1, p3.

Row 3 K2, p3, k4, tw2, p2, tw2, p4, k3, p4, tw2, (p2, tw2) twice, k4, p3, k4, tw2, p2, tw2, p4, k3, p2.

Row 4 K1, p5, k3, p2, k2, p5, k5, p3, (p2, k2) twice, p2, k3, p5, k3, p2, k2, p5, k5, p1. These 4 rows establish patt. Cont in patt, inc 1 st at each end of next row and 4 foll 5th rows then on every foll 6th row until there are 96 sts, working extra sts into patt. Work 3 rows straight. Cast off.

Diamond pattern

22 ROWS

11 sts

NECKBAND

Join right shoulder seam. With right side facing and using $3\frac{3}{4}$mm needles, pick up and k 19 sts down left side neck, k across 12 centre front sts, pick up and k 19 sts up right side neck and k across 30 centre back sts. *80 sts.* Work 6cm in k1, p1 rib. Cast off in rib.

FINISHING

Block each piece as given on p. 140. Join left shoulder and neckband seam. Fold neckband in half to wrong side and slip stitch in position. Mark positions of armholes 27cm down from shoulders on back and front. Sew in sleeves between markers. Join side and sleeve seams.

Designed by Gayle Crowther

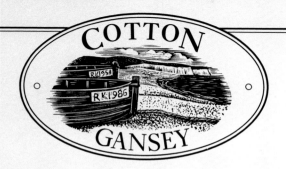

COTTON GANSEY

The texture of this stylish but simply shaped shirt is provided by a variation of a Broken diamonds pattern. The double knitting cotton used here highlights the design, but any other yarn of a similar thickness may be used instead.

MATERIALS

Yarn

Standard double knitting cotton

13 [13, 14] × 50g balls, cream

Needles

1 pair size 3¼mm

1 pair size 4mm

Notions

3 buttons, 1.5cm in diameter

MEASUREMENTS

To fit chest 86 [91, 97]cm

34 [36, 38]in

1 Actual chest size 96 [100, 104]cm

38 [39, 41]in

2 Length to back neck 60 [61, 62]cm

23¼ [24, 24½]in

3 Sleeve seam 15cm, 6in

Tension

20 sts and 32 rows measure 10cm over pattern on 4mm needles (or size needed to obtain given tension)

Designed by Debbie Scott

BACK

Using 3¼mm needles, cast on 98 [102, 106] sts. Work 3cm in k1, p1 rib. Change to 4mm needles. Commence patt.

Row 1 (Wrong side) P0 [2, 4], (p4, k6, p4) to last 0 [2, 4] sts, p0 [2, 4].

Row 2 Knit.

Rows 3 and 4 As rows 1 and 2.

Row 5 As row 1.

Row 6 K3 [5, 7], (p1, k6) to last 4 [6, 8] sts, p1, k3 [5, 7].

Row 7 P0 [0, 1], k0 [0, 1], p0 [2, 2], (p2, k1, p8, k1, p2) to last 0 [2, 4] sts, p0 [2, 2], k0 [0, 1], p0 [0, 1].

Row 8 K0 [0, 2], p0 [1, 1], k0 [1, 1], (k1, p1, k10, p1, k1) to last 0 [2, 4] sts, k0 [1, 1], p0 [1, 1], k0 [0, 2].

Row 9 P0 [1, 3], k0 [1, 1], (k1, p12, k1) to last 0 [2, 4] sts, k0 [1, 1], p0 [1, 3].

Row 10 As row 8.

Row 11 As row 7.

Row 12 As row 6.

These 12 rows form patt. Cont in patt until work measures 60 [61, 62]cm from beg, ending with a wrong side row.

Shape shoulders Cast off 34 [36, 38] sts at beg of next 2 rows. Cast off rem 30 sts.

FRONT

Work as given for back until work measures 39 [40, 41]cm from beg, ending with a right side row.

Divide for neck opening

Next row Patt 46 [48, 50], cast off 6, patt to end.

Complete left side of front first. Cont straight until front measures 52 [53, 54]cm from beg, ending at neck edge.

Shape neck Cast off 6 sts at beg of next row. Dec 1 st at neck edge on every right side row until 34 [36, 38] sts rem. Cont straight until front matches back to shoulder, ending at side edge. Cast off. With right side facing, rejoin yarn to rem sts and patt to end. Complete as given for first side of neck.

SLEEVES

Using 3¼mm needles, cast on 70 [74, 78] sts. Work 3cm in k1, p1 rib. Change to 4mm needles. Cont in patt as given for back, inc 1 st at each end of 3rd row and every foll alt row until there are 98 [102, 106] sts, working extra sts into patt. Cont straight until work measures 15cm from beg, ending with a wrong side row. Cast off.

BUTTON BANDS

Buttonhole band

With right side facing and using 3¼mm needles, pick up and k 28 sts evenly along right side of neck opening. Work 3 rows in k1, p1 rib.

Buttonhole row Rib 3, (cast off 2, rib 8 including st used in casting off) twice, cast off 2, rib to end.

Next row Rib to end, casting on 2 sts over those cast off in previous row.

Rib 2 rows. Cast off in rib.

Button band

Work as given for buttonhole band, picking up sts along left side of neck opening and omitting buttonholes.

COLLAR

Using 3¼mm needles, cast on 103 sts.

Row 1 (Right side) K1, (p1, k1) to end.

Row 2 P1, (k1, p1) to end.

Rep these 2 rows until collar measures 7cm, ending with a wrong side row. Cast off in rib.

FINISHING

Block each piece as given on p. 140. Overlap buttonhole band over button border and catch down at base of opening. Join shoulder seams. Sew on collar. Mark position of armholes 24 [25, 26]cm down from shoulder on back and front. Sew in sleeves between markers. Join side and sleeve seams. Sew on buttons.

JACOB'S LADDER GANSEY

This summer-weight sweater features a saddle-shoulder and traditional gansey stitches. There is a central panel of delicate cables and a Jacob's ladder pattern, which is also repeated on the sleeves.

MATERIALS

Yarn

Standard 4 ply cotton

7 [8, 9] × 50g balls, peach

Needles

1 pair size 2¼mm

1 pair size 3¼mm

1 cable needle

MEASUREMENTS

To fit chest 86 [91, 97]cm

34 [36, 38]in

1 Actual chest size 92 [100, 110]cm

36¼ [39¼, 43¼]in

2 Length to back neck 55 [56, 57]cm

21½ [22, 22½]in

3 Sleeve seam 44 [45, 46]cm

17¼ [17¾, 18]in

Tension

28 sts and 40 rows measure 10cm over stocking stitch on 3¼mm needles (or size needed to obtain given tension)

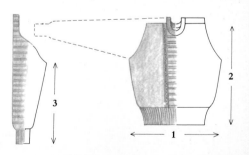

BACK

Using 2¼mm needles, cast on 109 [119, 127] sts.
Row 1 (Right side) K1, (p1, k1) to end.
Row 2 P1, (k1, p1) to end.
Rep these 2 rows until rib measures 10cm, ending with row 1.
Next row Rib 10 [12, 10], (pick up loop lying between sts and work tbl – referred to as m1, rib 3) to last 6 [8, 6] sts, rib to end. *140 [152, 164] sts.*
Change to 3¼mm needles. Commence patt.
Row 1 K45 [51, 57], k1 tbl, p2, k6, p2, k1 tbl, k26, k1 tbl, p2, k6, p2, k1 tbl, k45 [51, 57].
Row 2 P46 [52, 58], k2, p6, k2, p28, k2, p6, k2, p46 [52, 58].
Row 3 K45 [51, 57], k1 tbl, p2, c6f, p2, k1 tbl, k26, k1 tbl, p2, c6b, p2, k1 tbl, k45 [51, 57].
Row 4 As row 2.
Rows 5 to 8 Rep rows 1 and 2 twice.
Row 9 As row 3.
Row 10 P46 [52, 58], k2, p6, k2, p1, k26, p1, k2, p6, k2, p46 [52, 58].
Row 11 As row 1.
Row 12 As row 10.
These 12 rows form patt. Cont in patt until work measures 35 [36, 37]cm from beg, ending with a wrong side row.
Shape armholes Cast off 8 sts at beg of next 2 rows. Dec 1 st at each end of next row and every foll alt row until 102 [106, 110] sts rem. Cont straight until armholes measure 18cm, ending with a wrong side row.
Shape shoulders Cast off 8 [8, 9] sts at beg of next 6 rows and 7 [9, 8] sts at beg of foll 2 rows. Leave rem 40 sts on a spare needle.

FRONT

Work as given for back until armholes measure 13cm, ending with a wrong side row.
Shape neck
Next row Patt 45 [47, 49] sts and turn; leave rem sts on a spare needle.
Complete left side of neck first. Cast off 4 sts at beg of next row and foll alt row and 2 sts at beg of foll alt row. Dec 1 st at neck edge on foll 4 alt rows. *31 [33, 35] sts.* Cont straight until front matches back to shoulder, ending at armhole edge.
Shape shoulder Cast off 8 [8, 9] sts at beg of next row and foll 2 alt rows. Work 1 row. Cast off rem 7 [9, 8] sts.
With right side facing, sl centre 12 sts on to a safety pin, rejoin yarn to rem sts and patt to end. Patt 1 row. Complete as given for first side of neck.

SLEEVES

Using 2¼mm needles, cast on 60 sts. Work 8cm in k1, p1 rib.
Next row Rib 4, (m1, rib 4) to end. *74 sts.*
Change to 3¼mm needles. Commence patt.
Rows 1 to 8 Beg with a k row, work 8 rows st st.
Rows 9 to 12 Knit.
These 12 rows form patt. Cont in patt, inc 1 st at each end of next row and every foll 7th row until there are 106 sts. Cont straight until sleeve measures 44 [45, 46]cm from beg, ending with a wrong side row.

Shape top Cast off 8 sts at beg of next 2 rows. Dec 1 st at each end of next row and every foll alt row until 28 sts rem. Work 10 [11, 12]cm straight on these sts for saddle shoulder, ending with a wrong side row. Leave these sts on a spare needle.

NECKBAND

Join right sleeve saddle shoulder to back and front and left sleeve saddle shoulder to front. With right side facing and using 2¼mm needles, k across 28 sts from left saddle shoulder, pick up and k 24 sts down left front neck, k across 12 centre front sts, pick up and k 24 sts up right front neck, k across 28 sts from right saddle shoulder and 40 centre back sts. *156 sts.* Work 7 rows in k1, p1 rib. Cast off in rib.

FINISHING

Block pieces as given on p. 140. Join left saddle shoulder to back then join neckband. Sew in sleeves. Join side and sleeve seams.

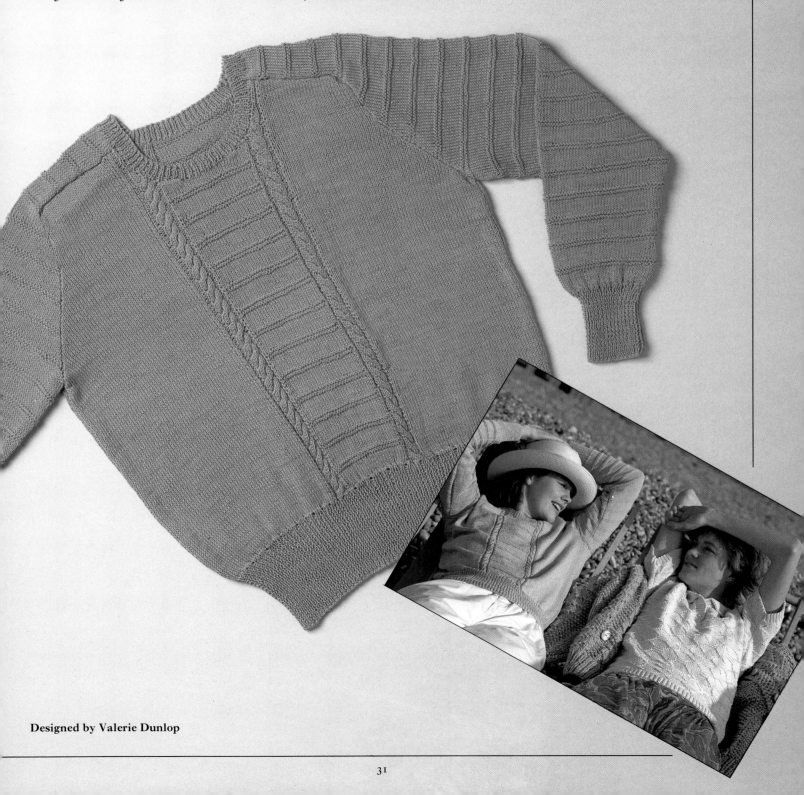

Designed by Valerie Dunlop

FIFE BANDED GANSEY

A simple version of an old classic –
found as far afield as Scotland,
Yorkshire, Norfolk and Cornwall –
the yoke of this banded gansey is
decorated with Garter stitch and
Seed stitch. The buttoned neckband
is typical of a Scottish gansey.

MATERIALS

Yarn

Standard double knitting wool

9 [10, 11, 12, 13] × 50g balls, brown

Needles

1 circular needle size 3¾mm, 80cm long

1 set of double-pointed needles size 3¾mm

Notions

2 buttons, 1.5cm in diameter

2 stitch holders

MEASUREMENTS

To fit chest 91 [97, 102, 107, 112]cm

36 [38, 40, 42, 44]in

1 Actual chest size 102 [107, 112, 116, 121]cm

40 [42, 44, 45¾, 47¾]in

2 Length to back neck 59 [62, 64, 68, 70]cm

23¼ [24¼, 25¼, 26¾, 27½]in

3 Sleeve seam 46 [47, 48, 49, 50]cm

18 [18½, 19, 19¼, 19¾]in

Tension

26 sts and 34 rows measure 10cm over

stocking stitch on 3¾mm needles (or size

needed to obtain given tension)

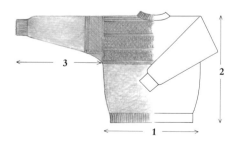

BACK and FRONT

This is knitted in one piece up to the armholes.
Using 3¾mm circular needle, cast on 232 [240,
256, 264, 280] sts. Work in rounds as follows:
Round 1 (K2, p2) to end of round.
Rep this round until rib measures 6 [6, 7, 7,
8]cm.
Next round **K7 [5, 8, 5, 9], *pick up loop
lying between sts and k tbl – referred to as m1,
k10 [9, 11, 10, 12]; rep from * 9 [11, 9, 11, 9]
times more, m1, k7 [5, 8, 5, 9], p1, m1, p1**;
rep from ** to ** once more. *256 [268, 280,
292, 304] sts.* Cont in st st as follows:
Round 1 *K125 [131, 137, 143, 149], p3; rep
from * once more.
Round 2 *K125 [131, 137, 143, 149], p1, k1,
p1; rep from * once more.
Rep these 2 rounds until work measures 31
[32, 34, 36, 38]cm from beg, ending with
round 2.
Change to yoke patt.
Round 1 Purl.
Round 2 *P126 [132, 138, 144, 150], k1, p1;
rep from * once more.
Round 3 Purl.
Round 4 *K125 [131, 137, 143, 149], p1, k1,
p1; rep from * once more.
Round 5 *K125 [131, 137, 143, 149], p3; rep
from * once more.
Round 6 As round 4.
Rep rounds 1 to 3.
Shape for gusset
Round 1 *K125 [131, 137, 143, 149], p1, m1,
k1, m1, p1; rep from * once more.
Round 2 *K125 [131, 137, 143, 149], p1, k3,
p1; rep from * once more.
Round 3 *K1 [0, 1, 0, 1], (p3, k1) 31 [32, 34,
35, 37] times, p0 [3, 0, 3, 0], p1, k3, p1; rep
from * once more.
Round 4 As round 2.
Round 5 *K125 [131, 137, 143, 149], p1, k1,
(m1, k1) twice, p1; rep from * once more.
Round 6 *P2 [1, 2, 1, 2], k1, (p3, k1) 30 [32,
33, 35, 36] times, p3 [2, 3, 2, 3], k5, p1; rep
from * once more.
Round 7 *K125 [131, 137, 143, 149], p1, k5,
p1; rep from * once more.
Round 8 As round 7.
Round 9 *K1 [0, 1, 0, 1], (p3, k1) 31 [32, 34,
35, 37] times, p0 [3, 0, 3, 0], p1, k1, m1, k3,
m1, k1, p1; rep from * once more.
Round 10 *K125 [131, 137, 143, 149], p1, k7,
p1; rep from * once more.
Round 11 As round 10.
Round 12 *P2 [1, 2, 1, 2], k1, (p3, k1) 30 [32,
33, 35, 36] times, p3 [2, 3, 2, 3], k7, p1; rep
from * once more.
Cont in this way, keeping cont of patt and inc
1 st inside border of 1 st at each end of each
gusset on next round and 3 foll 4th rounds.
Work 1 round.
Next round *P126 [132, 138, 144, 150], k15,

p1; rep from * once more.
Rep last round once.
Next round *P126 [132, 138, 144, 150], k1,
m1, k13, m1, p1; rep from * once more.
Next round *K125 [131, 137, 143, 149], p1,
k17, p1; rep from * once more.
Rep last round twice.
Next round *P126 [132, 138, 144, 150], k1,
m1, k15, m1, k1, p1; rep from * once more.
Next round *P126 [132, 138, 144, 150], k19,
p1; rep from * once more.
Rep last round once more.
Next round *K125 [131, 137, 143, 149], p1,
k19, p1; rep from * once more.
Next round *K125 [131, 137, 143, 149], p1,
k1, m1, k17, m1, k1, p1; rep from * once more.
Next round *P1, (k1, p1) 62 [65, 68, 71, 74]
times, p1, k21, p1; rep from * once more.
Next round *K125 [131, 137, 143, 149], p1,
k21, p1; rep from * once more.
Rep last round once.
Next round *K1, (p1, k1) 62 [65, 68, 71, 74]

times, p1, k21, p1; rep from * once more.
Next round *K125 [131, 137, 143, 149], p1,
k21, p1; rep from * once more.
Divide for back and front
Next row K125 [131, 137, 143, 149] sts and
turn; leave rem sts on a spare needle.
Complete back first.
***Work backwards and forwards as follows:
Row 1 (Wrong side) K1, (p1, k1) to end.
Row 2 Knit.
Row 3 Purl.

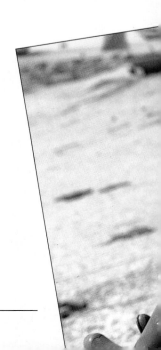

Row 4 As row 1.
Row 5 Purl.
Row 6 Knit.
Rep these 6 rows 2 [3, 3, 4, 4] times.
K 1 row. P 1 row. K 2 rows. P 1 row. K 2 rows. P 1 row. K 1 row.
Row 1 Knit.
Row 2 Purl.
Row 3 K1 [0, 1, 0, 1], (p3, k1) to last 0 [3, 0, 3, 0], p0 [3, 0, 3, 0].
Row 4 Purl.
Row 5 Knit.
Row 6 K2 [1, 2, 1, 2], (p1, k3) to last 3 [2, 3, 2, 3] sts, p1, k2 [1, 2, 1, 2].
Rep these 6 rows 3 times.
K 1 row. P 2 rows. K 1 row. P 1 row.
Shape neck
Next row P46 [48, 50, 52, 54], cast off 33 [35, 37, 39, 41], p to end.
Complete right shoulder first.
Next row K to last 2 sts, k2 tog.
Next row Purl.

Next row P to last 2 sts, p2 tog.
Next row Knit.
Next row P to last 2 sts, p2 tog.
Next row Purl.
Next row K to last 2 sts, k2 tog.
P 2 rows. K 1 row. P 2 rows. K 1 row.
Leave rem 42 [44, 46, 48, 50] sts on a stitch holder. With right side of back facing, rejoin yarn to rem sts, k2 tog, k to end.
Next row Purl.
Next row P2 tog, p to end.
Next row Knit.
Next row P2 tog, p to end.
Next row Purl.
Next row K2 tog, k to end.
P 2 rows. K 1 row. P 2 rows. K 1 row.
Leave rem 42 [44, 46, 48, 50] sts on a stitch holder.
With right side of front facing, sl 23 sts on to a safety pin, rejoin yarn to rem sts, k to last 23 sts and sl these sts on to a safety pin. Work as given for back from *** to *** but leave sts on

needle.
Graft shoulders With back and front right sides together, cast off 42 [44, 46, 48, 50] sts taking 1 st from each needle and working into them tog. Work other shoulder in same way.

NECKBAND

With right side facing, using circular needle size 3¾mm and beg 5 rows down from left shoulder, pick up and k 4 sts to shoulder, 10 sts down left front neck, 33 [35, 37, 39, 41] sts from centre front, 10 sts up right front neck, 10 sts down right back neck, 33 [35, 37, 39, 41] sts from centre back and 6 sts up left back neck then cast on 4 sts. *110 [114, 118, 122, 126] sts.* Work backwards and forwards as follows:
Row 1 (Wrong side) K6, (p2, k2) to last 4 sts, k4.
Row 2 K4, (p2, k2) to last 6 sts, p2, k4.
Row 3 As row 1.

Designed by Rae Compton

Row 4 K2, yfwd, k2 tog, rib to last 4 sts, k4. Rep rows 1 and 2 twice, then work rows 3 and 4. Work 1 row. Cast off in rib. Overlap the first 4 sts over the cast on sts and catch down the cast on sts to wrong side. Sew on buttons.

SLEEVES

With right side facing and using set of double-pointed needles size 3¾mm, pick up and k 88 [96, 96, 104, 104] sts evenly around armhole then p1, k21, p1 from safety pin. Work in rounds as follows:
Next round P89 [97, 97, 105, 105], k21, p1. Rep last round once.
Next round P89 [97, 97, 105, 105], skpo, k17, k2 tog, p1.
Commence patt.
Round 1 K88 [96, 96, 104, 104], p1, k19, p1.
Round 2 (P1, k1) to last 21 sts, p1, k19, p1.
Round 3 As round 1.
Round 4 (K1, p1) to last 21 sts, p1, skpo, k15, k2 tog, p1.
These 4 rounds establish patt.
Next round Patt 88 [96, 96, 104, 104], p1, k17, p1.
Rep last round twice.
Next round Patt 88 [96, 96, 104, 104], p1, skpo, k13, k2 tog, p1.
Next round Patt 88 [96, 96, 104, 104], p1, k15, p1.
Rep last round twice.
Cont in this way, keeping cont of patt and dec 1 st inside border of 1 st at each end of gusset on next round and 3 foll 4th rounds. Work 3 rounds.
Next round P89 [97, 97, 105, 105], skpo, k3, k2 tog, p1.
Next round P89 [97, 97, 105, 105], k5, p1.
Rep last round once.
Next round K88 [96, 96, 104, 104], p1, k5, p1.
Next round K88 [96, 96, 104, 104], p1, skpo, k1, k2 tog, p1.
Next round K88 [96, 96, 104, 104], p1, k3, p1.
Next round P89 [97, 97, 105, 105], k3, p1.
Rep last round once.
Next round P89 [97, 97, 105, 105], sl 1, k2 tog, psso, p1.
Cont in st st as follows:
Next round K88 [96, 96, 104, 104], p3.
Next round K88 [96, 96, 104, 104], p1, k1, p1.
Work 2 rounds.
Next round Skpo, k84 [92, 92, 100, 100], k2 tog, p3.
Cont in this way, dec 1 st at beg and end of st st part on every foll 11th [9th, 10th, 7th, 8th] round until 73 [75, 77, 79, 81] sts rem. Cont straight until sleeve measures 40 [41, 41, 41, 42]cm from beg.
Next round K6 [5, 5, 7, 7], *k2 tog, k6 [10, 7, 10, 7]; rep from * 6 [4, 6, 4, 6] times more, k2 tog, k6 [5, 4, 7, 6], p2 tog, p1. *64 [68, 68, 72, 72] sts.* Work 6 [6, 7, 8, 8]cm in rounds of k2, p2 rib. Cast off in rib.

FINISHING

Block as given on p. 140.

Shown opposite are the Fife banded gansey, the Sanquhar gansey and the Eriskay gansey.

SANQUHAR GANSEY

The Sanquhar pattern is one of the oldest knitting patterns in Scotland. It originates from the small and ancient town of that name in Dumfrieshire. In the eighteenth century the town of Sanquhar was famous for its knitted stockings and gloves made from very fine yarn in contrasting colours, mainly black and white, using patterns like the stitches from a sampler. The bold sweater shown here features a traditional Sanquhar pattern known as the Duke's pattern, but a heavyweight wool has been used instead of the traditional fine yarn.

MATERIALS

Yarn

Standard Aran-weight wool

A 5 [5, 6, 6, 7, 7] × 100g balls, brown

B 4 [5, 5, 6, 6, 7] × 100g balls, cream

Needles

1 pair size 4mm

1 pair size 4½mm

1 set of four double-pointed needles size 4½mm

Notions

2 stitch holders

MEASUREMENTS

To fit chest 86 [91, 97, 102, 107, 112]cm

34 [36, 38, 40, 42, 44]in

1 Actual chest size 104 [110, 116, 122, 128, 134]cm

41 [43¼, 45¾, 48, 50½, 52¾]in

2 Length to back neck 62 [62, 62, 66, 66, 66]cm

24½ [24½, 24½, 26, 26, 26]in

3 Sleeve seam 45 [45, 46, 49, 49, 50]cm

17½ [17½, 18, 19¼, 19¼, 19¾]in

Tension

20 sts and 22 rows measure 10cm over pattern on 4½mm needles (or size needed to obtain given tension)

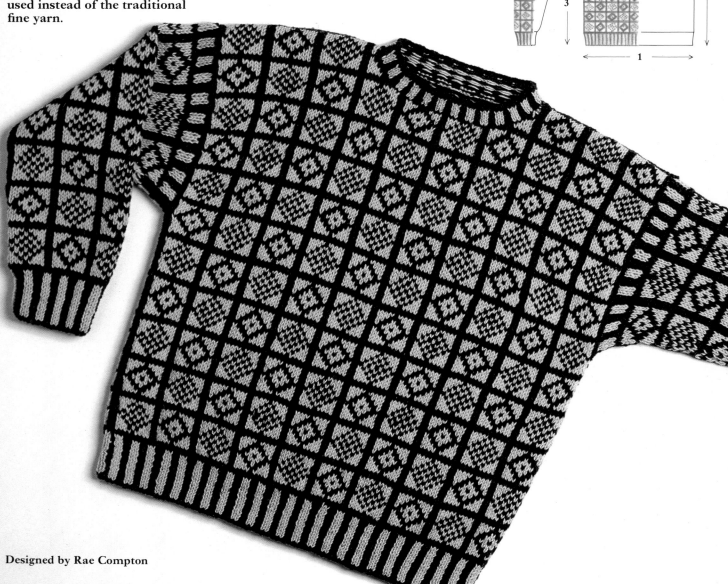

Designed by Rae Compton

BACK

Using 4mm needles and yarn A, cast on 96 [100, 108, 112, 120, 124] sts.
Note Carry yarn not in use loosely across wrong side of work. Cont as follows:
Row 1 (Right side) (K2B, p2A) to end.
Row 2 (K2A, p2B) to end.
Rep these 2 rows until rib measures 6cm, ending with row 2. Change to 4½mm needles.
Next row Using yarn A, k7 [6, 9, 6, 6, 7], *inc in next st, k8 [7, 9, 8, 11, 9]; rep from * to last 8 [6, 9, 7, 6, 7] sts, inc in next st, k to end. *106 [112, 118, 124, 130, 136] sts.*
P 1 row in yarn A. Beg with a k row, cont in st-st and patt from chart for back, working odd-numbered (k) rows from right to left and even-numbered (p) rows from left to right until work measures approximately 62 [62, 62, 66, 66, 66]cm from beg, ending with row 10 [10, 10, 22, 22, 22]. Leave these sts on a spare needle.

FRONT

Work as given for back, until front measures 12 rows less than back.
Shape neck
Next row Patt 44 [46, 48, 50, 52, 54] sts and turn; leave rem sts on a spare needle. Complete left side of neck first. Cast off 3 sts at beg of next row and foll alt row and 2 sts at beg of foll 2 alt rows. Patt 4 rows straight. *34 [36, 38, 40, 42, 44] sts.*
Graft left shoulder With back and front wrong sides together and using yarn A, cast off 34 [36, 38, 40, 42, 44] sts taking 1 st from each needle and working them tog. Sl next 38 [40, 42, 44, 46, 48] sts on back on to a stitch holder. With right side of front facing, sl centre 18 [20, 22, 24, 26, 28] sts on to a stitch holder, rejoin yarns to rem sts and patt to end. Patt 1 row. Cast off 3 sts at beg of next row and foll alt row and 2 sts at beg of foll 2 alt rows. Patt 3 rows straight. *34 [36, 38, 40, 42, 44] sts.*
Graft right shoulder Work as given for left shoulder.

SLEEVES

Using 4mm needles and yarn A, cast on 44 [44, 48, 48, 52, 52] sts. Work 6cm in rib as given for back welt, ending with row 2. Change to 4½mm needles.
Next row Using yarn A, k4 [4, 4, 6, 5, 5], *inc in next st, k2 [2, 4, 1, 2, 2]; rep from * to last 4 [4, 4, 6, 5, 5] sts, inc in next st, k to end. *57 [57, 57, 67, 67, 67] sts.*

P 1 row in A. Beg with a k row, cont in st-st and patt, working from chart for sleeve, inc 1 st at each end of every 7th [6th, 5th, 7th, 6th, 5th] row until there are 75 [79, 83, 87, 91, 95] sts, working extra sts into patt. Patt 13 [10, 11, 17, 15, 19] rows straight.
1st, 2nd and 3rd sizes
Next row Using yarn A, k4 [6, 8], (inc in next st, k10) to last 5 [7, 9] sts, inc in next st, k to end. *82 [86, 90] sts.*
Next row P2 [0, 2] B, (k2A, p2B) to last 0 [2, 0] sts, k0 [2, 0] A.
Next row P0 [2, 0] A, (k2B, p2A) to last 2 [0, 2] sts, k2 [0, 2] B.
4th, 5th and 6th sizes
Next row Using yarn A, p [10, 12, 14], (inc in next st, p10) to last [11, 13, 15] sts, inc in next st, p to end. *[94, 98, 102] sts.*
Next row P [2, 0, 2] A, (k2B, p2A) to last [0, 2, 0] sts, k [0, 2, 0] B.
Next row P [0, 2, 0] B, (k2A, p2B) to last [2, 0, 2] sts, k [2, 0, 2] A.
All sizes
Rep last 2 rows until sleeve measures 45 [45, 46, 49, 49, 50]cm from beg, ending with a wrong side row. Using yarn A, cast off in rib.

NECKBAND

With right side of work facing using double-pointed needles and yarn A, pick up and k 16 sts down left front neck, k18 [20, 22, 24, 26,

28] centre front sts, pick up and k 16 sts up right front neck, k38 [40, 42, 44, 46, 48] centre back sts. *88 [92, 96, 100, 104, 108] sts.* Divide sts on to three needles. Work 5 rounds of k2B, p2A rib. Using yarn A, rib 1 round. Cast off in rib.

FINISHING

Block each piece as given on p. 140. Mark positions of armholes 21 [22, 23, 24, 25, 26]cm down from shoulders on back and front. Sew in sleeves. Join side and sleeve seams.

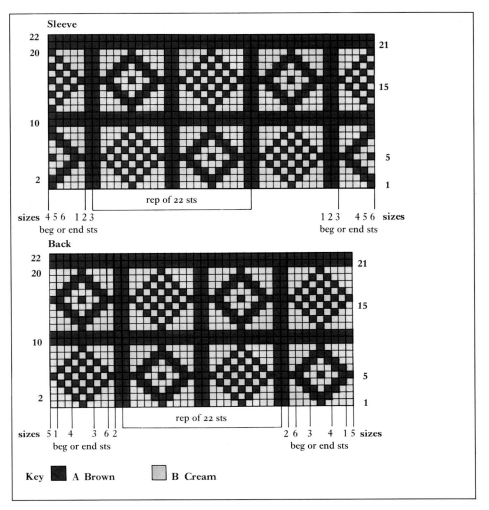

Sleeve

22
20
21
15
10
5
2
1
rep of 22 sts
sizes 4 5 6 1 2 3   1 2 3   4 5 6 sizes
beg or end sts   beg or end sts

Back

22
20
21
15
10
5
2
1
rep of 22 sts
sizes 5 1 4   3 6 2   2 6   3   4   1 5 sizes
beg or end sts   beg or end sts

Key   ■ A Brown   ▨ B Cream

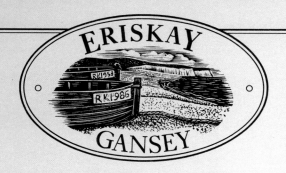

MATERIALS

Yarn

Standard 5 ply Guernsey wool

The smaller size gansey has been knitted in grey wool, the larger size gansey has been knitted in cream wool.

7 [8] × 100g balls, grey or cream

Needles

1 circular needle size 2¾mm, 80cm long

Set of four double-pointed needles size 2¾mm

1 cable needle

Notions

2 [3] buttons, 1.5cm in diameter

2 stitch holders

The Eriskay gansey is perhaps the most beautiful and intricately patterned of all the fishermen's ganseys. The patterns below the chest band of Fishing nets include Diamonds, Marriage lines and Waves. The yoke contains Anchor, Tree of life, Horseshoe, Cables, Open tree and Starfish.

Traditional design by Margaret MacInnes

MEASUREMENTS

Traditionally these ganseys are worn close-fitting.

To fit chest 81-91 [97-102]cm

32-36 [38-42]in

1 Actual chest size 92 [102]cm

$36\frac{1}{4}$ [42]in

2 Length to back neck 65 [67]cm

$25\frac{1}{2}$ [$26\frac{1}{4}$]in

3 Sleeve seam 47 [55]cm

$18\frac{1}{2}$ [$21\frac{1}{2}$]in

Tension

28 sts and 37 rows measure 10cm over bodice pattern on $2\frac{3}{4}$mm needles (or size needed to obtain given tension)

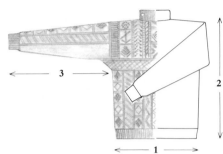

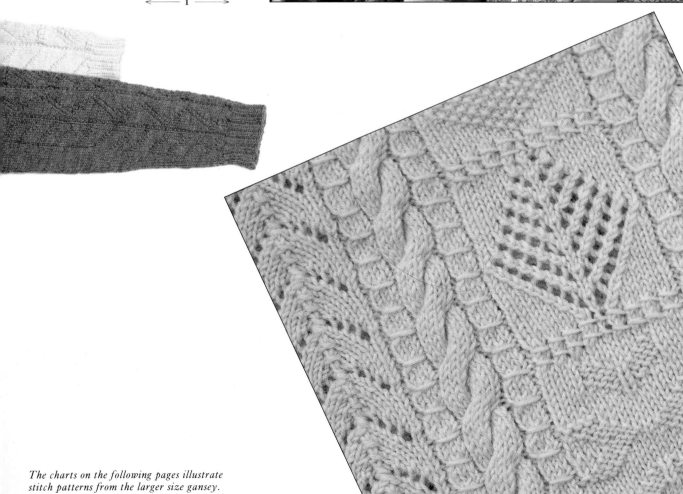

The charts on the following pages illustrate stitch patterns from the larger size gansey.

Bodice panel A

Double moss stitch and plain diamonds
Repeat of 11 [13] sts
Rounds 1 and 2 K5 [6], p1, k5 [6].
Rounds 3 and 4 K4 [5], p1, k1, p1, k4 [5].
Rounds 5 and 6 K3 [4], (p1, k1) twice, p1, k3 [4].
Rounds 7 and 8 K2 [3], (p1, k1) 3 times, p1, k2 [3].
Rounds 9 and 10 K1 [2], (p1, k1) 4 times, p1, k1 [2].
2nd size only
Rounds 11 and 12 K1, (p1, k1) 6 times.
Rounds 13 and 14 K2 (p1, k1) 4 times, p1, k2.
Both sizes
Rounds 11 [15] and 12 [16] As rounds 7 and 8.
Rounds 13 [17] and 14 [18] As rounds 5 and 6.
Rounds 15 [19] and 16 [20] As rounds 3 and 4.
Rounds 17 [21] and 18 [22] As rounds 1 and 2.
1st size only
Round 19 (Bind 2) twice, yfwd, k3, pass yfwd over k3, (bind 2) twice.
2nd size only
Round 23 (Bind 2) 3 times, k1, (bind 2) 3 times.
Both sizes
Round 20 [24] Knit.
Rounds 21 [25] and 22 [26] As rounds 19 [23] and 20 [24].
Rounds 23 [27] to 26 [30] As rounds 1 to 4.
Rounds 27 [31] and 28 [32] K3 [4], p1, k3, p1, k3 [4].
Rounds 29 [33] and 30 [34] K2 [3], p1, k5, p1, k2 [3].
Rounds 31 [35] and 32 [36] K1 [2], p1, k7, p1, k1 [2].
2nd size only
Rounds 37 and 38 K1, p1, k9, p1, k1.
Rounds 39 and 40 K2, p1, k7, p1, k2.
Both sizes
Rounds 33 [41] and 34 [42] As rounds 29 [33] and 30 [34].
Rounds 35 [43] and 36 [44] As rounds 27 [31] and 28 [32].
Rounds 37 [45] and 38 [46] As rounds 3 and 4.
Rounds 39 [47] and 40 [48] As rounds 1 and 2.
Rounds 41 [49] to 44 [52] As rounds 19 [23] to 22 [26].
These 44 [52] rounds form panel A.

Bodice panel B

Marriage lines
Repeat of 11 [13] sts
Round 1 K1, p1, k9 [11].
Round 2 K1, p2, k8 [10].
Round 3 K2, p2, k7 [9].
Round 4 K3, p2, k6 [8].
Round 5 K4, p2, k5 [7].
Round 6 K5, p2, k4 [6].
Round 7 K6, p2, k3 [5].
Round 8 K7, p2, k2 [4].
Round 9 K8, p2, k1 [3].
2nd size only
Round 10 K9, p2, k2.
Round 11 K10, p2, k1.
Both sizes
Round 10 [12] K9 [11], p1, k1.
Round 11 [13] Knit.
These 11 [13] rounds form panel B.

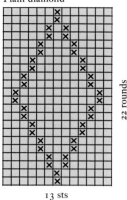

Part of bodice panel A
Plain diamond

22 rounds
13 sts

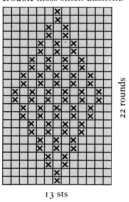

Part of bodice panel A
Double moss stitch diamond

22 rounds
13 sts

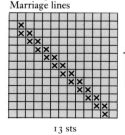

Bodice panel B
Marriage lines

13 rounds
13 sts

Bodice panel C

Wave
Repeat of 11 [13] sts
Rounds 1 and 2 (K1, p1) twice, k7 [9].
Rounds 3 and 4 K2, p1, k1, p1, k6 [8].
Rounds 5 and 6 K3, p1, k1, p1, k5 [7].
Rounds 7 and 8 K4, p1, k1, p1, k4 [6].
Rounds 9 and 10 K5, p1, k1, p1, k3 [5].
Rounds 11 and 12 K6, p1, k1, p1, k2 [4].
Rounds 13 and 14 K7, p1, k1, p1, k1 [3].
2nd size only
Rounds 15 and 16 K8, p1, k1, p1, k2.
Rounds 17 and 18 K9, (p1, k1) twice.
Rounds 19 and 20 As rounds 15 and 16.
Rounds 21 and 22 As rounds 13 and 14.
Both sizes
Rounds 15 [23] and 16 [24] As rounds 11 and 12.
Rounds 17 [25] and 18 [26] As rounds 9 and 10.
Rounds 19 [27] and 20 [28] As rounds 7 and 8.
Rounds 21 [29] and 22 [30] As rounds 5 and 6.
Rounds 23 [31] and 24 [32] As rounds 3 and 4.
These 24 [32] rounds form panel C.

Bodice panel D

Small starfish and diamond
Repeat of 13 sts
Round 1 K1, p1, k9, p1, k1.
Round 2 K1, p2, k7, p2, k1.
Round 3 K2, p2, k5, p2, k2.
Round 4 K3, (p2, k3) twice.
Round 5 K4, p2, k1, p2, k4.
Round 6 K5, p3, k5.
Round 7 K6, p1, k6.
Round 8 Knit.
Round 9 As round 7.
Round 10 As round 6.
Round 11 As round 5.
Round 12 As round 4.
Round 13 As round 3.
Round 14 As round 2.
Round 15 As round 1.
Round 16 As round 7.
Round 17 K5, p1, k1, p1, k5.
Round 18 K4, (p1, k1) twice, p1, k4.
Round 19 K3, (p1, k1) 3 times, p1, k3.
Round 20 K2, (p1, k1) 4 times, p1, k2.
Round 21 K1, (p1, k1) 6 times.
Round 22 As round 20.
Round 23 As round 19.
Round 24 As round 18.
Round 25 As round 17.
Round 26 As round 7.
Round 27 Knit.
These 27 rounds form panel D.

Bodice panel C
Wave

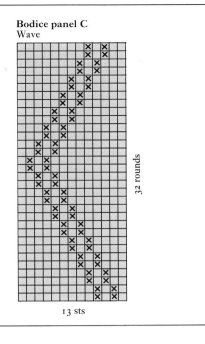

32 rounds

13 sts

Bodice panel D
Small starfish and diamond

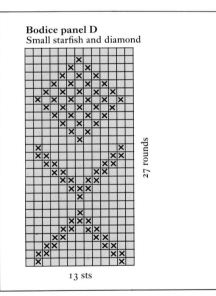

27 rounds

13 sts

Yoke panel E

Tree of life, anchor, open diamond
Repeat of 17 sts
Row 1 (Right side) K7, p1, k1, p1, k7.
Row 2 P6, k2, p1, k2, p6.
Row 3 K5, p2, k3, p2, k5.
Row 4 P4, k2, p5, k2, p4.
Row 5 K3, p2, k2, p1, k1, p1, k2, p2, k3.
Row 6 (P2, k2) twice, p1, (k2, p2) twice.
Row 7 K1, p2, k2, p2, k3, p2, k2, p2, k1.
Row 8 P1, k1, p2, k2, p5, k2, p2, k1, p1.
Rows 9 and 10 As rows 5 and 6.
Row 11 K2, p1, k2, p2, k3, p2, k2, p1, k2.
Rows 12 and 13 As rows 4 and 5.
Row 14 P3, k1, p2, k2, p1, k2, p2, k1, p3.
Rows 15 and 16 As rows 3 and 4.
Row 17 K4, p1, k2, p1, k1, p1, k2, p1, k4.
Rows 18 and 19 As rows 2 and 3.
Row 20 P5, (k1, p5) twice.
Rows 21 and 22 As rows 1 and 2.
Row 23 K6, p1, k3, p1, k6.
Row 24 Purl.
Row 25 As row 1.
Row 26 P7, k1, p1, k1, p7.
Row 27 (Bind 2) 4 times, yfwd, k1, pass yfwd over k1 – referred to as bind 1, (bind 2) 4 times.
Row 28 Purl.
Rows 29 and 30 As rows 27 and 28.
Row 31 K8, p1, k8.
Row 32 P7, k3, p7.
Row 33 K6, p5, k6.
Row 34 P5, k2, p1, k1, p1, k2, p5.
Row 35 K4, p2, k2, p1, k2, p2, k4.
Row 36 P3, k2, p3, k1, p3, k2, p3.
Row 37 K2, p2, k4, p1, k4, p2, k2.
Row 38 P1, k2, p5, k1, p5, k2, p1.
Row 39 K1, p1, (k6, p1) twice, k1.
Row 40 P2, k1, p5, k1, p8.
Row 41 K8, p1, k4, p2, k2.
Row 42 P3, k2, p3, k1, p8.
Row 43 K8, p1, k2, p2, k4.
Row 44 P5, k2, p1, k1, p8.
Row 45 K8, p3, k6.
Row 46 P7, k2, p8.
Row 47 K7, p2, k8.
Row 48 P8, k3, p6.
Row 49 K5, p2, k1, p1, k8.
Row 50 P8, k1, p2, k2, p4.
Row 51 K3, p2, k3, p1, k8.
Row 52 P8, k1, p4, k2, p2.
Row 53 K1, p2, k5, p1, k8.
Row 54 P8, k1, p6, k1, p1.
Row 55 K6, p5, k6.
Row 56 P6, k5, p6.
Rows 57 to 60 As rows 27 to 30.
Row 61 K6, k2 tog, yfwd, k1, yfwd, skpo, k6.
Row 62 and every foll alt row Purl.
Row 63 K5, k2 tog, yfwd, k3, yfwd, skpo, k5.
Row 65 K4 (k2 tog, yfwd) twice, k1, (yfwd, skpo) twice, k4.
Row 67 K3, (k2 tog, yfwd) twice, k3, (yfwd, skpo) twice, k3.
Row 69 K2, (k2 tog, yfwd) twice, k5, (yfwd, skpo) twice, k2.
Row 71 K4, (yfwd, skpo) twice, k1, (k2 tog, yfwd) twice, k4.
Row 73 K5, yfwd, skpo, yfwd, sl 1, k2 tog, psso, yfwd, k2 tog, yfwd, k5.
Row 75 K6, yfwd, skpo, k1, k2 tog, yfwd, k6.
Row 77 K7, yfwd, sl 1, k2 tog, psso, yfwd, k7.
Row 78 Purl.
These 78 rows form panel E.

Part of yoke panel E
Tree of life

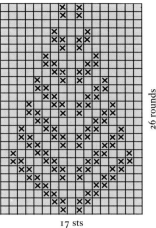

26 rounds

17 sts

Part of yoke panel E
Anchor

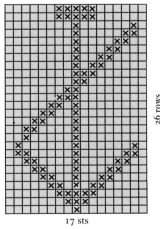

26 rows

17 sts

Yoke panel F

Horseshoe
Repeat of 9 [11] sts
2nd size only
Row 1 K1, yfwd, k3, sl 1, k2 tog, psso, k3, yfwd, k1.
Row 2 Purl.
Both sizes
Row 1 [3] (Right side) K1 [2], yfwd, k2, sl 1, k2 tog, psso, k2, yfwd, k1 [2].
Row 2 [4] **and foll alt row** Purl.
Row 3 [5] K2 [3], yfwd, k1, sl 1, k2 tog, psso, k1, yfwd, k2 [3].
Row 5 [7] K3 [4], yfwd, sl 1, k2 tog, psso, yfwd, k3 [4].
Row 6 [8] Purl.
These 6 [8] rows form panel F.

Yoke panel G

Cable
Repeat of 6 [8] sts
Row 1 (Right side) K6 [8].
Row 2 P6 [8].
Rows 3 to 4 [6] Rep rows 1 and 2 once [twice].
Row 5 [7] Sl next 3 [4] sts onto cable needle and leave at back, k3 [4], k3 [4] sts from cable needle.
Row 6 [8] As row 2.
These 6 [8] rows form panel G.

Yoke panel H

Starfish, open tree, diamond
Repeat of 17 sts
Row 1 (Right side) K4, p1, k7, p1, k4.
Row 2 P4, k2, p5, k2, p4.
Row 3 K4, p3, k3, p3, k4.
Row 4 P4, k4, p1, k4, p4.
Row 5 K5, p3, k1, p3, k5.
Row 6 P6, k2, p1, k2, p6.
Row 7 K7, p1, k1, p1, k7.
Row 8 Purl.
Row 9 P4, k9, p4.
Row 10 P1, k4, p7, k4, p1.
Row 11 K2, p4, k5, p4, k2.
Row 12 P3, (k4, p3) twice.
Row 13 K4, p4, k1, p4, k4.
Row 14 As row 12.
Row 15 As row 11.
Row 16 As row 10.
Row 17 As row 9.
Row 18 Purl.
Row 19 As row 7.
Row 20 As row 6.
Row 21 As row 5.
Row 22 As row 4.
Row 23 As row 3.
Row 24 As row 2.
Row 25 As row 1.
Row 26 Purl.
Row 27 (Bind 2) 4 times, bind 1, (bind 2) 4 times.
Row 28 Purl.
Rows 29 and 30 As rows 27 and 28.
Row 31 K6, k2 tog, yfwd, k1, yfwd, skpo, k6.
Row 32 and 11 foll alt rows Purl.
Row 33 K5, k2 tog, yfwd, k3, yfwd, skpo, k5.
Row 35 K4, (k2 tog, yfwd) twice, k1, (yfwd, skpo) twice, k4.
Row 37 K3, (k2 tog, yfwd) twice, k3, (yfwd, skpo) twice, k3.
Row 39 K2, (k2 tog, yfwd) 3 times, k1, (yfwd, skpo) 3 times, k2.
Row 41 K1, (k2 tog, yfwd) 3 times, k3, (yfwd, skpo) 3 times, k1.
Row 43 (k2 tog, yfwd) 4 times, k1, (yfwd, skpo) 4 times.
Row 45 As row 41.
Row 47 As row 39.
Row 49 As row 37.
Row 51 As row 35.
Row 53 As row 33.
Row 55 As row 31.
Row 56 Purl.
Rows 57 to 60 As rows 27 to 30.
Row 61 K8, p1, k8.
Row 62 P7, k1, p1, k1, p7.
Row 63 K6, (p1, k1) twice, p1, k6.
Row 64 P5, (k1, p1) 3 times, k1, p5.
Row 65 K4, (p1, k1) 4 times, p1, k4.
Row 66 P3, (k1, p1) 5 times, k1, p3.
Row 67 K2, (p1, k1) 6 times, p1, k2.
Row 68 P1, (k1, p1) 8 times.
Rows 69 and 70 Rep row 68 twice.
Row 71 As row 67.
Row 72 As row 66.
Row 73 As row 65.
Row 74 As row 64.
Row 75 As row 63.
Row 76 As row 62.
Row 77 As row 61.
Row 78 Purl.
These 78 rows form panel H.

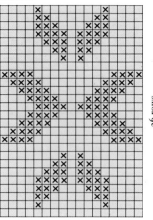

Part of yoke panel H
Starfish

26 rows

17 sts

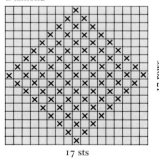

Part of yoke panel H
Diamond

17 rows

17 sts

BACK and FRONT

This garment is knitted in one piece to the armholes. Using circular needle size 2¾mm, cast on 256 [280] sts. Work in rounds as follows:
Round 1 (P1, k2 tbl, p1) to end.
Rep this round 13 times more.
Next round **K31 [23], *inc in next st, k63 [45]; rep from * 0 [1] times more, inc in next st, k32 [24]; rep from ** once more. *260 [286] sts.*
Next round (Yfwd, k2, pass yfwd over k2 – referred to as bind 2) to end.
Next round Knit.
Rep last 2 rounds once more. Commence patt.
Round 1 *P1 [0], k1 [0], p1, work 11 [13] sts as round 1 of panel A, p1, k1, p1, work 11 [13]

sts as round 1 of panel B, p1, k1, p1, work 11 [13] sts as round 1 of panel C, p1, k1, p1, work 11 [13] sts as round 1 of panel A, p1, k1, p1, work 13 sts as round 1 of panel D, p1, k1, p1, work 11 [13] sts as round 1 of panel A, p1, k1, p1, work 11 [13] sts as round 1 of panel C, p1, k1, p1, work 11 [13] sts as round 1 of panel B, p1, k1, p1, work 11 [13] sts as round 1 of panel A, p1, k1 [0]; rep from * once more.
Round 2 *P1 [0], k1 [0], p1, work 11 [13] sts as round 2 of panel A, p3, work 11 [13] sts as round 2 of panel B, p3, work 11 [13] sts as round 2 of panel C, p3, work 11 [13] sts as round 2 of panel D, p3, work 13 sts as round 2 of panel A, p3, work 11 [13] sts as round 2 of panel C, p3, work 11 [13] sts as round 2 of panel B, p3, work 11 [13] sts as round 2 of panel A, p1, k1 [0]; rep from * once more.
These 2 rounds establish patt for bodice. Cont in patt as set working appropriate rounds of panels until 126 [125] rounds in all have been worked.
Shape for gussett
2nd size only
Next round *Pick up loop lying between sts and p tbl, (k1, p1) all in next st, patt 141, (p1, k1) all in next st; rep from * once more.
Both sizes
Next round *P1, k1, p1, (bind 2) 61 [69] times, yfwd, k3, pass yfwd over k3 – referred to as bind 3, p1, k1; rep from * once more.
Next round *P1, k1, p1, k125 [141], p1, k1; rep from * once more.
Next round *P1, k twice in next st, p1, (bind 2) 61 [69] times, bind 3, p1, k twice in next st; rep from * once more.
Next round *P1, k2, p1, k125 [141], p1, k2; rep from * once more.
Next round *P1, k twice in next st, k1, p1, k2, (p1, k7) 15 [17] times, p1, k2, p1, k twice in next st, k1; rep from * once more.
Next round *P1, k3, p1, k3, (p1, k5, p1, k1) 15 [17] times, k2, p1, k3; rep from * once more.
Next round *P1, k3, p1, k3, (p1, k5, p1, k1) 15 [17] times, k2, p1, k3; rep from * once more.
Next round *P1, k1, k twice in next st, k1, p1, k4, (p1, k3) 30 [34] times, k1, p1, k twice in next st, k2; rep from * once more.
Next round *P1, k4, p1, k5, (p1, k1, p1, k5) 15 [17] times, p1, k4; rep from * once more.
Next round *P1, k2, k twice in next st, k1, p1, k6, (p1, k7) 14 [16] times, p1, k6, p1, k twice in next st, k3; rep from * once more.
Next round *P1, k5, p1, k5, (p1, k1, p1, k5) 15 [17] times, p1, k5; rep from * once more.
Next round *P1, k3, k twice in next st, k1, p1, k4, (p1, k3) 30 [34] times, k1, p1, k twice in next st, k4; rep from * once more.
Next round *P1, k6, p1, k3, (p1, k5, p1, k1) 15 [17] times, k2, p1, k6; rep from * once more.
Next round *P1, k4, k twice in next st, k1, p1, k2, (p1, k7) 15 [17] times, p1, k2, p1, k twice in next st, k5; rep from * once more.
2nd size only
Next round *P1, k7, p1, k3, (p1, k5, p1, k1) 17 times, k2, p1, k7; rep from * once more.
Next round *P1, k5, k twice in next st, k1, p1, k4, (p1, k3) 34 times, k1, p1, k twice in

next st, k6; rep from * once more.
Next round *P1, k8, p1, k5, (p1, k1, p1, k5) 17 times, p1, k8; rep from * once more.
Next round *P1, k8, p1, k6, (p1, k7) 16 times, p1, k6, p1, k8; rep from * once more.
Next round *P1, k8, p1, k5, (p1, k1, p1, k5) 17 times, p1, k8; rep from * once more.
Next round *P1, k8, p1, k4 (p1, k3) 34 times, k1, p1, k8; rep from * once more.
Next round *P1, k8, p1, k3, (p1, k5, p1, k1) 17 times, k2, p1, k8; rep from * once more.
Next round *P1, k8, p1, k2, (p1, k7) 17 times, p1, k2, p1, k8; rep from * once more. *284 [320] sts.*
Both sizes
Next round *P1, k7 [8], p1, (bind 2) 61 [69] times, bind 3, p1, k7 [8]; rep from * once more.
Next round **P1, k7 [8], p1, k9 [10], *inc in next st, k14 [16]; rep from * 6 times more, inc in next st, k10 [11], p1, k7 [8]; rep from ** once more. *300 [336] sts.*
Divide for front
Next round P1, k7 [8], p1 and sl these 9 [10] sts on to safety pin, (bind 2) 65 [73] times, bind 3, sl next 8 [9] sts on to safety pin and turn; leave rem sts on needle.
Complete front first. Work backwards and forwards. P 1 row. ***Commence yoke patt.
Row 1 K2, p9, k2 [3], p1, work 17 sts as row 1 of panel E, p1, k2 [3], p1, work 9 [11] sts as row 1 of panel F, p1, k2 [3], p1, work 6 [8] sts as row 1 of panel G, p1, k2 [3], p1, work 17 sts as row 1 of panel H, p1, k2 [3], p1, work 6 [8] sts as row 1 of panel G, p1, k2 [3], p1, work 9 [11] sts as row 1 of panel F, p1, k2 [3], p1, work 17 sts as row 1 of panel E, p1, k2 [3], p9, k2.
Row 2 P2, k9, p2 [3], k1, work 17 sts as row 2 of panel E, k1, p2 [3], k1, work 9 [11] sts as row 2 of panel F, k1, p2 [3], k1, work 6 [8] sts as row 2 of panel G, k1, p2 [3], k1, work 17 sts as row 2 of panel H, k1, p2 [3], k1, work 6 [8] sts as row 2 of panel G, k1, p2 [3], k1, work 9 [11] sts as row 2 of panel F, k1, p2 [3], k1, work 17 sts as row 2 of panel E, k1, p2 [3], k9, p2.
Row 3 K10, p1, bind 2 [3], p1, work 17 sts as row 3 of panel E, p1, bind 2 [3], p1, work 9 [11] sts as row 3 of panel F, p1, bind 2 [3], p1, work 6 [8] sts as row 3 of panel G, p1, bind 2 [3], p1, work 17 sts as row 3 of panel H, p1, bind 2 [3], p1, work 6 [8] sts as row 3 of panel G, p1, bind 2 [3], p1, work 9 [11] sts as row 3 of panel F, p1, bind 2 [3], p1, work 17 sts as row 3 of panel E, p1, bind 2 [3], p1, k10.
Row 4 P10, k1, p2 [3], k1, work 17 sts as row 4 of panel E, k1, p2 [3], k1, work 9 [11] sts as row 4 of panel F, k1, p2 [3], k1, work 6 [8] sts as row 4 of panel G, k1, p2 [3], k1, work 17 sts as row 4 of panel H, k1, p2 [3], k1, work 6 [8] sts as row 4 of panel G, k1, p2 [3], k1, work 9 [11] sts as row 4 of panel F, k1, p2 [3], k1, work 17 sts as row 4 of panel E, k1, p2 [3], k1, p10.
These 4 rows establish patt for yoke. Cont in patt as set, working appropriate rows of panels until 78 rows in all have been worked***.
Shape neck
Next row K2, (bind 2) 20 [23] times, k2 and turn; leave rem sts on needle. Complete left front neck first.
Next row Purl.

Row 1 K2, (bind 2) to last 2 sts, k2.
Row 2 Purl.
Row 3 K2, (p1, k7) to last 2 [8] sts, p1, k1 [7].
Row 4 P2 [0], (k1, p5, k1, p1) to last 2 sts, p2.
Row 5 K4, (p1, k3) to last 4 [2] sts, p1, k3 [1].
Row 6 P4 [2], (k1, p1, k1, p5) to end.
Row 7 K6, (p1, k7) to last 6 [4] sts, p1, k5 [3]. Mark end of this row.
Row 8 As row 6.
Row 9 As row 5.
Row 10 As row 4.
Row 11 As row 3.
Row 12 Purl.
Rows 13 to 16 Rep rows 1 and 2 twice. Leave these sts on a spare needle. With right side of front facing, sl centre 45 [49] sts on to a stitch holder, rejoin yarn to rem sts and k2, (bind 2) to last 2 sts, k2.
Next row Purl.
Row 1 K2, (bind 2) to last 2 sts, k2.
Row 2 Purl.
Row 3 K1 [7], (p1, k7) to last 3 sts, p1, k2.
Row 4 P3, (k1, p5, k1, p1) to last 1 [7] sts, p1 [6], k0 [1].
Row 5 K3 [1], (p1, k3) to last st, k1.
Row 6 (P5, k1, p1, k1) to last 4 [2] sts, p4 [2].
Row 7 K5 [3], (p1, k7) to last 7 sts, p1, k6.
Row 8 As row 6.
Row 9 As row 5.
Row 10 As row 4.
Row 11 As row 3.
Row 12 Purl.
Rows 13 to 16 Rep rows 1 and 2 twice. Leave these sts on a spare needle. With right side of back facing, rejoin yarn to rem sts, p1, k7 [8], p1 and sl these 9 [10] sts on to safety pin, (bind 2) 65 [73] times, bind 3, sl last 8 [9] sts on to safety pin. P 1 row. Work as given for front from *** to ***.
Graft shoulder With right sides of back and front together, cast off 44 [50] sts, taking 1 st from each needle and working them together, sl next 45 [49] centre back sts on to stitch holder, rejoin yarn to rem sts and complete to match first shoulder.

NECKBAND

With right side facing, using circular needle size 2¾mm and beg at marker, pick up and k 7 sts down front neck, k 45 [49] centre front sts, pick up and k 10 sts up right front neck, k 45 [49] centre back sts, pick up and k 5 sts to marker and 2 sts behind the first 2 picked up sts. *114 [122] sts.* Work backwards and forwards as follows:
Row 1 (Wrong side) P2, k3, (p2 tbl, k2) to last 5 sts, k3, p2.
Row 2 K5, (p2, k2 tbl) to last 5 sts, k5.
Row 3 As row 1.
Row 4 K2, cast off 2, k1 (st used in casting off) (p2, k2 tbl) to last 5 sts, k5.
Row 5 P2, k3, (p2 tbl, k2) to last 3 sts, k1, cast on 2, k2.
Rep rows 2 and 3, 4 [3] times then rows 4 and 5 once.
2nd size only
Rep last 8 rows once more.
Both sizes
Rep rows 2 and 3 once. Cast off k-wise. Sew on buttons.

SLEEVES

With right side facing and using set of four double-pointed needles size 2¾mm, sl 9 [10] sts on safety pin on to needle, rejoin yarn and pick up and k 89 sts evenly around armhole edge, p1, k7 [8]. Work in rounds as follows:
Next round P1, k4 [5], k2 tog, k1, p91, k1, skpo, k4 [5].
Next round P1, k3 [4], k2 tog, k1, p91, k1, skpo, k3 [4].
1st size only
Next round P1, k2, k2 tog, k1, p1, k9, p2, work 11 sts as round 1 of panel B, p1, k1, p1, work 11 sts as round 1 of panel C, p1, k1, p1, work 11 sts as round 1 of panel A, p1, k1, p1, work 11 sts as round 1 of panel C, p1, k1, p1, work 11 sts as round 1 of panel B, p2, k9, p1, k1, skpo, k2.
Next round P1, k1, k2 tog, k1, p1, k9, p2, work 11 sts as round 2 of panel B, p3, work 11 sts as round 2 of panel C, p3, work 11 sts as round 2 of panel A, p3, work 11 sts as round 2 of panel C, p3, work 11 sts as round 2 of panel B, p2, k9, p1, k1, skpo, k1.
These 2 rounds establish patt.
2nd size only
Next round P1, k3, k2 tog, k1, p1, k19, p1, k1, p1, work 13 sts as round 1 of panel B, p1, k1, p1, work 13 sts as round 1 of panel A, p1, k1, p1, work 13 sts as round 1 of panel B, p1, k1, p1, k19, p1, k1, skpo, k3.
Next round P1, k2, k2 tog, k1, p1, k19, p3, work 13 sts as round 2 of panel B, p3, work 13 sts as round 2 of panel A, p3, work 13 sts as round 2 of panel B, p3, k19, p1, k1, skpo, k2.
These 2 rounds establish patt.
Next round P1, k1, k2 tog, k1, p1, patt to last 5 sts, p1, k1, skpo, k1.
Both sizes
Cont in patt as set, working appropriate rounds of panels, work as follows:
Next round P1, k1, k2 tog, p1, patt to last 4 sts, p1, skpo, k1.
Next round P1, k3, patt to last 3 sts, k3.
Rep last round 35 [39] times more.
Next round P1, k1, skpo, patt to last 3 sts, k2 tog, k1.
Patt 6 [7] rounds straight. Rep last 7 [8] rounds 14 times more. *66 sts.* Work a further 10 [18] rounds straight, dec 1 st at centre of last round. *65 sts.*
Next round P1, k3 [5], p2, (k2 tbl, p2) to last 3 [5] sts, k3 [5].
Rep last round 14 times more. Cast off knitwise.

FINISHING

Block as given on p. 140.

LADDER & CABLE
GANSEY

Ladder and Cable patterns traditionally found on Inverness ganseys are incorporated in this double knitting weight sweater. Knitted in panels, the chunky look is offset by a pretty picot edging on the neckband.

MATERIALS

Yarn

Standard double knitting wool

17 × 50g balls, pale apricot

Needles

1 pair size 3mm

1 pair size 3¾mm

Cable needle

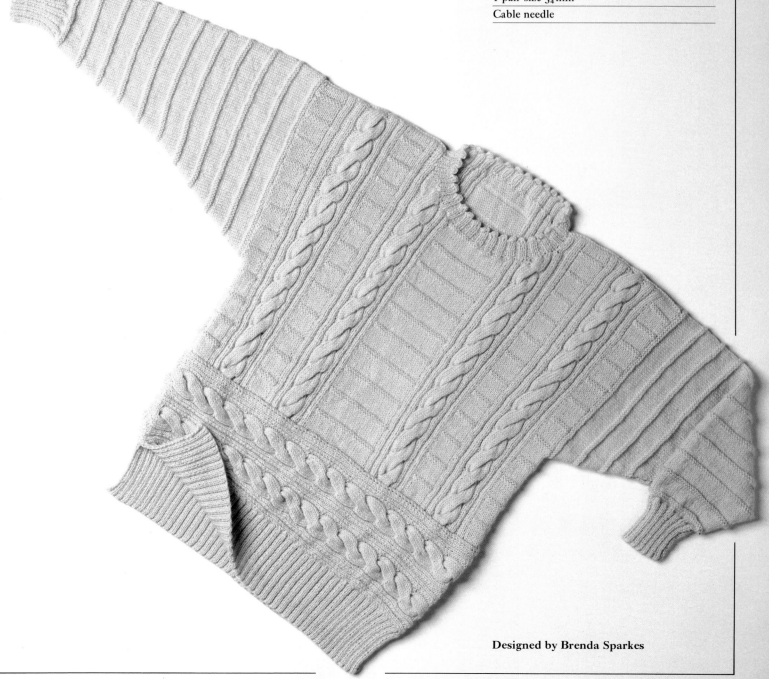

Designed by Brenda Sparkes

MEASUREMENTS

To fit chest 91–96cm, 34–36in	
1 Actual chest size 112cm, 44in	
2 Length to back neck 70cm, 27½in	
3 Sleeve seam 45cm, 17¾in	

Tension

24 sts and 34 rows measure 10cm over sleeve pattern on 3¾mm needles (or size needed to obtain given tension)

36 sts and 32 rows measure 10cm over cable and rib pattern (or size needed to obtain given tension)

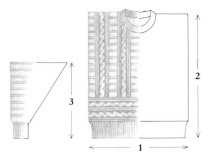

The back and the front of this gansey are made in the same way, each from two separate pieces; a yoke (the top part), and a bodice (the lower part), which are then sewn together.

BACK

Yoke

Using 3¾mm needles, cast on 178 sts.
Commence patt.
Row 1 (Right side) K9, p1, *(k2, p2) twice, k12, (p2, k2) twice, p1, k8, p1, (k2, p2) twice, k12, (p2, k2) twice*, p1, k24, p1; rep from * to * once, p1, k9.
Row 2 P9, k1, *(p2, k2) twice, p12, (k2, p2) twice, k1, p8, k1, (p2, k2) twice, p12, (k2, p2) twice*, k1, p24, k1; rep from * to * once, k1, p9.
Rows 3 and 4 As rows 1 and 2.
Row 5 K9, p1, *(k2, p2) twice, sl next 6 sts on to cable needle and leave at back, k6, k6 from cable needle – referred to as c12b, (p2, k2) twice, p1, k8, p1, (k2, p2) twice, c12b, (p2, k2) twice*, p1, k24, p1; rep from * to * once, p1, k9.
Row 6 As row 2.
Row 7 P10, *(k2, p2) twice, k12, (p2, k2) twice, p10, (k2, p2) twice, k12, (p2, k2) twice*, p26; rep from * to * once, p10.
Row 8 K10, *(p2, k2) twice, p12, (k2, p2) twice, k10, (p2, k2) twice, p12, (k2, p2) twice*, k26; rep from * to * once, k10.
Rows 9 to 12 Rep rows 1 and 2 twice.
These 12 rows form patt. Cont in patt until work measures approximately 46cm from beg, ending with row 6 of patt.

Shape shoulders

Next row K18, (k2 tog) 6 times, k24 and turn; leave rem sts on a spare needle. K 1 row. Cast off k-wise.
With right side facing, sl centre 70 sts on to a holder, rejoin yarn to rem sts, k24, (k2 tog) 6 times, k18. K 1 row. Cast off k-wise.

Bodice

This is knitted sideways.
Using 3¾mm needles, cast on 52 sts.
Commence cable and rib patt.
Row 1 (Right side) P1, *(k2, p2) twice, k12, p2; rep from * once, k2, p2, k2, p1.
Row 2 K1, *(p2, k2) twice, p12, k2; rep from * once, p2, k2, p2, k1.
Rows 3 and 4 As rows 1 and 2.
Row 5 P1, *(k2, p2) twice, c12b, p2; rep from * once, k2, p2, k2, p1.
Row 6 As row 2.
Rows 7 to 12 Rep rows 1 and 2, 3 times.
These 12 rows form patt. Cont in patt until work measures 56cm from beg, ending with a wrong side row. Cast off.

Welt

Join yoke and bodice together.
With right side facing and using 3mm needles, pick up and k 162 sts evenly along lower edge of back.
Row 1 (Wrong side) P2, (k2, p2) to end.
Row 2 K2, (p2, k2) to end.
Rep these 2 rows until rib measures 10cm, ending with row 1 of patt. Cast off in rib.

FRONT

Yoke

Work as given for yoke of back until work measures 38cm from beg, ending with a wrong side row.

Shape neck

Next row Patt 76 sts and turn; leave rem sts on a spare needle. Complete left side of neck first.
Dec 1 st at neck edge on every row until 54 sts rem. Cont straight until front matches back to shoulder, ending with row 6 of patt.

Shape shoulder

Next row K18, (k2 tog) 6 times, k to end. K 1 row. Cast off k-wise.
With right side facing, sl centre 26 sts on to a holder, rejoin yarn to rem sts and patt to end.
Dec 1 st at neck edge on every row until 54 sts rem. Cont straight until front matches back to shoulder, ending with row 6 of patt.

Shape shoulder

Next row K24, (k2 tog) 6 times, k to end. K 1 row. Cast off k-wise.

Bodice and welt

Work as given for bodice and welt of back.

SLEEVES

Using 3mm needles, cast on 56 sts. Work 8cm in k2, p2 rib. Change to 3¾mm needles. Cont in patt of 1 row k, 1 row p, 1 row k, 2 rows p, 2 rows k, 1 row p, 1 row k, 1 row p, 1 row k, 1 row p and at the same time inc 1 st at each end of every foll 3rd row until there are 102 sts, then on every foll alt row until there are 144 sts. Work a further 15 rows. Work should measure 45cm. Cast off.

NECKBAND

Join right shoulder seam. With right side facing and using 3mm needles, pick up and k 25 sts down left front neck, k 26 centre front sts, pick up and k 25 sts up right front neck, 2 sts down right back neck, then work across 70 centre back sts as follows: k2, (k1, k2 tog, k1) 3 times, k10, k2 tog, k18, k2 tog, k10, (k1, k2 tog, k1) 3 times, k2, then pick up and k 2 sts up left back neck. *142 sts.* Beg 2nd row, work 9 rows in rib as given for welt.
Next row *Cast off in rib 1, sl 1, cast on 4, place slipped sts back on to left hand needle, cast off in rib 7 sts; rep from * to last st, cast off rem st.

FINISHING

Block each piece as given on p. 140. Join left shoulder and neckband seam. Mark position of armholes 29cm down from shoulders on back and front. Sew in sleeves. Join sleeve and side seams to welt.

CHEVRON & CABLE GANSEY

Based on patterns from Inverness, Scotland, this designer's version of a gansey-style sweater makes clever use of horizontal cables, and to achieve this the body is knitted in four panels.

MATERIALS

Yarn

Standard double knitting wool

19×50g balls, grey

Needles

1 pair size 3mm

1 pair size $3\frac{3}{4}$mm

Cable needle

MEASUREMENTS

To fit chest 97–107cm, $38\frac{1}{4}$–$42\frac{1}{4}$in

1 Actual chest size 120cm, $47\frac{1}{4}$in

2 Length to back neck 77cm, $30\frac{1}{4}$in

3 Sleeve seam 48cm, 19in

Designed by Brenda Sparkes

Tension

24 sts and 32 rows measure 10cm over chevron pattern on 3¾mm needles (or size needed to obtain given tension)

36 sts and 32 rows measure 10cm over cable and rib pattern on 3¾mm needles (or size needed to obtain given tension)

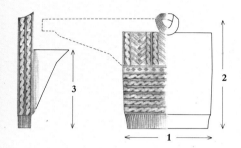

The back and the front of this gansey are made in the same way, each from two separate pieces; a yoke (the top part) and a bodice (the lower part) which are then sewn together.

BACK AND FRONT

Yoke

Using 3¾mm needles, cast on 144 sts.
Row 1 (Right side) Knit.
Rows 2 and 3 Purl.
Row 4 Knit.
Rows 5 and 6 Purl.
Row 7 Knit.
Row 8 P2, (p4, k2, p4) to last 2 sts, p2.
Row 9 K2, (k3, p4, k3) to last 2 sts, k2.
Row 10 P2, (p2, k6, p2) to last 2 sts, p2.
Row 11 K2, (k2, p6, k2) to last 2 sts, k2.
Row 12 P2, (p3, k4, p3) to last 2 sts, p2.
Row 13 K2, (k4, p2, k4) to last 2 sts, k2.
Row 14 Purl.
Rows 15 and 16 Knit.
Row 17 Purl.
Row 18 Knit.
Next row (K2, inc in next st, k1) to end. *180 sts.*
Commence chevron and cable patt.
Row 1 (Wrong side) K2, p2, k2, *p12, k2, (p11, k2) twice, p12, k2, p2, k2; rep from * twice more.
Row 2 P2, k2, p2, *k12, (p2, k10, p2) twice, k12, p2, k2, p2; rep from * twice more.
Row 3 K2, p2, k2, *p12, k2, p9, k6, p9, k2, p12, k2, p2, k2; rep from * twice more.
Row 4 P2, k2, p2, *k12, p2, k8, p3, k2, p3, k8, p2, k12, p2, k2, p2; rep from * twice more.
Row 5 K2, p2, k2, *p12, k2, p7, k3, p4, k3, p7, k2, p12, k2, p2, k2; rep from * twice more.
Row 6 P2, k2, p2, *k12, p2, (k6, p3) twice, k6, p2, k12, p2, k2, p2; rep from * twice more.

Row 7 K2, p2, k2, *p12, k2, p5, k3, p3, k2, p3, k3, p5, k2, p12, k2, p2, k2; rep from * twice more.
Row 8 P2, k2, p2, *sl next 6 sts on to cable needle and leave at front, k6, k6 from cable needle – referred to as c12f, p2, k4, p3, k3, p4, k3, p3, k4, p2, c12f, p2, k2, p2; rep from * twice more.
Row 9 K2, p2, k2, *p12, k2, p3, (k3, p3, k3) twice, p3, k2, p12, k2, p2, k2; rep from * twice more.
Row 10 P2, k2, p2, *k12, p2, k2, (p3, k4, p3) twice, k2, p2, k12, p2, k2, p2; rep from * twice more.
Row 11 K2, p2, k2, *p12, k2, p2, (k2, p6, k2) twice, p2, k2, p12, k2, p2, k2; rep from * twice more.
Row 12 P2, k2, p2, *k12, p2, k2, p2, (k7, p2) twice, k2, p2, k12, p2, k2, p2; rep from * twice more.
Row 13 K2, p2, k2, *(p12, k2, p12) twice, p2, k2; rep from * twice more.
Row 14 P2, k2, p2, *(k12, p2, k12) twice, p2, k2, p2; rep from * twice more.
These 14 rows form patt. Rep these 14 rows 4 times more. Cast off.

Bodice (knitted sideways)

Using 3¾mm needles, cast on 110 sts.
Commence cable and rib patt.
Row 1 (Right side) (P2, k12, p2, k2) to last 2 sts, p2.
Row 2 K2, (p2, k2, p12, k2) to end.
Rows 3 to 6 Rep rows 1 and 2 twice.
Row 7 (P2, c12f, p2, k2) to last 2 sts, p2.
Row 8 As row 2.
Rows 9 to 14 Rep rows 1 and 2, 3 times more.
These 14 rows form patt. Mark beg of next row. Cont in patt until work measures 60cm from beg, ending with a wrong side row. Cast off. Join marked edge of bodice to yoke.

Welt

With right side facing and using 3mm needles, pick up and k 144 sts evenly along lower edge. Work 9cm in k2, p2 rib. Cast off in rib.

LEFT SLEEVE

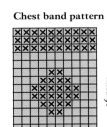

Using 3mm needles, cast on 60 sts. Work 8cm in k2, p2 rib.
Next row Inc in first 4 sts, (inc in next st, rib 1) to last 4 sts, inc in last 4 sts. *94 sts.* Change to 3¾mm needles.
Row 1 (Right side) (P2, k2) 3 times, (p2, k12, p2, k2) to last 10 sts, (p2, k2) twice, p2.
Row 2 K2, (p2, k2) twice, (p2, k2, p12, k2) to

last 12 sts, (p2, k2) 3 times.
These 2 rows establish cable and rib patt.
Cont in patt as set, inc 1 st at each end of every foll right side row until there are 220 sts, working extra sts into rib. Patt 1 row.
Shape saddle shoulder Cast off in rib 72 sts at beg of next 2 rows. *76 sts.* Cont straight in patt until saddle measures 21cm, ending with a wrong side row**.
Shape neck
Next row Patt 36 sts and turn; leave rem sts on a spare needle. Complete back neck first. Cont straight until saddle measures 30cm, ending with a wrong side row. Cast off. With right side facing, rejoin yarn to rem sts, cast off 16 sts, patt to end. Patt 1 row. Cast off 8 sts at beg of next row. Dec 1 st at neck edge on next 12 rows then on 3 foll alt rows. Fasten off.

RIGHT SLEEVE

Work as given for left sleeve to **.
Shape neck
Next row Patt 40 sts and turn; leave rem sts on a spare needle. Complete front neck first. Cast off 16 sts at beg of next row and 8 sts at beg of foll alt row. Dec 1 st at neck edge on next 12 rows then on 3 foll alt rows. Fasten off. With right side facing, rejoin yarn to rem sts, patt to end. Cont straight until saddle measures 30cm, ending with a wrong side row. Cast off.

NECKBAND

Join saddle shoulders to front.
With right side facing and using 3mm needles, pick up and k 25 sts from left back neck, 44 sts down left front neck, 10 centre front sts, 44 sts up right front neck and 25 sts from right back neck. *148 sts.* Work 12 rows in k2, p2 rib. Cast off in rib.

FINISHING

Block each piece as given on p. 140. Join back saddles and neckband seam. Join saddle shoulder to back. Sew sleeves to yoke. Join side and sleeve seams.

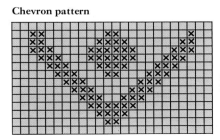

Chest band pattern   Chevron pattern

10 sts   24 sts   16 rows   14 rows

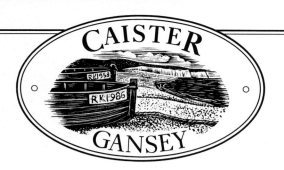

CAISTER GANSEY

This traditional Norfolk gansey has a yoke patterned with Seed stitch above a band of Rig' and furrow, which is repeated on the shoulder straps. The Cables are unusual in having Garter stitch panels at each side which makes them stand out in higher relief.

MATERIALS

Yarn

Standard 5 ply Guernsey wool

8 [8, 9, 10, 10, 11] × 100g balls, grey

Needles

1 circular needle size 3mm, 80cm long

1 set of four double-pointed needles size 3mm

1 cable needle

Notions

2 stitch holders

Chest bands and seed stitch

Pattern repeat 4 rows

Chest bands worked once only

8 sts

Traditional design by Rae Compton

MEASUREMENTS

To fit chest 87 [91, 97, 102, 107, 112]cm

34 [36, 38, 40, 42, 44]in

1 Actual chest size 100 [106, 111, 117, 122,

128]cm

39¼ [41¾, 43¾, 46, 48, 50¼]in

2 Length to back neck 57 [59, 61, 63, 65, 67]cm

22½ [23, 24, 24¾, 25½, 26¼]in

3 Sleeve seam 43 [44, 45, 46, 47, 48]cm

17 [17¼, 17¾, 18, 18½, 19]in

Tension

28 sts and 30 rows measure 10cm over

stocking stitch on 3mm needles (or size

needed to obtain given tension)

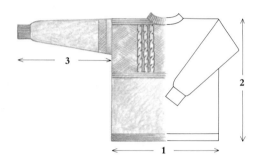

BACK and FRONT

This garment is knitted in one piece to the armholes.

Back welt Using circular needle size 3mm, cast on 124 [132, 140, 148, 156, 164] sts. K 20 rows. Leave these sts on needle. Work front welt as back welt and turn.

Next round **P1, k8 [4, 8, 5, 9, 5], *inc in next st, k6 [7, 7, 8, 8, 9]; rep from * 14 times more, inc in next st, k8 [5, 9, 5, 9, 6], p1**; now work from ** to ** across back welt sts. *280 [296, 312, 328, 344, 360] sts.*

Work in rounds as follows:

Round 1 *P1, k138 [146, 154, 162, 170, 178], p1; rep from * once more.

Rep last round until work measures 31 [32, 33, 34, 35, 36]cm from beg. Commence yoke patt.

Rounds 1 and 2 Purl.

Rounds 3 and 4 *P1, k138 [146, 154, 162, 170, 178], p1; rep from * once more.

Rounds 5 to 8 As rounds 1 to 4.

Rounds 9 and 10 As rounds 1 and 2.

Round 11 P1, k33 [37, 41, 45, 49, 53], (pick up loop lying between sts and k tbl – referred to as m1, k2, m1, k6) 3 times, k30, (m1, k2, m1, k6) 3 times, k27 [31, 35, 39, 43, 47], p1; rep from * once more. *304 [320, 336, 352, 368, 384] sts.*

Round 12 *P3, (k2, p2) 7 [8, 9, 10, 11, 12] times, k30, p2, (k2, p2) 7 times, k30, (p2, k2) 7 [8, 9, 10, 11, 12] times, p3; rep from * once more.

Round 13 *P1, k30 [34, 38, 42, 46, 50], (p2, k6, p2) 3 times, k30, (p2, k6, p2) 3 times, k30 [34, 38, 42, 46, 50], p1; rep from * once more.

Round 14 *P1, k2, (p2, k2) 7 [8, 9, 10, 11, 12] times, k32, (p2, k2) 7 times, k32, (p2, k2) 7 [8,

9, 10, 11, 12] times, p1; rep from * once more.

Round 15 As round 13.

Rounds 16 to 23 Rep rounds 12 to 15 twice.

Rounds 24 and 25 As rounds 12 and 13.

Round 26 *P1, k2, (p2, k2) 7 [8, 9, 10, 11, 12] times, (k2, c6b, k2) 3 times, k2, (p2, k2) 7 times, (k2, c6b, k2) 3 times, k2, (p2, k2) 7 [8, 9, 10, 11, 12] times, p1; rep from * once more.

Round 27 As round 13.

Rep rounds 12 to 27 once more.

Divide for front

Next row P1 and sl this st on to safety pin, m1, p2, (k2, p2) 7 [8, 9, 10, 11, 12] times, k30, p2, (k2, p2) 7 times, k30, (p2, k2) 7 [8, 9, 10, 11, 12] times, p2, m1 and turn; leave rem sts on needle.

***Work backwards and forwards.

Row 1 (Wrong side) K1, p30 [34, 38, 42, 46, 50], (k2, p6, k2) 3 times, p30, (k2, p6, k2) 3 times, p30 [34, 38, 42, 46, 50], k1.

Row 2 K3, (p2, k2) 7 [8, 9, 10, 11, 12] times, k32, (p2, k2) 7 times, k32, (p2, k2) 7 [8, 9, 10, 11, 12] times, k1.

Row 3 As row 1.

Row 4 K1, p2, (k2, p2) 7 [8, 9, 10, 11, 12] times, k30, p2, (k2, p2) 7 times, k30, (p2, k2) 7 [8, 9, 10, 11, 12] times, p2, k1.

Rows 5 to 12 Rep rows 1 to 4 twice.

Row 13 As row 1.

Row 14 K3, (p2, k2) 7 [8, 9, 10, 11, 12] times, (k2, c6b, k2) 3 times, k2, (p2, k2) 7 times, (k2, c6b, k3) 3 times, k2, (p2, k2) 7 [8, 9, 10, 11, 12] times, k1.

Row 15 As row 1.

Row 16 As row 4.

These 16 rows form patt. Cont in patt until armholes measure 17 [18, 19, 20, 21, 22]cm, ending with a wrong side row.

Next row Patt 33 [37, 41, 45, 49, 53], (k2 tog, k1, k2 tog, k5) 3 times, patt 30, (k2 tog, k1, k2 tog, k5) 3 times, patt 29 [33, 37, 41, 45, 49]. *140 [148, 156, 164, 172, 180] sts***.*

Next row K1, p to last st, k1.

Shape neck

Next row Patt 46 [49, 52, 55, 58, 61] sts and turn; leave rem sts on needle.

Complete left front neck first.

Row 1 Purl.

Rows 2 and 3 Knit.

Row 4 Purl.

Rep these 4 rows 5 times more then rows 1 and 2 once. Leave these sts on spare needle. With right side of front facing, sl centre 48 [50, 52, 54, 56, 58] sts on to stitch holder, rejoin yarn to rem sts and p to end. Complete to match left front neck.

With right side of back facing, rejoin yarn to rem sts, p1 and sl this st on to safety pin, m1, p2, (k2, p2) 7 [8, 9, 10, 11, 12] times, k30, p2, (k2, p2) 7 times, k30, (p2, k2) 7 [8, 9, 10, 11, 12] times, p2, m1. Work as given for front from *** to ***.

Graft shoulders With right sides of back and front together, cast off 46 [49, 52, 55, 58, 61] sts taking 1 st from each needle and working them tog. Sl next 48 [50, 52, 54, 56, 58] centre back sts on to stitch holder, rejoin yarn to rem sts and complete to match first shoulder.

NECKBAND

With right side facing and using set of four double-pointed needles size 3mm, pick up and k 18 sts down left front neck, k across 48 [50, 52, 54, 56, 58] centre front sts, pick up and k 18 sts up right front neck and k across 48 [50, 52, 54, 56, 58] centre back sts. *132 [136, 140, 144, 148, 152] sts.* Work 12 rounds in k1, p1 rib. Cast off in rib.

SLEEVES

With right side facing and using set of four double-pointed needles size 3mm, p1 from safety pin, pick up and k 108 [116, 120, 128, 132, 140] sts evenly around armhole edge then p1 from safety pin. Work in rounds as follows:

Round 1 P1, k to last st, p1.

Round 2 P1, skpo, k to last 3 sts, k2 tog, p1.

Rep last 2 rounds 4 times more. Commence band patt.

Round 1 Purl.

Round 2 P1, k to last st, p1.

Round 3 P3, (k2, p2) to last st, p1.

Round 4 As round 2.

Round 5 P1, (k2, p2) to last 3 sts, k2, p1.

Rounds 6 and 7 As rounds 2 and 3.

Round 8 P1, skpo, k to last 3 sts, k2 tog, p1.

Round 9 P1, k1, (p2, k2) to last 4 sts, p2, k1, p1.

Round 10 As round 2.

Round 11 P2, (k2, p2) to end.

Round 12 As round 2.

Round 13 As round 9.

Round 14 As round 8.

Round 15 P1, k2, (p2, k2) to last st, p1.

Round 16 As round 2.

Round 17 Purl.

Next round P1, k to last st, p1.

Rep this round once more.

Next round P1, skpo, k to last 3 sts, k2 tog, p1.

Next round P1, k to last st, p1.

Rep last round 4 [3, 3, 2, 2, 2] times more.

Rep last 6 [5, 5, 4, 4, 4] rounds until 62 [62, 64, 64, 66, 68] sts rem, ending with dec round. Cont straight until sleeve measures 36 [37, 38, 39, 40, 41]cm, ending 1 st before end of last round.

Next round P2 tog, k9 [9, 10, 10, 9, 8], *k2 tog, k8 [8, 8, 8, 9, 6]; rep from * to last 11 [11, 12, 11, 11, 10] sts, k2 tog, k to end. *56 [56, 58, 58, 60, 60] sts.*

Work 7cm in rounds of k1, p1 rib. Cast off in rib.

FINISHING

Block as given on p. 140.

FAIR ISLE

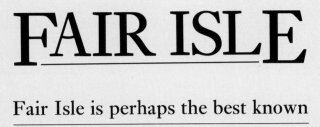

Fair Isle is perhaps the best known
of traditional British knitting. The beautifully
muted colours and soft Shetland wool
combine in the folk art patterns of Britain's
most northerly islands, to produce
sweaters that are now accepted
as classics of fashion.

The Shetland group, which consists of over 100 islands, lies about 200 miles off the coast of Norway. Only fourteen of the Shetland Islands are actually inhabited, and of these the largest are Mainland, Yell and Unst. Fair Isle is one of the more isolated islands. It lies to the south, between the main group and the northern coast of Scotland.

The Shetland Islands may be remote from both mainland Norway and Scotland, but because they have a large, safe harbour at Lerwick, sheltered by the island of Bressay, they have always been a thriving centre for traders and fishermen. Many sea-going routes converged on Shetland and the harbour was a haven for hundreds of ships and boats, of all nationalities, in their journeys from the south of Europe to the Baltic, Scandinavia, the Faeroe Islands and Iceland.

Over the centuries the Islanders relied on crofting and fishing to make a living, but for much of their history they were exploited by ruthless landlords and their lives were often full of struggle and hardship. To supplement their meagre living from the sea and land, the Islanders built up a cottage industry of hand-knitting, which has been sustained for more than 500 years, and as one knitter recently said "Without the knitting I shudder to think what would have happened to the Islands".

The earliest-known examples of patterned knitting found in Shetland which may be related to the later Fair Isle patterns were found on the body of the "Gunnister Man". His body was found preserved in a peat bog in 1951, and on it were knitted stockings, gloves and cap, along with a patterned purse containing coins dating from between 1681 and 1690. However, no one knows whether this man was a Shetland Islander or a trader from abroad, and no other patterned Fair Isle knitting has been discovered dating from before 1850. Before that there was a flourishing trade in hand-knitted, plain, coarse, woollen stockings and this was the main activity of the Shetland knitters throughout the eighteenth century. In the first half of the nineteenth century the mainstay of the knitting industry was the production of Shetland lace (see p. 114), and it seems that the rise in popularity of what we now know as Fair Isle started as the demand for lace declined.

The earliest existing examples of Fair Isle patterned knitting as we now know it, with its large geometric shapes and alternating coloured bands, are a beautiful cap and purse, dating from 1850, which can now be seen in the National Museum of Antiquities of Scotland in Edinburgh. These are hand-knitted in silk, and may well have been made for the Victorian tourist trade in the Islands. The Shetlanders tried to spice up the story behind their knitting with a little romance, and in 1856 a Miss Eliza Edmondston from Shetland related the tale that the Islanders had copied the patterns from the sailors of the Spanish Armada ship *El Gran Griffon*, which was wrecked

on their shores in 1588. This myth was popular and boosted sales of the knitting to the visitors, but there does not seem to be any foundation in fact. It seems much more likely that when the fifty or so Islanders were faced with 300 Spanish sailors from the wrecked Armada ship, knowing that they had no surplus food stores to feed them during the winter, they not only refused them food but in some cases hastened their deaths by pushing them over the steep cliffs!

As with any folk art, it is difficult to ascertain the exact origins of the Fair Isle patterns, but they seem to be related to patterns found in Estonia and Russia and could easily have been brought to Shetland by traders. In Fair Isle the tale is told that a local man brought home a patterned shawl as a gift from that area and the local women tried to copy the patterns in their knitting. This may be less romantic but is likely to be nearer the truth.

The patterns of the mid-nineteenth century Fair Isle knitting consisted of large hexagonal shapes with different crosses and shapes within them, and with vertical and diagonal lines between each one, these are described as the traditional "oxo" patterns. In between are different "peerie" (small) patterns, each one having a different background colour, or in the larger bands, two background colours. The ingenuity of the individual knitters led to the invention of a large variety of patterns. Knitters would pride themselves on never using the same one twice on a garment. All these designs were achieved by using just two colours of yarn in a row, with the colour not being knitted stranded along the back of the knitting.

The colours used in the old Fair Isle patterns were the natural shades of the sheep's wool, ranging through natural black, "moorit" brown, to greys, fawn and cream. Also used were a gold obtained from onions, and madder red and indigo blue. The madder and indigo dyes were imported and were first used in Shetland around 1840. These were the colours used in all Fair Isle knitting until about 1920 when mill-dyed yarns from the mainland of Scotland began to be more generally used.

All the Fair Isle garments in existence from before the turn of the century are small items such as caps, scarves, hats, gloves and stockings, but around 1900 the first all-over patterned Fair Isle sweaters appeared. Like fisher ganseys, they were seamless garments, knitted in the round, with the sleeves being knit down from the shoulders. These sweaters were originally made as everyday workwear for the local fishermen. However Fair Isle knitting became generally popular when the Prince of Wales (later Edward VIII) was presented with a Fair Isle sweater and wore it on the golf course at St. Andrews in 1921. He also had his portrait painted by Sir Henry Lander wearing the sweater, and as a result, Fair Isle became very fashionable.

During the Second World War Shetland and Fair Isle knitting was again very popular. It was frequently bought by soldiers who were stationed in the Islands as gifts for their wives or sweethearts. Later on the influence of Norwegian patterns overtook the old traditional Fair Isle, and a lot of sweaters were knitted with vertical, rather than horizontal bands, and with the star and tree motifs which are usually associated with Norwegian knitting. These are still popular with Shetland fishermen.

By the 1960s the old Fair Isle patterns had almost disappeared. Margaret Stuart, whose mother was from Shetland, became aware of this and encouraged knitters to go back to the strong bands of pattern and traditional colours. Since then there has been a general revival of interest in the hand-knitting of Shetland, including Fair Isle, and the revenue earned from the discovery of oil is being ploughed back into the knitwear industry. This ensures that Shetland knitting will remain an important part of the Islands' economy in the years to come.

Left: The tiny harbour on Fair Isle
Above: Shetland sheep keeping warm
Below: An old Fair Isle pattern interpreted in a new colour combination

CROSS & FLOWER
FAIR ISLE

A traditional pattern takes on a new and bolder look when double knitting wool is used, in rich, earthy shades. Knitted in separate pieces and then seamed, this pattern would make a warm sweater for either men or women. The design is a variation of the O.X.O. pattern and dates from the 1920s.

MATERIALS

Yarn

Standard double knitting wool

A 2 [2, 2, 3, 3] × 50g balls, sage

B 2 [2, 2, 3, 3] × 50g balls, violet

C 2 [2, 2, 2, 3] × 50g balls, beige

D 2 [3, 3, 3, 3] × 50g balls, airforce blue

E 2 [2, 2, 2, 3] × 50g balls, lilac

F 3 [3, 3, 3, 4] × 50g balls, brown

Needles

1 pair size 3¾mm

1 pair size 4½mm

Notions

1 stitch holder

**Designed by Margaret Stuart
and Madeline Weston**

Special note
If you have not knitted with two colours of yarn in a row before, please see p. 139.

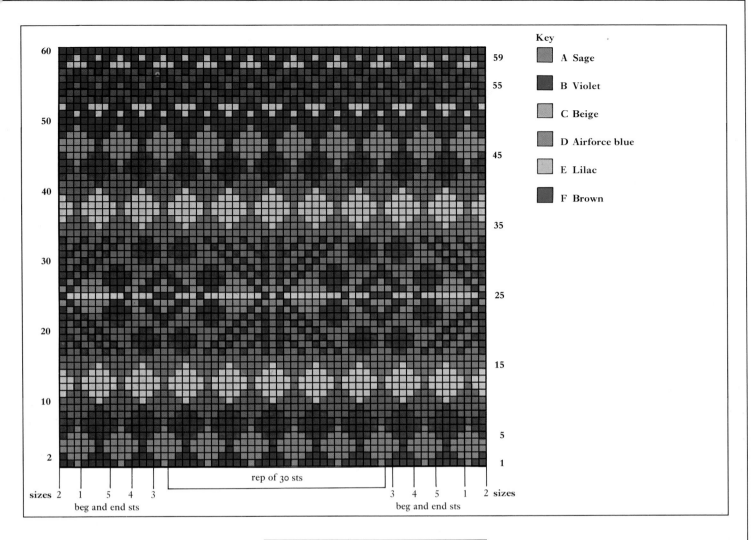

Key

A	Sage
B	Violet
C	Beige
D	Airforce blue
E	Lilac
F	Brown

rep of 30 sts

sizes 2 1 5 4 3

beg and end sts

3 4 5 1 2 sizes

beg and end sts

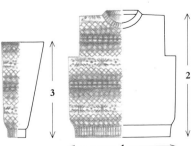

MEASUREMENTS

To fit chest 86 [91, 97, 102, 107]cm

34 [36, 38, 40, 42]in

1 Actual chest size 96 [102, 106, 110, 116]cm

37¾ [40, 41¼, 43¼, 45½]in

2 Length to back neck 55 [59, 60, 62, 65]cm

21½ [23¼, 23½, 24¼, 25½]in

3 Sleeve seam 41 [42, 45, 48, 50]cm

16 [16½, 17¾, 19, 19¾]in

Tension

23 sts and 26 rows measure 10cm over pattern

on 4½mm needles (or size needed to obtain

given tension)

BACK

Carry yarn not in use loosely across wrong
side of work. Using 3¾mm needles and yarn
A, cast on 106 [110, 114, 118, 122] sts.
Row 1 (Right side) P2A, (k2B, p2A) to end.
Row 2 K2A, (p2B, k2A) to end.
Row 3 P2A, (k2C, p2A) to end.
Row 4 K2A, (p2C, k2A) to end.
Row 5 P2A, (k2D, p2A) to end.
Row 6 K2A, (p2D, k2A) to end.

Row 7 P2A, (k2E, p2A) to end.
Row 8 K2A, (p2E, k2A) to end.
Row 9 P2A, (k2F, p2A) to end.
Row 10 K2A, (p2F, k2A) to end.
Rows 11 and 12 As rows 7 and 8.
Rows 13 and 14 As rows 5 and 6.
Rows 15 and 16 As rows 3 and 4.
Rows 17 and 18 As rows 1 and 2.
Change to 4½mm needles.
Next row Using yarn A, k5 [7, 9, 9, 7], *pick
up loop lying between sts and k tbl – referred
to as m1, k16 [12, 12, 10, 9]; rep from * to
last 5 [7, 9, 9, 7] sts, m1, k to end. 113 [119,
123, 129, 135] sts.
P 1 row in A. Reading odd numbered (k) rows
from right to left and even numbered (p) rows
from left to right, cont in st st and patt from
chart until work measures 35 [37, 38, 40,
40]cm from beg ending with a wrong side row.
Shape armholes Cast off 12 [14, 14, 16, 16]
sts at beg of next 2 rows. 89 [91, 95, 97, 103]
sts.
Cont straight in patt until armholes measure
20 [22, 22, 22, 25]cm, ending with a wrong
side row.
Shape shoulders
Next row Cast off 25 [25, 27, 27, 30] sts, patt
to last 25 [25, 27, 27, 30], cast off these sts.
Leave rem 39 [41, 41, 43, 43] sts on a spare
needle.

FRONT

Work as given for back until armholes measure 10 [11, 11, 11, 13]cm, ending with a wrong side row.
Shape neck
Next row Patt 38 [38, 40, 41, 44] sts and turn; leave rem sts on a spare needle.
Complete left side of neck first. Cast off 2 sts at beg of next row and foll 3 alt rows then 1 st on every alt row until 25 [25, 27, 27, 30] sts rem. Cont straight until front matches back to shoulder, ending with a wrong side row.
Cast off.
With right side facing, sl centre 13 [15, 15, 15, 15] sts on to stitch holder, rejoin appropriate yarn to rem sts and patt to end. Patt 1 row. Complete to match first side of neck.

SLEEVES

Using 3¾mm needles and yarn A, cast on 46 [46, 46, 50, 54] sts. Work 18 rows in rib as given for back welt. Change to 4½mm needles.
Next row Using A, k5 [7, 7, 7, 6], *m1, k3 [2, 2, 2, 3]; rep from * to last 2 [5, 5, 5, 3] sts, k to end. *59 [63, 63, 69, 69] sts.*
P 1 row in A. Cont in st st and patt from chart as given for 2nd [3rd, 3rd, 4th, 4th] sizes, inc 1 st at each end of 9th [1st, 9th, 9th, 3rd] row and every foll 4th [4th, 4th, 5th, 4th] row until there are 95 [103, 103, 103, 117] sts, working extra sts into patt. Cont straight until sleeve measures 41 [42, 45, 48, 50]cm. Mark each end of last row. Work a further 5 [6, 6, 7, 7]cm in patt, ending with a wrong side row. Cast off.

NECKBAND

Join right shoulder seam. With right side facing, using 3¾mm needles and yarn A, pick up and k 23 [25, 27, 28, 30] sts down left side neck, k across 13 [15, 15, 15, 15] centre front sts, pick up and k 23 [25, 27, 28, 30] sts up right side neck, k across 39 [41, 41, 43, 43] centre back sts. *98 [106, 110, 114, 118] sts.*
Next row (Wrong side) K2A, (p2D, k2A) to end. Now rep rows 13 to 18 as given for back welt. Using A, cast off in rib.

FINISHING

Block each piece as given on page 140. Join left shoulder and neckband seam. Sew in sleeves, sewing rows above markers to cast off sts at armholes. Join side and sleeve seams.

CROSS & SQUARE
FAIR ISLE

This sleeveless slipover combines a bold, traditional pattern – a repeating cross motif – with contemporary colours. This Fair Isle is knitted in the round.

Traditional design by Margaret Stuart

MATERIALS

This design has been knitted in two different colour combinations, the main one using seven colours of Shetland 2 ply jumper weight wool, the alternative, shown on page 61, using four colours of 4 ply Botany wool. Separate yarn quantities are given for both. Although the same basic pattern is used on each sweater, the yarn sequence is not the same, so two different colour charts have been provided, as well as separate pattern instructions where necessary.

Yarn for main colour combination

This garment is knitted in Shetland 2 ply jumper weight wool, which is the equivalent of standard 4 ply wool.

A 2 [2, 2, 2] × 2oz hanks, navy
B 1 [1, 1, 1] × 2oz hank, purple mix
C 1 [1, 1, 1] × 2oz hank, red
D 1 [1, 1, 1] × 2oz hank, brown
E 1 [1, 1, 1] × 2oz hank, blue mix
F 2 [2, 2, 2] × 2oz hanks, cream
G 1 [1, 1, 1] × 2oz hank, red mix

Yarn for alternative colour combination

4 ply Botany wool

A 6 [6, 7, 7] × 25g hanks, blue mix
B 3 [3, 4, 4] × 25g hanks, green
C 3 [3, 4, 4] × 25g hanks, turquoise
D 2 [2, 2, 2] × 25g hanks, yellow mix

Needles

Circular needle size 2¾mm, 60cm long
Circular needle size 2¾mm, 40cm long
Circular needle size 3mm, 80cm long

Main colour combination

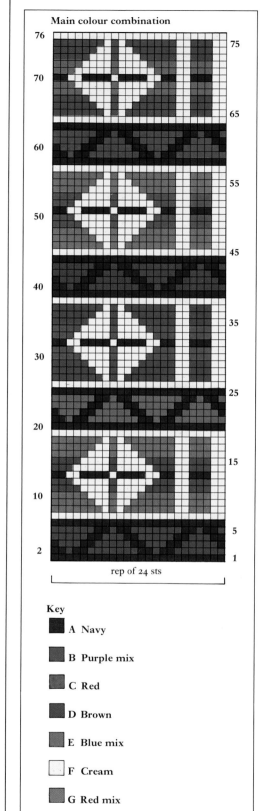

76
75
70
65
60
55
50
45
40
35
30
25
20
15
10
5
2
1

rep of 24 sts

Key

■ A Navy

■ B Purple mix

■ C Red

■ D Brown

■ E Blue mix

□ F Cream

■ G Red mix

MEASUREMENTS

To fit chest 86 [91, 97, 102]cm

34 [36, 38, 40]in

1 Actual chest size 97 [101, 109, 116]cm

38 [39¾, 43, 45¾]in

2 Length to back neck 55 [58, 61, 63]cm

21½ [22¾, 24, 24¾]in

Tension

33 sts and 38 rows measure 10cm over pattern
on 3mm needles (or size needed to obtain
given tension)

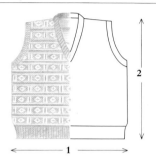

Special note

If you have not knitted with two colours of
yarn in a row before, please see p. 139.

BACK and FRONT

This garment is knitted in one piece to the
armholes. Carry yarn not in use loosely across
wrong side of work. Using circular needle
size 2¾mm, 60cm long and yarn A, cast on 276
[300, 320, 336] sts. Cont in rounds as follows:-

Main colour combination

Rounds 1 to 3 (K2B, p2A) to end.

Rounds 4 to 6 (K2C, p2A) to end.

Rounds 7 to 9 (K2D, p2A) to end.

Rounds 10 to 12 (K2E, p2A) to end.

Alternative colour combination

Rounds 1 to 3 (K2C, p2A) to end.

Rounds 4 to 6 (K2B, p2A) to end.

Rounds 7 to 9 (K2D, p2A) to end.

Rounds 10 to 12 (K2C, p2A) to end.

Both colour combinations

Rounds 13 to 15 As rounds 7 to 9.

Rounds 16 to 18 As rounds 4 to 6.

Rounds 19 to 21 As rounds 1 to 3.

Change to circular needle size 3mm.

Next round Using A, *(k8, pick up loop
lying between sts and k tbl – referred to as
m1) 2 [2, 1, 1] times, k7 [9, 8, 6], m1; rep
from * to end. *312 [336, 360, 384] sts.*
Reading rounds from right to left cont in st st
and patt from appropriate chart.
Cont in patt until work measures 35 [35, 38,
38]cm from beg, ending 1 [7, 14, 20] sts
before end of last round.

Divide for back and front

Next round *Cast off 21 [21, 23, 23], patt 135
[147, 157, 169] including st used in casting
off; rep from * once more.
Complete back first. Keeping continuity of
patt, work backwards and forwards in st st,
reading p rows from left to right from chart.

Next row Patt to end.

Next row K1, skpo, patt to last 3 sts, k2 tog,
k1.

Rep last 2 rows until 109 [117, 127, 137] sts
rem.

Next 3 rows Patt to end.

Next row K1, skpo, patt to last 3 sts, k2 tog,
k1.

Rep last 4 rows 5 times more. *97 [105, 115,
125] sts.* Cont straight until armhole measures
20 [23, 23, 25]cm, ending with a wrong side
row.

Shape shoulders

Next row Cast off 30 [32, 35, 40] sts, patt to
last 30 [32, 35, 40] sts, cast off these sts. Leave
rem 37 [41, 45, 45] sts on a spare needle.
With wrong side of front facing, rejoin
appropriate yarn to rem sts.

Next row Patt 67 [73, 78, 84] sts and turn;
leave rem sts on needle.
Complete right side of neck first.

Next row Skpo, patt to last 3 sts, k2 tog, k1.

Next row Patt to end.

Rep last 2 rows 4 [4, 4, 5] times more.

Next row Patt to last 3 sts, k2 tog, k1.

Next row Patt to end.

Next row Skpo, patt to last 3 sts, k2 tog, k1.

Next row Patt to end.

Rep last 4 rows 3 [4, 4, 4] times more.

Next 2 rows Patt to end.

Next row Skpo, patt to last 3 sts, k2 tog, k1.

Next row Patt to end.

Rep last 4 rows 5 times more. Keeping
armhole edge straight, cont to dec at neck
edge as before until 30 [32, 35, 40] sts rem.
Cont straight until front matches back to
shoulder, ending with wrong side row. Cast
off.
With wrong side of front facing, sl next st on
to safety pin, rejoin appropriate yarn to rem
sts and patt to end.

Next row K1, skpo, patt to last 2 sts, k2 tog.

Next row Patt to end.

Rep last 2 rows 4 [4, 4, 5] times more.

Next row K1, skpo, patt to end.

Next row Patt to end.

Next row K1, skpo, patt to last 2 sts, k2 tog.

Next row Patt to end.

Rep last 4 rows 3 [4, 4, 4] times more.

Next 2 rows Patt to end.

Next row K1, skpo, patt to last 2 sts, k2 tog.

Next row Patt to end.

Complete as given for right side neck.

NECKBAND

Join shoulder seams. With right side facing,
using circular needle size 2¾mm, 60cm long
and yarn A, pick up and k 76 [84, 84, 88] sts
down left side neck, k centre front st, pick up
and k 76 [84, 84, 88] sts up right side neck, k
18 [20, 22, 22], inc in next st, k 18 [20, 22, 22]
across centre back sts. *191 [211, 215, 223] sts.*

Round 1 (K2D, p2A) 18 [20, 20, 21] times,
k2D, using A, skpo, k1, k2 tog, (k2D, p2A) 28
[31, 32, 33] times.

Round 2 (K2D, p2A) 18 [20, 20, 21] times,
using D, k1, skpo, k1A, using D, k2 tog, k1D,
p2A, (k2D, p2A) 27 [30, 31, 32] times.

Round 3 (K2D, p2A) 18 [20, 20, 21] times,
using D, skpo, k1A, using D, k2 tog, p2A,
(k2D, p2A) 27 [30, 31, 32] times.

Main colour combination

Round 4 (K2C, p2A) 17 [19, 19, 20] times,
k2C, using A, p1, yb, skpo, k1, k2 tog, p1,
(k2C, p2A) 27 [30, 31, 32] times.

Alternative colour combination

19
15

18

10

5

2

1

rep of 24 sts

Key

A Blue mix

C Turquoise

B Green

D Yellow mix

Round 5 (K2C, p2A) 17 [19, 19, 20] times,
k2C, using A, skpo, k1, k2 tog, (k2C, p2A) 27
[30, 31, 32] times.
Round 6 (K2C, p2A) 17 [19, 19, 20] times,
using C, k1, skpo, k1A, using C, k2 tog, k1C,
p2A, (k2C, p2A) 26 [29, 30, 31] times.
Round 7 (K2B, p2A) 17 [19, 19, 20] times,
using B, skpo, k1A, using B, k2 tog, p2A,
(k2B, p2A) 26 [29, 30, 31] times.
Round 8 (K2B, p2A) 16 [18, 18, 19] times,
k2B, using A, p1, yb, skpo, k1, k2 tog, p1,
(k2B, p2A) 26 [29, 30, 31] times.
Round 9 (K2B, p2A) 16 [18, 18, 19] times,
k2B, using A, skpo, k1, k2 tog, (k2B, p2A) 26
[29, 30, 31] times.
Using A, cast off in rib.

Alternative colour combination
Round 4 (K2B, p2A) 17 [19, 19, 20] times,
k2B, using A, p1, yb, skpo, k1, k2 tog, p1,
(k2B, p2A) 27 [30, 31, 32] times.
Round 5 (K2B, p2A) 17 [19, 19, 20] times,
k2B, using A, skpo, k1, k2 tog, (k2B, p2A) 27
[30, 31, 32] times.
Round 6 (K2B, p2A) 17 [19, 19, 20] times,
using B, k1, skpo, k1A, using B, k2 tog, k1B,
p2A, (k2B, p2A) 26 [29, 30, 31] times.
Round 7 (K2C, p2A) 17 [19, 19, 20] times,
using C, skpo, k1A, using C, k2 tog, p2A,
(k2C, p2A) 26 [29, 30, 31] times.
Round 8 (K2C, p2A) 16 [18, 18, 19] times,
k2C, using A, p1, yb, skpo, k1, k2 tog, p1,
(k2C, p2A) 26 [29, 30, 31] times.
Round 9 (K2C, p2A) 16 [18, 18, 19] times,
k2C, using A, skpo, k1, k2 tog, (k2C, p2A) 26
[29, 30, 31] times.
Using A, cast off in rib.

ARMBANDS

With right side facing, using circular needle
size 2¾mm, 40cm long, yarn A and beg at
centre of cast off sts at armhole, pick up and k
156 [168, 172, 184] sts evenly around armhole
edge. Work in rounds as follows:-
Main colour combination
Rounds 1 to 3 (K2D, p2A) to end.
Rounds 4 to 6 (K2C, p2A) to end.
Rounds 7 to 9 (K2B, p2A) to end.
Using A, cast off in rib.
Alternative colour combination
Rounds 1 to 3 (K2D, p2A) to end.
Rounds 4 to 6 (K2B, p2A) to end.
Rounds 7 to 9 (K2C, p2A) to end.
Using A, cast off in rib.

FINISHING

Darn in any loose ends. Block as given on
p. 140.

CHILD'S SET FAIR ISLE

The charming hearts pattern used on this child's hat, scarf and mitts set shows that Fair Isle is really the "folk art" of the Shetland Isles. Knitted in two sizes, the hat has "lug pieces" to keep tiny ears warm in the coldest weather.

Traditional design by Margaret Stuart

MATERIALS

Yarn

These items are knitted in Shetland 2 ply jumper weight wool, which is the equivalent of standard 4 ply wool

A 2 [2] × 2oz hanks, blue

B 1 [2] × 2oz hanks, red

C 1 [1] × 2oz hanks, white

D 1 [1] × 2oz hanks, mustard

Needles

1 pair size 3¼mm

1 set of double-pointed needles size 3mm

1 set of double-pointed needles size 3¼mm

Crochet hook

Notions

1 button, 1.3cm in diameter

MEASUREMENTS

To fit child aged 2 to 4 years [4 to 6 years]

Scarf

1 Width 13.5 [15.5]cm, 5¼ [6]in

2 Length, including fringe 117 [120]cm, 46 [47]in

Lug Hat

3 Width 23 [25]cm, 9 [9¾]in

Mitts

4 Width 8 [8]cm, 3 [3]in

5 Length 19.5 [21]cm, 7½ [8¼]in

Tension

31 sts and 35 rows measure 10cm over pattern on 3¼mm needles (or size needed to obtain given tension)

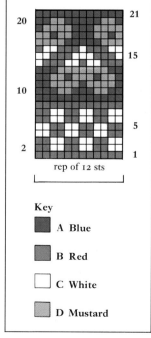

Special note

If you have not knitted with two colours of yarn in a row before, please see p. 139.

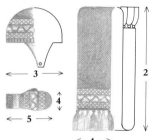

Key

A Blue

B Red

C White

D Mustard

rep of 12 sts

SCARF

Carry yarn not in use loosely across wrong side of work. Using set of double-pointed needles size 3¼mm and yarn A, cast on 84 [96] sts. Work 3 rounds in k1, p1 rib. Reading rounds from right to left, work 29 rounds in st st and patt from chart. Then cont in yarn A only.

Next round K3 [2], *k2 tog, k2 [4]; rep from * 18 [14] times more, k2 tog, k3 [2]. *64 [80] sts.*

Knit 268 [278] rounds.

Next round K3 [2], *inc in next st, k2 [4]; rep from * 18 [14] times more, inc in next st, k3 [2]. *84 [96] sts.*

Work 29 rounds in patt from chart. Using A, work 3 rounds in k1, p1 rib. Cast off in rib.

Finishing

Flatten tube in half, so that the round ends fall along one fold. Block as given on p. 140. To make fringe, cut yarns into 22cm lengths in colours as desired. Using 10 strands together, crochet hook and working through double thickness, make 7 fringes at each end of scarf.

LUG HAT

Carry yarn not in use loosely across wrong side of work.

Crown

Using set of double-pointed needles size 3¼mm and yarn A, cast on 132 [144] sts. Mark the 14th [15th] and 42nd [45th] st at beg (for left ear flap) and at end (for right ear flap) of cast on row. Cont in rounds as follows:

Round 1 (K2B, p2A) to end.
Rep this round 7 [9] times more.

Next round Using A, *k10 [11], inc in next st; rep from * to end. *144 [156] sts.*

Reading rounds from right to left, cont in st st and patt from chart until 28 rounds have been worked.

Shape crown

Next round Using B, k7, *k2 tog, k14 [12]; rep from * 7 [9] times more, k2 tog, k7. *135 [145] sts.*

Cont in A only.

Next round *K12 [13], k3 tog, k12 [13]; rep from * to end.

Next round Knit.

Next round *K11 [12], k3 tog, k11 [12]; rep from * to end.

Next round Knit.

Next round *K10 [11], k3 tog, k10 [11]; rep from * to end.

Next round Knit.

Cont dec in this way on next round and every foll alt round until 15 sts rem.

Next round (K3 tog) to end. *5 sts.*

Break off yarn, thread end through rem sts, pull up and fasten off.

Right ear flap

With right side facing, using 3¼mm needles and yarn A, pick up and k 28 [30] sts between markers. Work backwards and forwards as follows:

Row 1 (Wrong side) K3A, (p1A, 1B) to last 3 sts, k3A.

Row 2 K3A, (1A, 1B) to last 3 sts, k3A.

These 2 rows form patt. Work 0 [2] rows in patt.

Cont in patt shaping ear flap as follows:

Next row K3A, skpo, patt to last 5 sts, k2 tog, k3A.

Next row K3A, patt to last 3 sts, k3A.

Rep last 2 rows until 8 sts rem, ending with a wrong side row**. Using A only, k 22 [26] rows.

Next row K3, cast off 2, k to end.

Next row K to end, casting on 2 sts over those cast off in previous row.

K 6 rows. Cast off.

Left ear flap

Work as given for right ear flap to **.

Using A only k 8 rows. Cast off.

Finishing

Block as given on p. 140. Sew on button.

MITTS

Carry yarn not in use loosely across wrong side of work.

Left mitt

Using set of four double-pointed needles size 3mm and yarn A, cast on 36 sts. Work 8 rounds in k1, p1 rib. Change to yarn B and rib 4 rounds. Change to yarn C and rib 4 rounds. Change to yarn A and rib 8 rounds.

Next round (Inc in next st, k2) to end. *48 sts.*

K 2 [5] rounds. Change to set of double-pointed needles size 3¼mm. Reading rounds from right to left, cont in st st and patt from chart, work 7 rounds**.

Divide for thumb

Next round Patt 17 [16] sts, sl next 7 [8] sts on to a safety pin, cast on 7 [8], patt to end.

Work a further 21 rows in patt. Cont in yarn A only. K 2 [5] rounds.

Next round (K2, skpo, k16, k2 tog, k2) twice.

Next round (K2, skpo, k14, k2 tog, k2) twice.

Next round (K2, skpo, k12, k2 tog, k2) twice.

Cont dec in this way on every round until 16 sts rem. With 8 sts on first and last needle, graft top seam.

Thumb

With right side facing and using A, k 7 [8] sts on a safety pin, then pick up and k 7 [8] sts along cast on sts. K 16 [18] rounds on these 14 [16] sts.

Next round (K1, k2 tog) to last 2 [1] sts, k2 [1] sts.

Next round (K2 tog, k1) to last 1 [2] sts, k1 [2].

Next round Sl 1, k2 tog, psso, k1, sl 1, k2 tog, psso, k 0 [1] st.

Break off yarn, thread end through rem sts, pull up and fasten off.

Right mitt

Work as given for left mitt to **.

Divide for thumb

Next round Patt 24, sl next 7 [8] sts on to safety pin, cast on 7 [8] sts, patt to end.

Complete to match left mitt.

Finishing

Darn in any loose ends. Block as given on p. 140.

DIAMOND FAIR ISLE

A pretty waistcoat in a pastel colour scheme, the pattern of "peaks" or "shaded diamonds" was very popular in Shetland knitting of the 1940s. An alternative colour combination in 4 ply cotton is shown opposite.

Traditional design by Margaret Stuart

MATERIALS

This design has been knitted in two different colour combinations, the main one using Shetland 2 ply jumper weight wool, the alternative using 4 ply cotton. Although separate yarn quantities are given for both, the colour chart shows just the main colour combination. In order to use the chart for the second colour combination, substitute the alternative colours for each yarn (A, B, C etc) for those on the chart.

Yarn for main colour combination

This garment is knitted in Shetland 2 ply jumper weight wool, which is the equivalent of standard 4 ply wool

A 2 [2, 2, 3] × 2oz hanks, blue
B 1 [2, 2, 2] × 2oz hanks, raspberry
C 2 [2, 2, 2] × 2oz hanks, mustard
D 2 [2, 2, 2] × 2oz hanks, white

Yarn for alternative colour combination

Mercerised 4 ply cotton

A 3 [3, 3, 4] × 50g balls, dark green
B 1 [2, 2, 2] × 50g balls, brick
C 2 [2, 2, 2] × 50g balls, light green
D 2 [2, 2, 2] × 50g balls, white

Shown opposite are alternative colour combinations for Diamond Fair Isle and Katie's Fair Isle.

Needles

1 pair size 2¾mm

1 pair size 3mm

1 circular needle size 2¾mm, 80cm long

1 circular needle size 2¾mm, 40cm long

1 circular needle size 3mm, 80cm long

Notions

5 buttons, 1.7cm in diameter

2 stitch holders

MEASUREMENTS

To fit chest 86 [91, 97, 102]cm

34 [36, 38, 40]in

1 Actual chest size 97 [105, 112, 119]cm

38 [41¼, 44, 46¾]in

2 Length to back neck 56 [59, 62, 64]cm

22 [23¼, 24¼, 25¼]in

Tension

33 sts and 38 rows measure 10cm over pattern
on 3mm needles (or size needed to obtain
given tension)

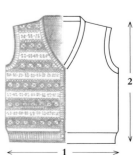

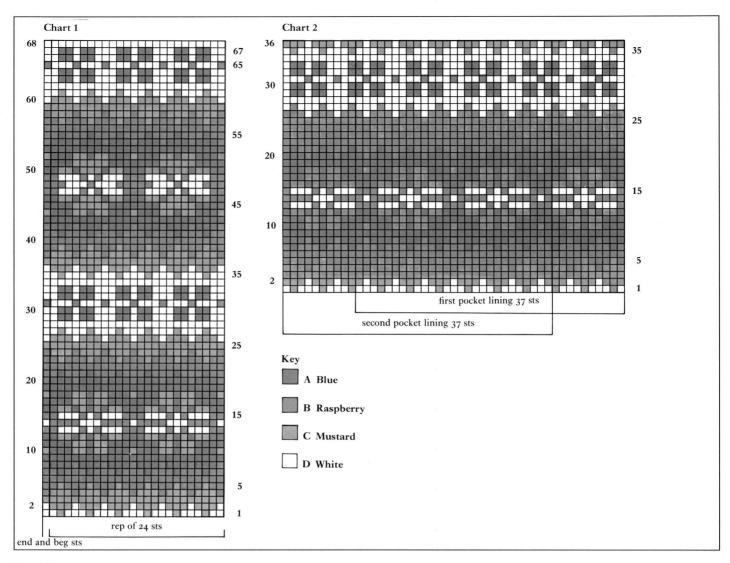

Chart 1

68
67
65
60
55
50
45
40
35
30
25
20
15
10
5
2
1

rep of 24 sts

end and beg sts

Chart 2

36
35
30
25
20
15
10
5
2
1

first pocket lining 37 sts

second pocket lining 37 sts

Key

A Blue

B Raspberry

C Mustard

D White

Special note

If you have not knitted with two colours of yarn in a row before, please see p. 139.

POCKET LININGS

Carry yarn not in use loosely across wrong side of work. Using 3mm needles and yarn A, cast on 37 sts. P 1 row in D. Reading odd numbered (k) rows from right to left and even numbered (p) rows from left to right and beg k row, cont in st st, work 36 rows from chart 2. Leave these sts on a spare needle. Make another pocket lining to match.

MAIN PART

Using circular needle size 2¾mm, 80cm long and A, cast on 310 [334, 358, 382] sts. Work backwards and forwards as follows:-
Row 1 (Right side) K2B, (p2A, k2B) to end.
Row 2 P2B, (k2A, p2B) to end.
Rows 3 and 4 As rows 1 and 2.
Row 5 K2C, (p2A, k2B) to end.
Row 6 P2C, (k2A, p2C) to end.
Rows 7 and 8 As rows 5 and 6.
Row 9 K2D, (p2A, k2D) to end.
Row 10 P2D, (k2A, p2D) to end.

Rows 11 and 12 As rows 9 and 10.
Rows 13 to 16 As rows 5 to 8.
Rows 17 to 20 As rows 1 to 4.
Change to circular needles size 3mm. K 1 row in A, inc 3 sts evenly. *313 [337, 361, 385] sts.* P 1 row in D. Cont in st st and patt from chart 1, work 36 rows.
Place pocket
Next row Patt 25 sts, sl next 37 sts on to stitch holder, patt across first pocket lining, patt to last 62 sts, sl next 37 sts on to stitch holder, patt across second pocket lining, patt to end.
Cont in patt until work measures 35 [35, 38, 38]cm from beg, ending with a wrong side row.
Divide for armholes
Next row Patt 66 [72, 75, 81] sts, cast off 20 [20, 24, 24], patt 141 [153, 163, 175] sts including st used in casting off, cast off 20 [20, 24, 24], patt to end.
Complete left front first. Keep continuity of patt.
Next row Patt to end.
Next row K1, skpo, patt to last 2 sts, k2 tog.
Rep last 2 rows 4 [5, 5, 5] times more.
Next row Patt to end.
Next row Patt to last 2 sts, k2 tog.

Next row Patt to end.
Next row K1, skpo, patt to last 2 sts, k2 tog.
Rep last 4 rows 3 times more. Keeping armhole edge straight, cont dec at neck edge as set on every foll alt row until 35 [39, 42, 47] sts rem, then on every foll 4th row until 29 [31, 34, 38] sts rem. Cont straight until armhole measures 20 [23, 23, 25]cm, ending at armhole edge.
Shape shoulder Cast off 10 [10, 11, 13] sts at beg of next row and foll alt row. Work 1 row.
Cast off rem 9 [11, 12, 12] sts.
With wrong side facing, rejoin appropriate yarn to 141 [153, 163, 175] sts for back.
Next row Patt to end.
Next row K1, skpo, patt to last 3 sts, k2 tog, k1.
Rep last 2 rows 4 [5, 5, 5] times more.
Next 3 rows Patt to end.
Next row K1, skpo, patt to last 3 sts, k2 tog, k1.
Rep last 4 rows 3 times more. *123 [133, 143, 155] sts.* Cont straight until armholes measure 20 [23, 23, 25]cm, ending with a wrong side row.
Shape shoulders Cast off 10 [10, 11, 13] sts at beg of next 4 rows and 9 [11, 12, 12] sts at beg of foll 2 rows. Leave rem 65 [71, 75, 79]

sts on a spare needle.

With wrong side facing, rejoin appropriate
yarn to rem 66 [72, 75, 81] sts for right front.

Next row Patt to end.

Next row Skpo, patt to last 3 sts, k2 tog, k1.

Rep last 2 rows 4 [5, 5, 5] times more.

Next row Patt to end.

Next row Skpo, patt to end.

Next row Patt to end.

Next row Skpo, patt to last 3 sts, k2 tog, k1.

Complete as given for left front.

BUTTON BAND

Join shoulder seams. With right side facing,
using circular needle size 2¾mm, 80cm long
and yarn A, pick up and k 112 [112, 120, 120]
sts up right front to front shaping, 73 [82, 82,
90] sts up shaped edge to shoulder, k 32 [35,
37, 39], k2 tog, k 31 [34, 36, 38] across back
neck sts, pick up and k 73 [82, 82, 90] sts
down shaped edge of left front and 112 [112,
120, 120] sts down left front. *434 [458, 478,
498] sts*. Work backwards and forwards as
follows:-

Row 1 (Wrong side) P2D, (k2A, p2D) to end.

Row 2 K2D, (p2A, k2D) to end.

Row 3 As row 1.

The last 2 rows form rib. Using C instead of
D, cont in rib.

Row 4 Rib 4, *cast off 2, rib 24 [24, 26, 26];
rep from * 4 times more, rib to end.

Row 5 Rib to end, casting on 2 sts over those
cast off in previous row.

Rib 1 row. Using B instead of D, rib 3 rows.
Using A, cast off in rib.

ARMBANDS

With right side facing, using circular needle
size 2¾mm, 40cm long, yarn A and beg at
centre of cast off sts for armhole, pick up and
k 156 [172, 172, 184] sts evenly around
armhole edge. Work in rounds as follows:-

Rounds 1 to 3 (K2D, p2A) to end.

Rounds 4 to 6 (K2C, p2A) to end.

Rounds 7 to 9 (K2B, p2A) to end.

Using A, cast off in rib.

POCKET EDGINGS

With right side facing, using 2¾mm needles,
rejoin yarn A to the 37 sts on pocket top. K 1
row, inc 1 st at centre. *38 sts*. Work 9 rows in
rib as given for front band, omitting buttonholes. Using A, cast off in rib.

FINISHING

Darn in any loose ends. Block as given on
p. 140. Catch down pocket linings and sides of
pocket edgings. Sew on buttons.

*Top: Diamond Fair Isle, main colour
combination.*
*Centre: Diamond Fair Isle, alternative colour
combination.*
*Bottom: Katie's Fair Isle, alternative colour
combination.*

KATIE'S FAIR ISLE

This intricate pattern comes from a sweater originally knitted early this century. Katie Williamson used to knit it for Margaret Stuart, hence it has become known as "Katie's pattern". The design features rows of O.X.O. patterns, including the Armada cross, with "peerie" patterns in between. The woollen slipover uses authentic Fair Isle colours, including madder red and indigo blue along with natural black and white. An alternative, summery version is also shown in cotton. This Fair Isle is knitted in the traditional way, in the round.

MATERIALS

This design has been knitted in two different colour combinations, the main one using Shetland 2 ply jumper weight wool, the alternative using 4 ply cotton. Although separate yarn quantities are given for both, the colour chart shows just the main colour combination. In order to use the chart for the second colour combination, substitute the alternative colours for each yarn (A, B, C etc) for those on the chart. On the cotton version shown on page 65, the two larger bands of pattern have been knitted in reverse order.

Yarn for main colour combination

This garment is knitted in Shetland 2 ply jumper weight wool, which is the equivalent of standard 4 ply wool

A 2 [2, 2, 2, 2] × 2oz hanks, blue

B 1 [1, 1, 1, 1] × 2oz hanks, mustard

C 1 [1, 1, 1, 1] × 2oz hanks, brown

D 1 [1, 1, 1, 1] × 2oz hanks, white

E 1 [1, 1, 2, 2] × 2oz hanks, red

F 1 [1, 1, 1, 1] × 2oz hanks, Shetland black

Yarn for alternative colour combination

Mercerised 4 ply cotton

A 2 [2, 2, 2, 3] × 50g balls, pale blue

B 1 [1, 1, 1, 1] × 50g balls, pale pink

C 1 [1, 1, 1, 1] × 50g balls, sage

D 2 [2, 2, 3, 3] × 50g balls, cream

E 2 [2, 2, 2, 2] × 50g balls, dark pink

F 1 [1, 1, 1, 1] × 50g balls, mustard

Needles

1 circular needle size 2¾mm, 40cm long

1 circular needle size 2¾mm, 60cm long

1 circular needle size 3mm, 80cm long

MEASUREMENTS

To fit chest 86 [91, 97, 102, 107]cm

34 [36, 38, 40, 42]in

1 Actual chest size 92 [98, 104, 109, 114]cm

36¼ [38½, 41, 43, 45]in

2 Length to back neck 55 [58, 58, 61, 63]cm

21½ [22¾, 22¾, 24, 24¾]in

Tension

33 sts and 38 rows measure 10cm over pattern on 3mm needles (or size needed to obtain given tension)

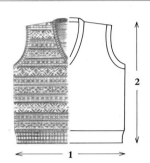

Special note

If you have not knitted with two colours of yarn in a row before, please see p. 139.

BACK and FRONT

This garment is knitted in one piece to the armholes. Carry yarn not in use loosely across wrong side of work. Using circular needle size 2¾mm, 60cm long and yarn A, cast on 284 [300, 316, 332, 348] sts. Cont in rounds as follows:

Rounds 1 to 4 (K2B, p2A) to end.

Rounds 5 to 8 (K2C, p2A) to end.

Rounds 9 to 12 (K2D, p2A) to end.

Rounds 13 to 16 (K2E, p2A) to end.

Rounds 17 to 24 As rounds 1 to 8.

Change to circular needle size 3mm.

Next round **Using A, k6 [9, 7, 5, 10], *pick up loop lying between sts and k tbl – referred to as m1, k13 [12, 12, 12, 11]; rep from * 9 [10, 11, 12, 13] times more, m1, k6 [9, 7, 5, 10]**; rep from ** to ** once more. *306 [324, 342, 360, 378] sts.*

Cont in st st and patt as given on chart reading rounds from right to left until work measures 35 [35, 35, 38, 38]cm from beg, finishing 10 [6, 11, 7, 12] sts before end of last round.

Divide for back and front

Next round *Cast off 20 [21, 22, 23, 24] sts, patt 133 [141, 149, 157, 165] sts including st used in casting off; rep from * once more.

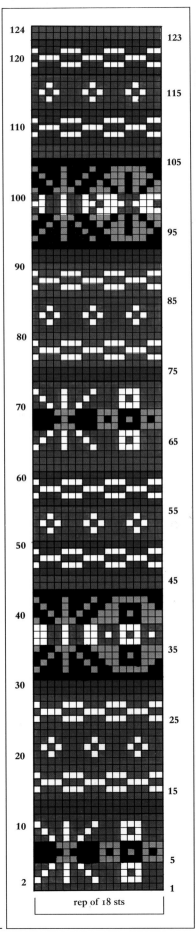

rep of 18 sts

Key

■ **A** Blue

■ **B** Mustard

■ **C** Brown

□ **D** White

■ **E** Red

■ **F** Shetland black

Complete back first. Cont in st st and patt from chart, reading p rows from left to right and working backwards and forwards as follows:

Next row Patt to end.
Next row K1, skpo, patt to last 3 sts, k2 tog, k1.
Rep last 2 rows until 97 [105, 111, 119, 125] sts rem. Cont straight until armholes measure 20 [23, 23, 23, 25]cm, ending with a wrong side row.

Shape shoulders
Next row Cast off 26 [30, 33, 37, 38] sts, patt to last 26 [30, 33, 37, 38] sts, cast off these sts. Leave rem 45 [45, 45, 45, 49] sts on a spare needle. With wrong side facing, rejoin appropriate yarn to rem sts.
Next row Patt 66 [70, 74, 78, 82] sts and turn leaving rem sts on a spare needle.
Complete right side of neck first.
Next row K2 tog, patt to last 3 sts, k2 tog, k1.
Next row Patt to end.
Rep last 2 rows 9 [5, 6, 6, 7] times more.
Next row Patt to last 3 sts, k2 tog, k1.
Next row Patt to end.
Next row K2 tog, patt to last 3 sts, k2 tog, k1.
Next row Patt to end.
Rep last 4 rows 3 [5, 5, 5, 5] times more.
Keeping armhole edge straight, cont dec at neck edge until 26 [30, 33, 37, 38] sts rem. Cont straight until front matches back to shoulder, ending with a wrong side row. Cast off.

Traditional design by Margaret Stuart

With wrong side of front facing, sl centre st on to a safety pin, rejoin appropriate yarn to rem sts and patt to end.
Next row K1, skpo, patt to last 2 sts, k2 tog.
Next row Patt to end.
Rep last 2 rows 9 [5, 6, 6, 7] times more.
Next row K1, skpo, patt to end.
Next row Patt to end.
Next row K1, skpo, patt to last 2 sts, k2 tog.
Next row Patt to end.
Complete as given for first side of neck.

NECKBAND

Join shoulder seams. With right side facing, using circular needle size 2¾mm, 60cm long and yarn A, pick up and k 76 [84, 84, 84, 88] sts down left side neck, k centre st on safety pin, pick up and k 76 [84, 84, 84, 88] sts up right side neck, k across 45 [45, 45, 45, 49] centre back sts inc 1 st at centre. *199 [215, 215, 215, 227] sts.* Work in rounds as follows:

Round 1 (K2E, p2A) 18 [20, 20, 20, 21] times, k2E, using A, skpo, k1, k2 tog, k2E, (p2A, k2E) 30 [32, 32, 32, 34] times.
Round 2 (K2E, p2A) 18 [20, 20, 20, 21] times, k1E, using E, skpo, k1A, using E, k2 tog, k1, (p2A, k2E) 30 [32, 32, 32, 34] times.
Round 3 (K2D, p2A) 18 [20, 20, 20, 21] times, using D, skpo, k1A, using D, k2 tog, (p2A, k2D) 30 [32, 32, 32, 34] times.
Round 4 (K2D, p2A) 17 [19, 19, 19, 20] times, k2D, using A, p1, yb, skpo, k1, k2 tog, p1, k2D, (p2A, k2D) 29 [31, 31, 31, 33] times.
Round 5 (K2C, p2A) 17 [19, 19, 19, 20] times, k2C, using A, skpo, k1, k2 tog, k2C, (p2A, k2C) 29 [31, 31, 31, 33] times.
Round 6 (K2C, p2A) 17 [19, 19, 19, 20] times, k1C, using C, skpo, k1A, using C, k2 tog, k1, (p2A, k2C) 29 [31, 31, 31, 33] times.
Round 7 (K2B, p2A) 17 [19, 19, 19, 20] times, using B, skpo, k1A, using B, k2 tog, (p2A, k2B) 29 [31, 31, 31, 33] times.
Round 8 (K2B, p2A) 16 [18, 18, 18, 19]

times, k2B, using A, p1, yb, skpo, k1, k2 tog, p1, k2B, (p2A, k2B) 28 [30, 30, 30, 32] times.
Using A, cast off in rib, dec as before.

ARMBANDS

With right side facing, using circular needle size 2¾mm, 40cm long, yarn A and beg at centre of cast off sts at armhole, pick up and knit 156 [168, 168, 168, 184] sts evenly around armhole edge. Work in rounds as follows:
Rounds 1 and 2 (K2E, p2A) to end.
Rounds 3 and 4 (K2D, p2A) to end.
Rounds 5 and 6 (K2C, p2A) to end.
Rounds 7 and 8 (K2B, p2A) to end.
Using yarn A, cast off in rib.

FINISHING

Darn in any loose ends. Block as given on p. 140.

THREE CROSS FAIR ISLE

An early Fair Isle pattern in a light-weight double knitting wool, and a modern colour scheme, retains a traditional look with its banded patterns and striped ribs. Knitted in pieces, and then seamed, the sweater is an easy, generous shape that suits both men and women.

MATERIALS

Yarn

Lightweight double knitting wool

A 8 [9, 9] × 25g hanks, olive green

B 8 [8, 9] × 25g hanks, dark red

C 4 [4, 4] × 25g hanks, pale mauve

D 3 [3, 3] × 25g hanks, blue/green

E 3 [3, 4] × 25g hanks, gold

F 3 [3, 3] × 25g hanks, light red

Needles

1 pair size 3¾mm

1 pair size 4mm

1 circular needle size 4mm, 40cm long

Notions

2 stitch holders

Designed by Audur Norris and Sarah Keogh

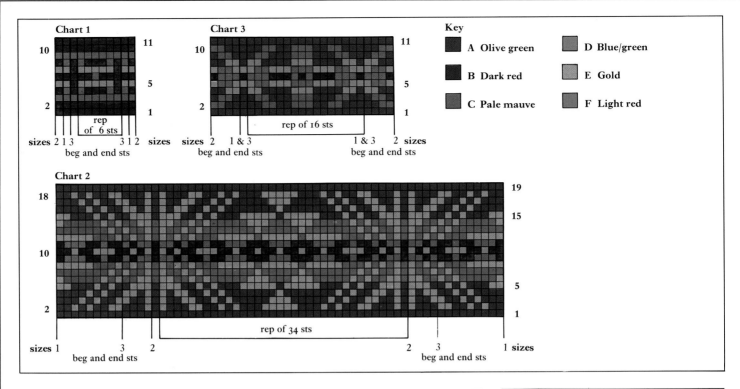

Key

■	A Olive green	▦	D Blue/green
■	B Dark red	▨	E Gold
▨	C Pale mauve	▨	F Light red

Chart 1 — rep of 6 sts
sizes 2 1 3 · 3 1 2 sizes
beg and end sts

Chart 3 — rep of 16 sts
sizes 2 1 & 3 · 1 & 3 2 sizes
beg and end sts · beg and end sts

Chart 2 — rep of 34 sts
sizes 1 · 3 · 2 · 2 · 3 · 1 sizes
beg and end sts · beg and end sts

MEASUREMENTS

To fit chest 91 [97, 102]cm

36 [38, 40]in

1 Actual chest size 98 [104, 110]cm

38½ [41, 43¼]in

2 Length to back neck 64 [65, 66]cm

25¼ [25½, 26]in

3 Sleeve seam 47 [47, 50]cm

18½ [18½, 19¾]in

Tension

26 sts and 28 rows measure 10cm over pattern

on 4mm needles (or size needed to obtain

given tension)

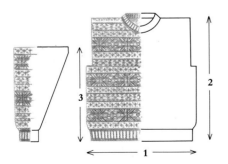

Special note

If you have not knitted with two colours of
yarn in a row before, please see p. 139.

BACK

Carry yarn not in use loosely across wrong
side of work. Using 3¾mm needles and yarn
A, cast on 128 [136, 144] sts.
Row 1 (Right side) (K2B, p2A) to end.
Row 2 (K2A, p2B) to end.
Row 3 (K2F, p2A) to end.
Row 4 (K2A, p2F) to end.
Row 5 (K2E, p2A) to end.
Row 6 (K2A, p2E) to end.
Row 7 (K2D, p2A) to end.
Row 8 (K2A, p2D) to end.
Row 9 (K2C, p2A) to end.
Row 10 (K2A, p2C) to end.
Rows 11 and 12 As rows 7 and 8.
Rows 13 and 14 As rows 5 and 6.
Rows 15 and 16 As rows 3 and 4.
Rows 17 and 18 As rows 1 and 2, inc 1 st at
centre of last row. *129 [137, 145] sts.*
Change to 4mm needles. Reading k rows from
right to left and p rows from left to right, beg
k row, cont in st st and patt as follows:-
Rows 1 to 11 Work rows 1 to 11 from chart 1.
Rows 12 to 30 Work rows 1 to 19 from chart 2.
Rows 31 to 41 Work rows 1 to 11 from chart 1.
Rows 42 to 52 Work rows 1 to 11 from chart 3.
These 52 rows form patt. Cont in patt until
work measures 40cm from beg, ending with
row 10 of chart 1.
Shape armholes
Next row Patt 8 and sl these sts on to safety
pin, patt to last 8 sts, sl these 8 sts on to safety
pin. *113 [121, 129] sts.*
Keeping continuity of patt, cont straight until
armholes measure 24 [25, 26]cm, ending with
a wrong side row.
Shape neck
Next row Patt 40 [44, 48] and turn; leave rem
sts on a spare needle.
Complete right side of neck first.
Next row P2, p2 tog, patt to end.
Next row Patt to last 4 sts, k2 tog, k2.

Rep last 2 rows once. Patt 1 row. Leave rem
36 [40, 44] sts on a spare needle. With right
side facing, sl next 33 sts on to stitch holder,
rejoin appropriate yarn to rem sts and patt to
end.
Next row Patt to last 4 sts, p2 tog tbl, p2.
Next row K2, skpo, patt to end.
Rep last 2 rows once. Patt 1 row. Leave rem
36 [40, 44] sts on a spare needle.

72

FRONT

Work as given for back until armholes measure 18 [19, 20]cm, ending with a wrong side row.
Shape neck
Next row Patt 46 [50, 54] and turn; leave rem sts on a spare needle.
Complete left side of neck first.
Next row P2, p2 tog, patt to end.
Next row Patt to last 4 sts, k2 tog, k2.
Rep last 2 rows 4 times more. *36 [40, 44] sts.*
Cont straight until front matches back to shoulder, ending with a wrong side row.
Graft shoulder With wrong sides of back and front together, cast off 36 [40, 44] sts, taking 1 st from each needle and working them tog. With right side of front facing, sl next 21 sts on to stitch holder, rejoin appropriate yarn to rem sts and patt to end.
Next row Patt to last 4 sts, p2 tog tbl, p2.
Next row K2, skpo, patt to end.
Complete as given for first side of neck.

SLEEVES

With right side facing, sl 8 sts on safety pin on to circular needle size 4mm, rejoin yarn B and pick up and k 133 [135, 141] sts evenly around armhole edge then k 8 from safety pin. *149 [151, 157] sts.* Work backwards and forwards. Beg p row, cont in st st and patt as given for 2nd [3rd, 3rd] sizes on back, dec 2 [1, 2] sts at each end of 2nd row and 1 st at each end of 4 [2, 4] foll 2nd [4th, 2nd] rows, then on 6 foll 3rd rows and 2 foll 5th rows. Keeping continuity of patt, dec 1 st at each end of 4th row and every foll 3rd [3rd, 4th] row until 77 [83, 89] sts rem. Work 7 [4, 2] rows straight.
Next row Using B, p7, (p2 tog, p1) to last 7 sts, p7. *56 [60, 64] sts.*
Change to 3¾mm needles. Work 18 rows in rib as given for back welt. Using A, cast off in rib.

NECKBAND

With right side facing, using circular needle size 4mm and yarn B, pick up and k 23 sts down left front neck, k across 21 centre front sts, pick up and k 23 sts up right front neck, 6 sts down right back neck, k across 33 centre back sts, pick up and k 6 sts up left back neck. *112 sts.* Work in rounds as follows:-
Rounds 1 and 2 (K2B, p2A) to end.
Rounds 3 and 4 (K2F, p2A) to end.
Rounds 5 and 6 (K2E, p2A) to end.
Rounds 7 and 8 (K2D, p2A) to end.
Rounds 9 and 10 (K2C, p2A) to end.
Rounds 11 and 12 As rounds 7 and 8.
Rounds 13 and 14 As rounds 5 and 6.
Rounds 15 and 16 As rounds 3 and 4.
Rounds 17 and 18 As rounds 1 and 2.
Using A, cast off in rib.

FINISHING

Darn in any loose ends. Block as given on p. 140. Join side and sleeve seams. Turn neckband in half to wrong side and slip stitch in position.

O·X·O
FAIR ISLE

This beautiful old pattern was taken from a sweater owned by Margaret's grandmother, Margaret Stout, dating from about 1915. All the undyed shades of the Shetland wool are used in the bold O.X.O. pattern. Also shown, overleaf, is an alternative version, knitted in 4 ply Botany wool. This Fair Isle is knitted in the traditional way, in the round.

MATERIALS

This design has been knitted in two different colour combinations, the main one using Shetland 2 ply jumper weight wool, the alternative using 4 ply Botany wool. Separate yarn quantities are given for both. Although the same pattern is used on each sweater, the yarn sequence is not the same, so two different colour charts have been provided.

Yarn for main colour combination

This garment is knitted in Shetland 2 ply jumper weight wool, which is the equivalent of standard 4 ply wool

A 2 [3, 3, 3] × 2oz hanks, Shetland black	
B 1 [1, 2, 2] × 2oz hanks, dark grey	
C 1 [1, 1, 1] × 2oz hank, mid grey	
D 1 [1, 1, 1] × 2oz hank, light grey	
E 3 [3, 3, 4] × 2oz hanks, fawn	
F 2 [2, 2, 2] × 2oz hanks, brown	

Yarn for alternative colour combination

4 ply Botany wool

A 4 [4, 5, 5] × 25g hanks, dark blue mix	
B 3 [3, 3, 3] × 25g hanks, mid blue	
C 1 [1, 1, 1] × 25g hanks, yellow	
D 3 [3, 3, 3] × 25g hanks, pink	
E 5 [6, 6, 6] × 25g hanks, pale blue	
F 3 [3, 4, 4] × 25g hanks, dark blue	

Needles

1 circular needle size 2¾mm, 60cm long

1 set of four double-pointed needles size 2¾mm

1 circular needle size 3mm, 80cm long

1 circular needle size 3mm, 40cm long

Notions

1 stitch holder

MEASUREMENTS

To fit chest 86 [91, 97, 102]cm

34 [36, 38, 40]in

1 Actual chest size 96 [103, 109, 115]cm

$37\frac{3}{4}$ [$40\frac{1}{2}$, 43, $45\frac{1}{4}$]in

2 Length to back neck 55 [58, 63, 65]cm

$21\frac{3}{4}$ [23, 25, $25\frac{1}{2}$]in

3 Sleeve seam 43 [45, 50, 50]cm

17 [$17\frac{3}{4}$, $19\frac{3}{4}$, $19\frac{3}{4}$]in

Tension

33 sts and 38 rows measure 10cm over pattern on 3mm needles (or size needed to obtain given tension)

Special note

If you have not knitted with two colours of yarn in a row before, please see p. 139.

Main colour combination

rep of 20 sts

Key

A Shetland black

B Dark grey

C Mid grey

D Light grey

E Fawn

F Brown

Traditional design by Margaret Stuart

BACK and FRONT

This garment is knitted in one piece to the armholes. Carry yarn not in use loosely across wrong side of work.

Using circular needle size 2¾mm and yarn A, cast on 280 [300, 320, 340] sts. Cont in rounds as follows:-

Rounds 1 to 3 (K2B, p2A) to end.
Rounds 4 to 6 (K2C, p2A) to end.
Rounds 7 and 8 (K2D, p2A) to end.
Rounds 9 and 10 (K2E, p2A) to end.
Rounds 11 and 12 As rounds 7 and 8.
Rounds 13 to 15 As rounds 4 to 6.
Rounds 16 to 18 As rounds 1 to 3.

Change to circular needle size 3mm, 80cm long.

Next round Using A, *k7 [7, 8, 8], pick up loop lying between sts and k tbl – referred to as m1, k7 [8, 8, 9], m1; rep from * to end. *320 [340, 360, 380] sts.*

Reading rounds from right to left and beg with round 19 [8, 1, 1] cont in st st and patt from chart until work measures 35 [38, 40, 40]cm from beg, ending with round 7 and 11 [7, 12, 8] sts before end of last round.

Divide for back and front

Next round *Cast off 23 [25, 25, 27], patt 137 [145, 155, 163] sts including st used in casting off; rep from * once more.

Complete back first. Keeping continuity of patt, work backwards and forwards in st st, reading p rows from left to right from chart.

Next row (Wrong side) Patt to end.
Next row K1, skpo, patt to last 3 sts, k2 tog, k1.

Rep last 2 rows until 107 [113, 123, 129] sts rem. Cont straight until armholes measure 20 [20, 23, 23]cm, ending with a wrong side row.

Shape shoulders

Next row Cast off 29 [31, 34, 36] sts, patt to last 29 [31, 34, 36] sts, cast off these sts. Leave rem 49 [51, 55, 57] sts on a spare needle.

With wrong side of front facing, rejoin appropriate yarn to rem sts.

Next row P1, p2 tog, patt to last 3 sts, p2 tog tbl, p1.
Next row K1, skpo, patt to last 3 sts, k2 tog, k1.

Rep last 2 rows 4 times more.

Next row Patt to end.

Next row K1, skpo, patt to last 3 sts, k2 tog, k1.

Rep last 2 rows until 107 [113, 123, 129] sts rem. Cont straight until armholes measure 13 [13, 15, 15]cm, ending with a wrong side row.

Shape neck

Next row Patt 36 [38, 42, 44] and turn; leave rem sts on needle.
Complete left side first.
Next row Patt to end.
Next row Patt to last 2 sts, k2 tog.
Rep last 2 rows until 29 [31, 34, 36] sts rem. Cont straight until front matches back to shoulder, ending with a wrong side row. Cast off.
With right side of front facing, sl centre 35 [37, 39, 41] sts on to stitch holder, rejoin appropriate yarn to rem sts and patt to end.

Next row Patt to end.
Next row Skpo, patt to end.
Complete as given for left side neck.

SLEEVES

With right side facing, using circular needle size 3mm, 40cm long, yarn A and beg at centre of cast off sts at armhole, pick up and k 140 [140, 160, 180] sts evenly around armhole edge. Cont in rounds of st st and patt from chart, working rounds in reverse order.

Rounds 1 to 7 As rounds 7 to 1.

Beg with round 40, cont in patt, work 15 [8, 15, 15] rounds.

Next round K1, k2 tog, patt to last 3 sts, skpo, k1.

Patt 5 [6, 6, 5] rounds straight. Keeping continuity of patt, rep last 6 [7, 7, 6] rounds until 100 [100, 120, 130] sts rem, ending with dec round. Patt 5 [0, 11, 0] rounds straight.

Next round Using A, k8 [8, 0, 2], (k2 tog, k1) to last 8 [8, 0, 2] sts, k to end. *72 [72, 80, 88] sts.*

Change to set of four double-pointed needles size 2¾mm. Work 18 rounds in rib as given for welt. Using A, cast off in rib.

NECKBAND

With right side facing, using set of four double-pointed needles size 2¾mm, pick up and k 22 [22, 25, 31] sts down left side neck, k across 35 [37, 39, 41] centre front sts, pick up and k 22 [22, 25, 31] sts up right side neck and k across 49 [51, 55, 57] centre back sts. *128 [132, 144, 160] sts.*

Round 1 (K2E, p2A) to end.
Rep this round 1 [1, 1, 2] times more.
Next round (K2D, p2A) to end.
Rep last round 1 [1, 2, 2] times more.
Next round (K2C, p2A) to end.
Rep last round 1 [2, 2, 2] times more.
Next 3 rounds (K2B, p2A) to end.
Using A, cast off in rib.

FINISHING

Darn in any loose ends. Block as given on p. 140.

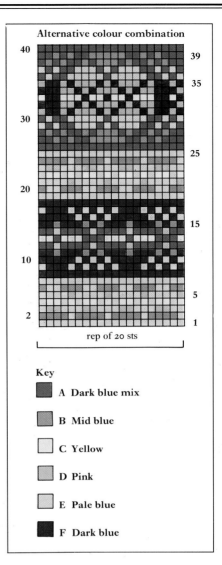

Alternative colour combination

rep of 20 sts

Key

■ A Dark blue mix
■ B Mid blue
□ C Yellow
■ D Pink
■ E Pale blue
■ F Dark blue

ADULT'S SET FAIR ISLE

Traditional design by Margaret Stuart

The lovely old pattern that Katie Williamson used on the slipover, p. 68, is used again on a warm, double thickness scarf. There is also a choice of tammy or beanie cap, and a pair of gloves or matching half finger gloves to complete the set.

MATERIALS

Yarn

These garments are knitted in Shetland 2 ply jumper weight wool, which is the equivalent of standard 4 ply wool.

The yarn quantities given below are sufficient for one set, consisting of a scarf, plus either the beanie or the tammy, and either the finger gloves or the half finger gloves. If you wish to make just one item, the gloves and the hats may be made from oddments of yarn, the scarf requires one hank each of yarns A, B, C and F, and two hanks of yarns D and E.

A $1\frac{1}{2} \times 2$oz hanks, blue

B $1\frac{1}{2} \times 2$oz hanks, mustard

C $1\frac{1}{2} \times 2$oz hanks, brown

D $2\frac{1}{2} \times 2$oz hanks, white

E $2\frac{1}{2} \times 2$oz hanks, red

F $1\frac{1}{2} \times 2$oz hanks, Shetland black

Needles

1 set of four double-pointed needles size $3\frac{1}{4}$mm

Crochet hook

Special note

If you have not knitted with two colours of yarn in a row before, please see p. 139.

MEASUREMENTS

All these items are to fit an average-sized woman.

Scarf

1 Width 18cm, 7in

2 Length, including fringe 180cm, 71in

Beanie

3 Width 24cm, 9½in

Tammy

4 Width of crown 32cm, 12½in

Finger gloves

5 Width 9.5cm, 3¾in

6 Length 29.5cm, 11½in

Half finger gloves

7 Width 9.5cm, 3¾in

8 Length 23cm, 9in

Tension

30 sts and 35 rows measure 10cm over pattern on 3¼mm needles (or size needed to obtain given tension)

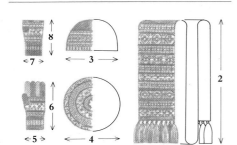

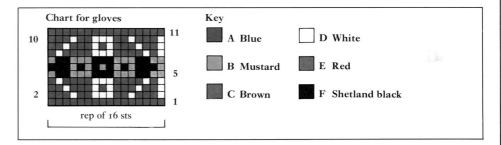

Chart for gloves

Key

A Blue   D White
B Mustard E Red
C Brown   F Shetland black

rep of 16 sts

FINGER GLOVES

Carry yarn not in use loosely across wrong side of work.

Left finger glove

Using set of four double-pointed needles size 3¼mm and yarn F, cast on 56 sts. Work 10 rounds in k2, p2 rib. Change to E and rib 10 rows. Change to C and rib 10 rows. Cont in patt as follows.

Round 1 Using A, (k6, inc in next st) to end. *64 sts.*

Round 2 K in A.

Rounds 3 to 7 As rounds 1 to 5 as given for tammy.

Round 8 Using A, (k31, inc in next st) twice. *66 sts.*

Rounds 9 to 12 As rounds 27 to 30 as given for tammy.

Round 13 Using C, (k31, k2 tog) twice. *64 sts.*

Round 14 K in C.

Rounds 15 to 19 Reading rounds from right to left, work rounds 1 to 5 from chart.

Divide for thumb

Round 20 Following round 6 from chart, patt 24, sl next 8 sts on to a safety pin, cast on 8, patt to end.

Rounds 21 to 25 Work rounds 7 to 11 from chart.

Rounds 26 and 27 K in A.

Round 28 Using C, (k31, inc in next st) twice. *66 sts.*

Rounds 29 to 32 As rounds 7 to 10 as given for tammy.

Round 33 Using E (k31, k2 tog) twice. *64 sts.*

Rounds 34 to 37 As rounds 2 to 5.

Rounds 38 to 39 K in A**.

Divide for fingers

1st finger Leave first 23 sts on first spare needle, using C, k 18, leave rem 23 sts on 2nd spare needle. K 29 rounds on these 18 sts.

Shape top

Next round *(K2 tog) twice, k1, (k2 tog) twice; rep from * once more. *10 sts.*

Next round (K2 tog, k1, k2 tog) twice. *6 sts.*

Next round (K2 tog, k1) twice. *3 sts.*

Break off yarn, thread end through rem sts, pull up and fasten off.

2nd finger Leave first 15 sts on first spare needle, using F, k8, pick up and k1 st from base of first finger, k8 from 2nd spare needle then cast on 1 st, k 32 rounds on these 18 sts. Complete as given for first finger.

3rd finger Leave first 7 sts on first spare needle, using C, k8, pick up and k 1 st from base of 2nd finger, k8 from 2nd spare needle then cast on 1 st. Complete as given for first finger.

4th finger Using F, k rem 7 sts on first spare needle, pick up and k 1 st from base of 3rd finger, k rem 7 sts from 2nd spare needle. K 27 rounds on these 15 sts.

Next round (K2 tog, k1) to end. *10 sts.* Complete as given for first finger.

Thumb With right side facing, using F, k 8 sts on safety pin, pick up and k 1 st from side, k 8 sts along cast on sts and 1 st from side. K 27 rounds on these 18 sts. Complete as given for first finger.

Right finger glove

Work as given for left finger glove, reversing position of thumb as follows:

Round 20 Following round 6 from chart, patt 32, sl next 8 sts on to safety pin, cast on 8, patt to end.

Finishing

Darn in any loose ends. Block as given on p. 140.

HALF FINGER GLOVES

Carry yarn not in use loosely across wrong side of work.

Left half finger glove

Work as given for left finger glove to ** using C instead of A on rounds 1 and 2, 8 to 12, 26 and 27, 38 and 39 and A instead of C on rounds 13 and 14, 28 to 32.

Divide for half fingers

1st half finger Leave first 23 sts on first spare needle, using C, k 18 sts, leave rem 23 sts on 2nd spare needle. K 7 rounds on these 18 sts. Work 3 rounds in k1, p1 rib. Cast off in rib.

2nd half finger Leave first 15 sts on first spare needle, using F, k8, pick up and k 1 st from base of first half finger, k8 then cast on 1 st. K 9 rounds on these 18 sts. Work 3 rounds in k1, p1 rib. Cast off in rib.

3rd half finger Leave first 7 sts on first spare needle, using C, k8, pick up and k1 st from base of 2nd half finger, k8 from 2nd spare needle then cast on 1 st. Complete as given for first half finger.

4th half finger Using F, k rem 7 sts on first spare needle, pick up and k 2 sts from base of 3rd half finger, k rem 7 sts from 2nd spare needle. K 5 rounds on these 16 sts. Work 3 rounds in k1, p1 rib. Cast off in rib.

Half thumb With right side facing and using F, k 8 sts from safety pin and k 1 st from side, 8 sts along cast on sts, 1 st from side. K 9 rounds on these 18 sts. Work 3 rounds in k1, p1 rib. Cast off in rib.

Right half finger glove

Work as given for left half finger glove, reversing position of thumb as follows:

Round 20 Following round 6 from chart, patt 32, sl next 8 sts on to safety pin, cast on 8, patt to end.

Finishing

Darn in any loose ends. Block as given on p. 140.

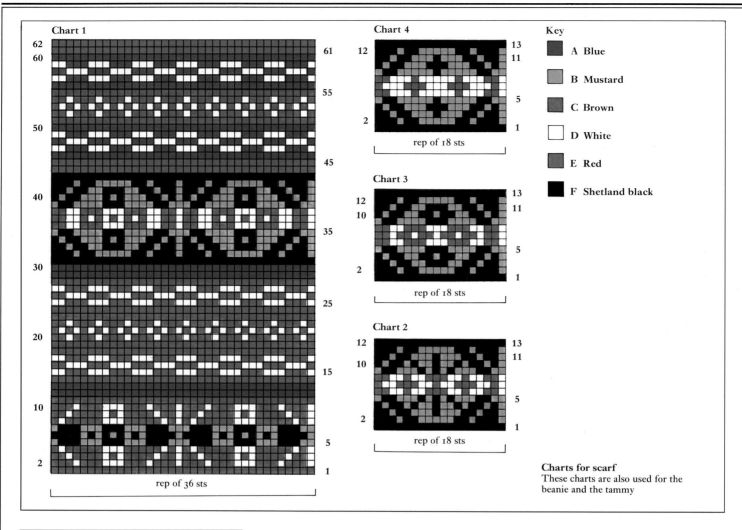

Chart 1

62 60 61
55
50
45
40
35
30
25
20
15
10
5
2 1

rep of 36 sts

Chart 4

12 13
11
5
2 1

rep of 18 sts

Chart 3

12 13
10 11
5
2 1

rep of 18 sts

Chart 2

12 13
10 11
5
2 1

rep of 18 sts

Key

A Blue
B Mustard
C Brown
D White
E Red
F Shetland black

Charts for scarf
These charts are also used for the beanie and the tammy

SCARF

Carry yarn not in use loosely across wrong side of work. Using set of four double-pointed needles and yarn A, cast on 108 sts. Work in rounds. K 8 rounds.

Reading rounds from right to left, cont in st st and patt from charts as follows:

Rounds 1 to 62 Work rounds 1 to 62 from chart 1.

Rounds 63 to 92 Work rounds 1 to 30 from chart 1.

Rounds 93 to 105 Work rounds 1 to 13 from chart 2.

Rounds 106 to 124 Work rounds 44 to 62 from chart 1.

Rounds 125 to 154 As rounds 63 to 92.

Rounds 155 to 167 Work rounds 1 to 13 from chart 3.

Rounds 168 to 186 As rounds 106 to 124.

Rounds 187 to 216 As rounds 63 to 92.

Rounds 217 to 229 Work rounds 1 to 13 from chart 4.

Rounds 230 to 248 As rounds 106 to 124.

Rounds 249 to 259 Work rounds 1 to 11 from chart 1.

Rounds 260 to 278 As rounds 106 to 124.

Rounds 279 to 291 Work rounds 1 to 13 from chart 4.

Rounds 292 to 310 Work rounds 12 to 30 from chart 1.

Rounds 311 to 321 Work rounds 1 to 11 from chart 1.

Rounds 322 to 340 As rounds 106 to 124.

Rounds 341 to 353 Work rounds 1 to 13 from chart 3.

Rounds 354 to 402 As rounds 292 to 340.

Rounds 403 to 415 Work rounds 1 to 13 from chart 2.

Rounds 416 to 464 As rounds 292 to 340.

Rounds 465 to 477 Work rounds 31 to 43 from chart 1.

Rounds 478 to 507 As rounds 292 to 321. Using yarn A, k 8 rounds. Cast off.

Finishing

Flatten tube in half, so that the round ends fall along one fold. Block as given on p. 140. To make fringe, cut yarn A into lengths of about 30cm. Using 14 strands together, crochet hook and working through double thickness, make 9 fringes at each end of scarf.

BEANIE

Carry yarn not in use loosely across wrong side of work. Using set of four double-pointed needles size 3¼mm and yarn F, cast on 144 sts. Work in rounds as follows:

Rounds 1 to 3 (K2E, p2F) to end.

Rounds 4 to 6 (K2C, p2F) to end.

Rounds 7 to 9 As rounds 1 to 3.

Round 10 Knit in F.

Reading rounds from right to left, cont in st st and patt from charts as follows:

Rounds 1 to 12 Work rounds 19 to 30 from chart 1 for scarf.

Rounds 13 to 23 Work rounds 1 to 11 from chart for gloves.

Rounds 24 to 35 Work rounds 44 to 55 from chart 1 for scarf.

Cont in F only. K 6 rounds, inc 1 st on last round. *145 sts.*

Shape crown

Next round (K26, k3 tog) to end.

Next round Knit.

Next round (K24, k3 tog) to end.

Next round Knit.

Next round (K22, k3 tog) to end.

Next round Knit.

Cont dec in this way on next round and every foll alt round until 15 sts rem.

Next round (K3 tog) to end.

Break off yarn, thread end through rem sts, pull up and fasten off.

Finishing

Darn in any loose ends. Block as given on p. 140.

TAMMY

Carry yarn not in use loosely across wrong side of work. Using set of four double-pointed needles size 3¼mm and yarn F, cast on 140 sts. Work 24 rounds in k1, p1 rib.
Next round *(K11, inc in next st) twice, k10, inc in next st; rep from * to end. *152 sts.*
Cont in patt as follows:
Round 1 K in E.
Round 2 (K1E, 1D, 2E) to end.
Round 3 (K1D, 1E) to end.
Round 4 As round 2.
Round 5 K in E.
Round 6 Using C, (k37, inc in next st) to end. *156 sts.*
Round 7 (K20D, 3C, 1D) to end.
Round 8 (K2C, 3D, 1C) to end.
Round 9 As round 7.
Round 10 K in C.
Round 11 Using A, (k38, inc in next st) to end. *160 sts.*
Round 12 K in A.
Rounds 13 to 23 Reading rounds from right to left, work rounds 1 to 11 from chart for gloves.
Round 24 Using C, (k19, inc in next st) to end. *168 sts.*
Round 25 K in C.
Round 26 K in A.
Rounds 27 to 30 Using A instead of C as rounds 7 to 10.
Rounds 31 to 35 As rounds 1 to 5.
Round 36 Using A, *(k2, inc in next st) 6 times, (k1, inc in next st) 5 times; rep from * to end. *234 sts.*
Round 37 K in A.
Rounds 38 to 50 Work rounds 1 to 13 from chart 2 for scarf.
Shape crown
Round 51 Using C, *(k4, k2 tog) 4 times, (k3, k2 tog) 3 times; rep from * to end. *192 sts.*
Round 52 K in C.
Rounds 53 to 57 As rounds 26 to 30.
Round 58 Using E, (k46, k2 tog) to end. *188 sts.*
Rounds 59 to 62 As rounds 2 to 5.
Round 63 Using A, *(k3, k2 tog) 3 times, (k2, k2 tog) 8 times; rep from * to end. *144 sts.*
Rounds 64 to 67 As rounds 27 to 30.
Round 68 Using C, (k7, k2 tog) to end. *128 sts.*
Round 69 K in C.
Rounds 70 to 80 Work rounds 1 to 11 from chart for gloves.
Round 81 Using A, *(k1, k2 tog) twice, (k2 tog) 13 times; rep from * to end. *68 sts.*
Round 82 K in A.
Rounds 83 to 86 As rounds 1 to 4.
Round 87 Using E, *k1, (k2 tog) 8 times; rep from * to end. *36 sts.*
Rounds 88 to 92 As rounds 26 to 30.
Round 93 Using E, *k1, (k2 tog) 4 times; rep from * to end. *20 sts.*
Round 94 (Using E, k3 tog, k1D) to end. *10 sts.*
Break off yarn, thread end through rem sts, pull up and fasten off.
Finishing
Fold rib in half to wrong side and slip stitch in position. Darn in any loose ends. Block as given on p. 140, using a large plate to shape the beret.

ARAN

Aran knitting has been popular
with hand knitters over the last fifty years.
The thick cream wool and the
heavy textured cables and trellis patterns
have become synonymous with
warm and practical sweaters for
country or town.

The Aran Islands lie off the west coast of Ireland in the mouth of Galway bay, and are exposed to the Atlantic Ocean to their west. This situation has moulded the lifestyle and culture of the islanders, and the knitting that is said to originate in this area.

There are three main islands: Inishmore (the big island), Inishmaan (the middle island) and Inisheer (the west island). The cliffs can be steep and dangerous, the soil poor, and the sea rough, but in spite of this, the islanders have for generations fished and farmed for a meagre livelihood. The landscape features tiny fields divided by dry stone walls, where the islanders raise cattle and sheep. Because they were isolated, the inhabitants had to be as self sufficient as possible. They spun their wool into yarn, and wove and knitted their own warm clothes.

Some scholars believe that knitting was introduced to the Aran Islands by early Christian missionaries, and that they brought the craft from the Coptic sect in Egypt. A monastery had been founded in Aran in the sixth century and the geographical position of the islands made them an important stopping place for travellers who journeyed by boat around the coast of Ireland. It is certainly perfectly feasible that the old sea routes from the Mediterranean carried the art of knitting as well as religious travellers and traders. There is also thought to be a connection between the plaits, cables and interlacing of Aran knitting and designs on both the Celtic stone crosses, and the early Irish monks' illuminated manuscripts. Historian Heinz Edgar Kiewe maintained that in the Book of Kells, which dates from AD 820, Daniel is depicted as wearing Aran-patterned stockings, breeches and sweater.

However, it is virtually impossible to ascertain the precise origins and meanings of the patterns since there is a surprising lack of any early knitted garments. Indeed the first supposed "Aran" sweater was actually discovered by Heinz Kiewe in Dublin in the early 1930s. In his book "The Sacred History of Knitting" he described it as "too odd for words, being hard as a board, shapeless as a Coptic priest's shirt and with an atmosphere of Stonehenge all around it". He showed it to Mary Thomas, knitting expert, who later published a pattern from the sweater in her "Book of Knitting Patterns", saying it was "traditional of Aran and worn by fishermen of that island". Unfortunately this garment has now disappeared. There is a collection of Irish knitting at the National Museum in Dublin, but it was only started in 1937, and it does not contain any garments older than that. What does seem sure, is that, whether or not the Aran patterns are as ancient as some maintain, they were rediscovered in the 1930s and reintroduced to the area. They have now become part of the folk knitting of Ireland and are today one of the most distinctive and recognisable knitting styles.

By examining the old garments from the National Museum in Dublin, it becomes apparent that patterns

were exchanged readily from different areas of the British Isles and Ireland. One of the museum's garments resembles a banded gansey with horizontal instead of vertical patterning – a design that was common to Norfolk, Yorkshire and the east coast of Scotland. There is another early garment in the museum that is knitted in the navy blue wool which is always associated with gansey knitting. Nowadays we think of Aran sweaters being made of the slightly greasy but undyed wool called bainin (natural), and certainly the intricate stitch patterns and textures are seen best in this. The wool does generally seem to be thicker than the closely spun guernsey wool, but not in every example. Originally handspun by the women of the islands, it would have been up to the individual spinner to decide on the weight of the wool she wanted to produce. Later, when mill-produced yarn was used, a standard, quite thick weight was the norm; no doubt the commercial consideration that this would knit up more quickly than a fine wool had some influence here.

Aran garments are now made up from separate pieces, quite unlike the traditional ganseys and Fair Isles which were always knitted in the round, but it seems that both methods were used by the earlier knitters.

One very attractive and unusual feature of Aran knitting, which does not appear to be found elsewhere, is that the old jerseys often have elaborately patterned welts at the hem and neck, containing cables and fancy stitches. The neck was often a high stand-up, or roll-over collar, which again is quite unlike the straight neck found on most British ganseys. Quite unusually, some Arans in the National Museum feature fancy openwork patterns, which may well be related to the openwork designs often used in the ganseys of the Western Isles of Scotland.

The Aran that has become so popular as a fashion garment today has a strong identity of its own, and with features that distinguish it from other types of knitting. Perhaps the most important of these is the fact that nearly all the cables, diagonals making trellis or lattice patterns, and other motifs, are composed of plain knit stitches travelling across a purl stitch background. This gives the effect of raising the pattern into an "embossed" texture with a considerable depth. These patterns are obviously functional as well as decorative. The more texture is worked into a garment, the more wool will be required. By using cables, bobbles and other raised patterns the sweaters become heavier and warmer.

The meanings of the patterns are shrouded in mystery, but it seems that they are related to the most important tools in the fisherman's life – the nets and ropes that, with his boat, enabled him to pursue his livelihood. The *Cable* is certainly the most basic of all Aran patterns and is found in many sizes and shapes. Since the rope could literally be the lifeline of any fisherman, it is not surprising that it features so predominantly. With other patterns, a lot of the meanings have been coloured by romantic imagination, but perhaps the *Diamonds* are related to the mesh of the nets, *Trellis* to the shape of the small enclosed fields, and the *Tree of life*, an ancient pre-Christian symbol that later took on a Christian meaning, may also be symbolic of the family "tree" of the fisherman himself.

Left: The rugged landscape of Inishmaan
Above: Typical Aran stitch patterns

CABLE & MOSS
ARAN

A contemporary design featuring traditional stitch patterns – Medallion cable and Moss stitch – this long, loose-fitting sweater is roomy enough to be worn over several layers of clothing.

MATERIALS

Yarn

Standard Aran-weight wool

9 [10, 11] × 100g hanks, blue

Needles

1 pair size 4½mm

1 pair size 5mm

1 cable needle

MEASUREMENTS

To fit chest 91 [96, 102]cm

36 [38, 40]in

1 Actual chest size 106 [110, 116]cm

41½ [43, 45½]in

2 Length to back neck 66 [69, 72]cm

26 [27, 28]in

3 Sleeve seam 45cm, 18in

Tension

22 sts and 26 rows measure 10cm over pattern

on 5mm needles (or size needed to obtain

given tension)

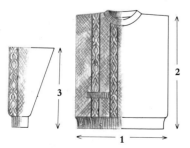

Cable panel

Repeat of 13 sts.

Row 1 (Right side) P2, k9, p2.

Row 2 K2, p9, k2.

Rows 3 and 4 As rows 1 and 2.

Row 5 P2, c4f, k1, c4b, p2.

Row 6 As row 2.

Rows 7 to 12 Rep rows 1 and 2, 3 times.

Row 13 As row 5.

Row 14 As row 2.

Rows 15 to 20 Rep rows 1 and 2, 3 times.

Row 21 P2, c4b, k1, c4f, p2.

Row 22 As row 2.

Rows 23 to 26 Rep rows 1 and 2 twice.

These 26 rows form cable panel.

BACK

Using 4½mm needles, cast on 119 [123, 131] sts.

Row 1 (Right side) K1, (p1, k1) to end.

Row 2 P1, (k1, p1) to end.

Rep these two rows until rib measures 5cm, ending with a 1st row. P1 row. Change to 5mm needles. Commence patt.

Row 1 K1, (p1, k1) 8 [9, 11] times, *work next 13 sts as 1st row of cable panel, k1, (p2, k1) 5 times; rep from * 3 times more, (p1, k1) 3 [4, 6] times.

Row 2 P1, (k1, p1) 8 [9, 11] times, *work next 13 sts as 2nd row of cable panel, p1, (k1, p1) 5 times; rep from * 3 times more, (k1, p1) 3 [4, 6] times.

Row 3 P1 (k1, p1) 8 [9, 11] times, *work next 13 sts as 3rd row of cable panel, p1, (k1, p1) 5 times; rep from * 3 times more, (k1, p1) 3 [4, 6] times.

Row 4 K1, (p1, k1) 8 [9, 11] times, *work next 13 sts as 4th row of cable panel, k1, (p1, k1) 5 times; rep from * 3 times more, (p1, k1) 3 [4, 6] times.

These 4 rows establish moss st patt.

Cont in patt as set, working appropriate rows of cable panel until work measures 64 [67, 70] cm from beg, ending with a right side row.

Shape neck

Next row Patt 42 [43, 46], cast off next 35 [37, 39] sts, patt to end.

Complete right side of back neck first. Dec 1 st at neck edge on every row until 37 [38, 41] sts rem. Patt 1 row. Cast off. With right side facing, rejoin yarn to rem sts, k2 tog, patt to end. Complete to match first side of neck.

POCKET LININGS

Using 5mm needles, cast on 31 sts. Beg k row, work 15cm in st st, ending with a p row. Leave these sts on a spare needle.

Make another pocket lining to match.

FRONT

Work as given for back until work measures 20cm from beg, ending with a wrong side row.

Place pockets

Next row Patt 10 [12, 16], sl next 31 sts on to a holder, patt across 31 sts of first pocket lining, patt 37, sl next 31 sts on to a holder, patt across 31 sts of second pocket lining, patt to end.

Cont in patt until front measures 59 [62, 65] cm from beg, ending with a right side row.

Shape neck

Next row Patt 46 [47, 50], cast off next 27 [29, 31] sts, patt to end.

Complete left side of neck first. Dec 1 st at neck edge on every row until 37 [38, 41] sts rem. Cont straight until front matches back to shoulder, ending with a wrong side row. Cast off. With right side facing, rejoin yarn to rem sts, k2 tog, patt to end. Complete to match first side of neck.

SLEEVES

Using 4½mm needles, cast on 59 sts. Work 5cm in rib as given for back welt, ending with a 1st row.

Next row P2, (inc in next st, p4) to last 2 sts, inc in next st, p1. *71 sts.* Change to 5mm needles. Commence patt.

Row 1 K1, (p1, k1) twice, *work next 13 sts as 1st row of cable panel, k1, (p1, k1) 5 times; rep from * once more, work next 13 sts as 1st row of cable panel, k1, (p1, k1) twice.
Row 2 P1, (k1, p1) twice, *work next 13 sts as 2nd row of cable panel, p1, (k1, p1) 5 times; rep from * once more, work next 13 sts as 2nd row of cable panel, p1, (k1, p1) twice.
Row 3 P1, (k1, p1) twice, *work next 13 sts as 3rd row of cable panel, p1, (k1, p1) 5 times; rep from * once more, work next 13 sts as 3rd row of cable panel, p1, (k1, p1) twice.
Row 4 K1, (p1, k1) twice, *work next 13 sts as 4th row of cable panel, k1, (p1, k1) 5 times; rep from * once more, work next 13 sts as 4th row of cable panel, k1, (p1, k1) twice.
These 4 rows establish moss st patt.
Cont in patt as set, working appropriate rows of cable panel. Inc 1 st at each end of next row and 8 foll 3rd rows, then on every foll 4th row until there are 117 sts, working extra sts into moss st patt. Cont straight until sleeve measures 44cm from beg, ending with a wrong side row. Beg p row, work 2 rows st st. Cast off.

NECKBAND

With right side facing, join right shoulder seam. With right side facing and using 4½mm needles, pick up and k 20 sts down left side of front neck, 25 [27, 29] sts from centre front, 20 sts up right side of front neck, 6 sts down right side of back neck, 32 [34, 36] sts from centre back and 63 sts up left side of back neck. *109 [113, 117] sts.* Beg 2nd row, work 12 rows in rib as for back welt. Cast off in rib.

POCKET EDGINGS

With right side facing and using 4½mm needles, rejoin yarn to the 31 sts left on holder. Beg with 1st row, work 6 rows in rib as given for back welt. Cast off in rib.

FINISHING

Block each piece as given on p. 140. With right side facing, join left shoulder seam. Join neckband in half to wrong side and slip stitch. Catch down pocket linings and sides of pocket edgings. Mark position of armholes 26cm down from shoulders on back and front. Sew in sleeves between markers. Join side and sleeve seams.

Designed by Sue Turton

Cable and moss Aran
Chevron Aran
Medallion Aran

MEDALLION
ARAN

A long, casual V-neck cardigan in a similar stitch pattern to the Cable and moss sweater produces an understated Aran look, where the simplicity of the pattern and the shape complement each other.

MATERIALS

Yarn
Standard Aran-weight wool

10 [10, 11] × 100g hanks, yellow

Notions
6 buttons, 2cm in diameter

Needles
1 pair size 4½mm

1 pair size 5mm

1 cable needle

Designed by Sue Turton

MEASUREMENTS

To fit chest 97 [102, 107]cm	
38 [40, 42]in	
1 Actual chest size 108 [115, 119]cm	
42½ [45¼, 47]in	
2 Length to back neck 68 [71, 74]cm	
26¾ [28, 29¼]in	
3 Sleeve seam 45cm, 17¾in	

Tension

22 sts and 26 rows measure 10cm over pattern on 5mm needles (or size needed to obtain given tension)

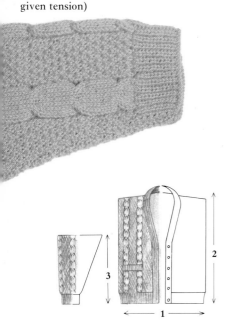

BACK

Using 4½mm needles, cast on 123 [131, 135] sts.

Row 1 (Right side) K1, (p1, k1) to end.

Row 2 P1, (k1, p1) to end.

Rep these 2 rows until rib measures 5cm, ending with a 1st row. P1 row. Change to 5mm needles. Commence patt.

Row 1 K1, (p1, k1) 3 [5, 6] times, *p2, k9, p2, (k1, p1) 5 times, k1; rep from * to last 20 [24, 26] sts, p2, k9, p2, (k1, p1) 3 [5, 6] times, k1.

Row 2 P1, (k1, p1) 3 [5, 6] times, *k2, p9, k2, (p1, k1) 5 times, p1; rep from * to last 20 [24, 26] sts, k2, p9, k2, (p1, k1) 3 [5, 6] times, p1.

Row 3 P1, (k1, p1) 3 [5, 6] times, *p2, k9, p2, (p1, k1) 5 times, p1; rep from * to last 20 [24, 26] sts, p2, k9, p2, (p1, k1) 3 [5, 6] times, p1.

Row 4 K1, (p1, k1) 3 [5, 6] times, *k2, p9, k2, (k1, p1) 5 times, k1; rep from * to last 20 [24, 26] sts, k2, p9, k2, (k1, p1) 3 [5, 6] times, k1.

Row 5 K1, (p1, k1) 3 [5, 6] times, *p2, c4f, k1, c4b, p2, (k1, p1) 5 times, k1; rep from * to last 20 [24, 26] sts, p2, c4f, k1, c4b, p2, (k1, p1) 3 [5, 6] times, k1.

Row 6 As row 2.

Rows 7 and 8 As rows 3 and 4.

Rows 9 to 12 As rows 1 to 4.

These 12 rows form patt. Cont in patt until work measures 68 [71, 74]cm from beg, ending with a wrong side row. Cast off.

POCKET LININGS

Using 5mm needles, cast on 37 sts. Beg k row, work 15cm in st st, ending with a p row. Leave these sts on a spare needle.

Make another pocket lining to match.

LEFT FRONT

Using 4½mm needles, cast on 55 [59, 61] sts. Work 5cm in rib as given for back welt, ending with a 1st row. P 1 row, inc 1 st at centre. *56 [60, 62] sts.

Change to 5mm needles. Commence patt.

Row 1 K1, (p1, k1) 3 [5, 6] times, *p2, k9, p2, (k1, p1) 5 times, k1; rep from * once more, p1.

Row 2 K1, *p1, (k1, p1) 5 times, k2, p9, k2; rep from * once more, (p1, k1) 3 [5, 6] times, p1.

Row 3 P1, (k1, p1) 3 [5, 6] times, *p2, k9, p2, (p1, k1) 5 times, p1; rep from * once more, k1.

Row 4 P1, *k1, (p1, k1) 5 times, k2, p9, k2; rep from * once more, (k1, p1) 3 [5, 6] times, k1.

Row 5 K1, (p1, k1) 3 [5, 6] times, *p2, c4f, k1, c4b, p2, (k1, p1) 5 times, k1; rep from * once more, p1.

Row 6 As row 2.

Rows 7 and 8 As rows 3 and 4.

Rows 9 to 12 As rows 1 to 4.

These 12 rows form patt. Cont in patt until work measures 20cm from beg, ending with a wrong side row.

Place pocket

Next row Patt 7 [11, 13], sl next 37 sts on to a holder, patt across 37 sts of pocket lining, patt to end.

Cont in patt until work measures 38 [41, 44] cm from beg, ending with a wrong side row.

Shape front Dec 1 st at end (front edge) of next row and every foll 4th row until 41 [44, 45] sts rem. Cont straight until front matches back to shoulder, ending with a wrong side row. Cast off.

RIGHT FRONT

Work as given for left front from ** to **.

Change to 5mm needles. Commence patt.

Row 1 P1, *k1, (p1, k1) 5 times, p2, k9, p2; rep from * once more, (k1, p1) 3 [5, 6] times, k1.

Row 2 P1, (k1, p1) 3 [5, 6] times, *k2, p9, k2, (p1, k1) 5 times, p1; rep from * once more, k1.

Row 3 K1, *p1, (k1, p1) 5 times, p2, k9, p2; rep from * once more, (p1, k1) 3 [5, 6] times, p1.

Row 4 K1, (p1, k1) 3 [5, 6] times, *k2, p9, k2 (k1, p1) 5 times, k1; rep from * once more, p1.

Row 5 P1, *k1, (p1, k1) 5 times, p2, c4f, k1, c4b, p2; rep from * once more, (k1, p1) 3 [5, 6] times, k1.

Row 6 As row 2.

Rows 7 and 8 As rows 3 and 4.

Rows 9 to 12 As rows 1 to 4.

These 12 rows form patt. Cont in patt until work measures 20cm from beg, ending with a wrong side row.

Place pocket

Next row Patt 12, sl next 37 sts on to a holder, patt across 37 sts of pocket lining, patt to end.

Complete as given for left front, reversing front shaping.

SLEEVES

Using 4½mm needles, cast on 59 sts. Work 5cm in rib as given for back welt, ending with a 1st row.

Next row P7, (inc in next st, p2) to last 4 sts, p4. *75 sts*. Change to 5mm needles. Cont in patt as given for 1st size on back, inc 1 st at each end of 3rd row and every foll 4th row until there are 119 sts, working extra sts into moss st patt. Cont straight until sleeve measures 44cm from beg, ending with a wrong side row. Beg p row, work 2 rows st st. Cast off.

BUTTON BAND

Mark right front with pins to indicate buttonholes, first one to come 2cm up from lower edge and last one 1cm below front shaping and rem 4 evenly spaced between.

Using 4½mm needles, cast on 11 sts. Work in rib as given for back welt, making buttonholes at pin positions as follows.

Buttonhole row Rib 4, cast off 2, rib to end.

Next row Rib to end, casting on 2 sts over those cast off in previous row.

Cont in rib until band when slightly stretched fits up right front, across back and down left front. Cast off in rib.

POCKET EDGINGS

With right side facing and using 4½mm needles, rejoin yarn to the 37 sts on holder. Work 6 rows in rib as given for back welt. Cast off in rib.

FINISHING

Block each piece as given on p. 140. Catch down pocket linings and sides of pocket edgings. Join shoulder seams. Sew on front band. Mark position of armholes 26cm down from shoulders on back and fronts. Sew in sleeves between markers. Join side and sleeve seams. Sew on buttons.

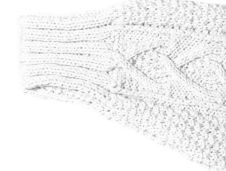

Classic Aran stitches – Crossover chevron and Moss stitch – are used on this roomy pullover. Shown here in traditional Aran wool, it would look just as effective in double knitting cotton.

MATERIALS

Yarn

Standard Aran-weight wool

9 [9, 10] × 100g hanks, cream

Needles

1 pair size 4mm

1 pair size 5mm

1 cable needle

MEASUREMENTS

To fit chest 91 [97, 102]cm

36 [38, 40]in

1 Actual chest size 112 [116, 124]cm

44 [45¾, 48¾]in

2 Length to shoulder 61 [64, 67]cm

24 [25¼, 26½]in

3 Sleeve seam 44cm, 17¼in

Tension

21 sts and 23 rows measure 10cm over pattern on 5mm needles (or size needed to obtain given tension)

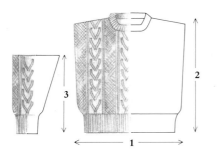

Pattern panel

Worked over 19 sts.

Row 1 (Right side) K1 tbl, p6, k2, p1, k2, p6, k1 tbl.

Row 2 P1, k6, p2, k1, p2, k6, p1.

Row 3 K1 tbl, p6, cr5, p6, k1 tbl.

Row 4 As row 2.

Row 5 K1 tbl, p5, cr3r, k1, cr3l, p5, k1 tbl.

Row 6 P1, k5, p2, k1, p1, k1, p2, k5, p1.

Row 7 K1 tbl, p4, cr3r, k1, p1, k1, cr3l, p4, k1 tbl.

Row 8 P1, k4, p2, (k1, p1) twice, k1, p2, k4, p1.

Row 9 K1 tbl, p3, cr3r, (k1, p1) twice, k1, cr3l, p3, k1 tbl.

Row 10 P1, k3, p2, (k1, p1) 3 times, k1, p2, k3, p1.

Row 11 K1 tbl, p2, cr3r, (k1, p1) 3 times, k1, cr3l, p2, k1 tbl.

Row 12 P1, k2, p2, (k1, p1) 4 times, k1, p2, k2, p1.

Row 13 K1 tbl, p1, cr3r, (k1, p1) 4 times, k1, cr3l, p1, k1 tbl.

Row 14 P1, k1, p2, (k1, p1) 5 times, k1, p2, k1, p1.

Row 15 K1 tbl, p1, k2, p3, k2, p1, k2, p3, k2, p1, k1 tbl.

Rows 2 to 15 form panel pattern.

BACK

Using 4mm needles, cast on 110 [114, 118] sts.

Row 1 (Right side) K2, (p2, k2) to end.

Row 2 P2, (k2, p2) to end.

Rep these 2 rows until rib measures 10cm, ending with row 1 of patt.

Next row Rib 5 [7, 3], *inc in next st, rib 9 [9, 7]; rep from * to last 5 [7, 3] sts, inc in next st, rib to end. *121 [125, 133] sts.*

Change to 5mm needles. Commence patt.

Row 1 K1, (p1, k1) 5 [6, 8] times, *p2, work row 1 of panel patt, p2, k1, (p1, k1) 7 times; rep from * once more, p2, work row 1 of panel patt, p2, (k1, p1) 5 [6, 8] times, k1.

Row 2 P1, (k1, p1) 5 [6, 8] times, *k2, work row 2 of panel patt, k2, p1, (k1, p1) 7 times; rep from * once more, k2, work row 2 of panel patt, k2, (p1, k1) 5 [6, 8] times, p1.

Row 3 P1, (k1, p1) 5 [6, 8] times, *p2, work 3rd row of panel patt, p3, (k1, p1) 7 times; rep from * once more, p2, work row 3 of panel patt, p2, (p1, k1) 5 [6, 8] times, p1.

Row 4 K1, (p1, k1) 5 [6, 8] times, *k2, work row 4 of panel patt, k3, (p1, k1) 7 times; rep from * once more, k2, work row 4 of panel patt, k2, (k1, p1) 5 [6, 8] times, k1.

These 4 rows establish moss st patt. Cont in patt as set, working appropriate rows of panel patt until work measures 58 [61, 64]cm from beg, ending with a wrong side row.

Shape neck

Next row Patt 49 [51, 53] sts and turn; leave rem sts on a spare needle. Complete right side of neck first. Dec 1 st at neck edge on next 5 rows. *44 [46, 48] sts.* Patt 2 rows. Cast off. With right side facing, sl centre 23 [23, 27] sts on to a holder, rejoin yarn to rem sts and patt to end. Complete to match first side of neck.

FRONT

Work as given for back until work measures 53 [56, 59]cm from beg, ending with a wrong side row.

Shape neck

Next row Patt 49 [51, 53] sts and turn; leave rem sts on a spare needle. Complete left side of neck first.

Dec 1 st at neck edge on next 5 rows. *44 [46, 48] sts.* Cont straight until front matches back to shoulder, ending with a wrong side row. Cast off.

With right side facing, sl centre 23 [23, 27] sts on to holder, rejoin yarn to rem sts and patt to end. Complete to match first side of neck.

SLEEVES

Using 4mm needles, cast on 54 sts. Work 10cm in rib as given for back welt, ending with a 1st row.

Next row Rib 3, (inc in next st, rib 2) to end. *71 sts.*

Change to 5mm needles. Commence patt.

Row 1 K1, (p1, k1) twice, p2, work row 1 of panel patt, p2, k1, (p1, k1) 7 times, p2, work row 1 of panel patt, p2, (k1, p1) twice, k1.

Row 2 P1, (k1, p1) twice, k2, work row 2 of panel patt, k2, p1, (k1, p1) 7 times, k2, work row 2 of panel patt, k2, (p1, k1) twice, p1.

Row 3 P1, (k1, p1) twice, p2, work row 3 of panel patt, p3, (k1, p1) 7 times, p2, work row 3 of panel patt, p2, (p1, k1) twice, p1.

Row 4 K1, (p1, k1) twice, k2, work row 4 of panel patt, k3, (p1, k1) 7 times, k2, work row 4 of panel patt, k2, (k1, p1) twice, k1.

These 4 rows establish moss st patt. Cont in patt as set, working appropriate rows of panel patt, inc 1 st at each end of next row and every foll 4th row until there are 109 sts, working extra sts into moss st patt. Patt 1 row. Work should measure 43cm. Purl 1 row. Knit 1 row. Cast off.

NECKBAND

Join right shoulder seam. With right side facing and using 4mm needles, pick up and k 20 sts down left side of front neck, k23 [23, 27] centre front sts, pick up and k 20 sts up right side of front neck, 8 sts down right side of back neck, k 23 [23, 27] centre back sts, pick up and k 8 sts up left side of back neck. *102 [102, 110] sts*. Beg 2nd row, work 15 rows in rib as given for back welt. Cast off in rib.

FINISHING

Block each piece as given on p. 140. Join left shoulder and neckband seam. Fold neckband in half to wrong side and slip stitch in position. Mark positions of armholes 25cm down from shoulders on back and front. Sew in sleeves. Join side and sleeve seams.

Designed by Sue Turton

PLAIT CABLE ARAN

The use of 4 ply wool produces a lightweight waistcoat, suitable for summer wear. The patterning is provided by two Aran stitches, Plait cable and Double seed stitch. The plait pattern is said to represent the "Holy Three", or Trinity.

MATERIALS

Yarn

Standard 4 ply wool

7 [8, 8] × 50g balls, pale blue

Needles

1 pair size 2¾mm

1 pair size 3¼mm

1 cable needle

Notions

4 buttons, 1.5cm in diameter

MEASUREMENTS

To fit chest 86 [91, 97]cm

34 [36, 38]in

1 Actual chest size 92 [97, 101]cm

36¼ [38, 39¾]in

2 Length to back neck 48cm, 19in

Tension

34 sts and 37 rows measure 10cm over pattern on 3¼mm needles (or size needed to obtain given tension)

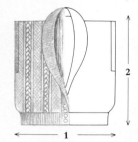

Cable panel

Repeat of 21 sts.

Row 1 (Right side) (K2 tog then k into first st again, sl both sts off needle tog – referred to as tw2) twice, p2, k9, p2, (tw2) twice.

Row 2 P4, k2, p9, k2, p4.

Row 3 (Tw2) twice, p2, c6f, k3, p2, (tw2) twice.

Row 4 As row 2.

Rows 5 and 6 As rows 1 and 2.

Row 7 (Tw2) twice, p2, k3, c6b, p2, (tw2) twice.

Row 8 As row 2.

These 8 rows form cable panel.

RIGHT FRONT

Using 2¾mm needles, cast on 64 [68, 72] sts. Work 5cm in k2, p2 rib.

Next row Rib 15, *inc in next st, rib 3, (inc in next st, rib 1) 3 times, rib 3, inc in next st, rib 10; rep from * once more, rib 1 [5, 9]. *74 [78, 82] sts.* Change to 3¼mm needles.

Foundation row (Wrong side) (P2, k2) 2 [3, 4] times, p2, *p4, k2, p9, k2, p4, (k2, p2) twice; rep from * once more, k2, p2, k2. Commence patt.

Row 1 P2, k2, p2, *(k2, p2) twice, work row 1 of cable panel; rep from * once more, k2, (p2, k2) 2 [3, 4] times.

Row 2 (K2, p2) 2 [3, 4] times, k2, *work row 2 of cable panel, (p2, k2) twice; rep from * once more, p2, k2, p2.

Row 3 K2, p2, k2, *(p2, k2) twice, work row 3 of cable panel; rep from * once more, p2, (k2,

Designed by Jenny Sandler

p2) 2 [3, 4] times.
Row 4 (P2, k2) 2 [3, 4] times, p2, *work row 4 of cable panel, (k2, p2) twice; rep from * once more, k2, p2, k2.
These 4 rows establish double moss stitch patt. Cont in patt as set, working appropriate rows of panel until work measures 10cm from beg, ending with a wrong side row.
Shape front Dec 1 st at beg of next row and 8 foll 6th rows. Patt 2 rows straight. Work should measure 24cm from beg.
Shape armhole Cast off 8 sts at beg of next row. Keeping armhole edge straight, cont to dec at neck edge on 3rd row and every foll 6th row until 44 [48, 52] sts rem. Cont straight until armhole measures 24cm, ending with a wrong side row. Cast off.

LEFT FRONT

Using 2¾mm needles, cast on 64 [68, 72] sts. Work 5cm in k2, p2 rib.
Next row Rib 11 [15, 19], *inc in next st, rib 3, (rib 1, inc in next st) 3 times, rib 3, inc in next st, rib 10; rep from * once more, rib 5. *74 [78, 82] sts.* Change to 3¼mm needles.
Foundation row (Wrong side) K2, p2, k2, *(p2, k2) twice, p4, k2, p9, k2, p4; rep from * once more, p2, (k2, p2) 2 [3, 4] times. Commence patt.
Row 1 (K2, p2) 2 [3, 4] times, k2, *work row 1 of cable panel, (p2, k2) twice; rep from * once more, p2, k2, p2.
Row 2 P2, k2, p2, *(k2, p2) twice, work row 2 of cable panel; rep from * once more, k2, (p2, k2) 2 [3, 4] times.
Row 3 (P2, k2) 2 [3, 4] times, p2, *work row 3 of cable panel, (k2, p2) twice; rep from * once more, k2, p2, k2.
Row 4 K2, p2, k2, *(p2, k2) twice, work row 4 of cable panel; rep from * once more, p2, (k2, p2) 2 [3, 4] times.
These 4 rows establish double moss stitch patt. Cont in patt as set, working appropriate rows of panel until work measures 10cm from beg, ending with a wrong side row.
Shape front Dec 1 st at end of next row and 8 foll 6th rows. Patt 1 row straight.
Shape armhole Cast off 8 sts at beg of next row. Patt 1 row. Complete as for right front.

BACK

Using 2¾mm needles, cast on 136 [144, 152] sts. Work 5cm in k2, p2 rib.
Next row Rib 13 [17, 21], *inc in next st, rib 3, (inc in next st, rib 1) 3 times, rib 3, inc in next st, rib 10; rep from * to last 3 [7, 11] sts, rib to end. *161 [169, 177] sts.* Change to 3¼mm needles.
Foundation row (Wrong side) (K2, p2) 3 [4, 5] times, *p4, k2, p9, k2, p4, (k2, p2) twice; rep from * to last 4 [8, 12] sts, (k2, p2) 1 [2, 3] times. Commence patt.
Row 1 (K2, p2) 3 [4, 5] times, *work row 1 of cable panel, (k2, p2) twice; rep from * to last 4 [8, 12] sts, (k2, p2) 1 [2, 3] times.
Row 2 (P2, k2) 3 [4, 5] times, *work row 2 of cable panel, (p2, k2) twice; rep from * to last 4 [8, 12] sts, (p2, k2) 1 [2, 3] times.
Row 3 (P2, k2) 3 [4, 5] times, *work row 3 of cable panel, (p2, k2) twice; rep from * to last 4 [8, 12] sts, (p2, k2) 1 [2, 3] times.

Row 4 (K2, p2) 3 [4, 5] times, *work row 4 of cable panel, (k2, p2) twice; rep from * to last 4 [8, 12] sts, (k2, p2) 1 [2, 3] times.
These 4 rows establish double moss st patt. Cont in patt as set, working appropriate rows of panel until back matches front to armhole shaping, ending with a wrong side row.
Shape armholes Cast off 8 sts at beg of next 2 rows. *145 [153, 161] sts.* Cont straight until back matches front to shoulder, ending with a wrong side row. Cast off.

BUTTON BANDS AND COLLAR

Button band and collar
Join shoulder seams. Using 3¼mm needles, cast on 10 sts. Cont in g st until band when slightly stretched fits along left front to beg of front shaping.
Shape collar
Next row K4, inc in next st, k to end.
K 5 rows.
Rep these last 6 rows until there are 30 sts. Cont straight until collar fits along shaped edge of front to centre back neck. Cast off. Sew in position.

Buttonhole band and collar
Mark button band with pins to indicate position of buttons, first one to come 1cm up from lower edge and last one in line with beg of front shaping, rem 2 spaced evenly between. Work as given for button band, making buttonholes at pin positions as follows:
Buttonhole row K4, cast off 2, k to end.
Next row K to end, casting on 2 sts over those cast off in previous row.
Sew band in position, then join back seam of collar.

ARMBANDS

Using 3¼mm needles, cast on 8 sts. Cont in g st until band when slightly stretched fits around armhole edge. Cast off.

FINISHING

Block each piece as given on p. 140. Sew in armbands, sewing cast on and cast off edges to cast off sts at armholes. Join side seams. Sew on buttons.

TREE OF LIFE

ARAN

Two famous Aran patterns, the Tree of life and Chain cable, are worked into this cardigan. The Tree of life is an ancient religious symbol which is also said to represent family connections; the Chain cable is related to the Honeycomb pattern, a very old, traditional pattern.

MATERIALS

Yarn

Standard Aran-weight wool

19 [19, 20, 22] × 50g balls, pink

Needles

1 pair size 3¾mm

1 pair size 4½mm

1 cable needle

Notions

3 buttons, 2.5cm in diameter

3 stitch holders

MEASUREMENTS

To fit chest 81-86 [91-96, 102-107, 112-116]cm

32-34 [36-38, 40-42, 44-46]in

1 Actual chest size 105 [114, 126, 138]cm

41¼ [45, 49½, 54]in

2 Length to back neck 65 [66, 67, 68]cm

25½ [26, 26¼, 26¾]in

3 Sleeve seam 42 [43, 43, 44]cm

16½ [17, 17, 17¼]in

Tension

20 sts and 26 rows measure 10cm over pattern on 4½mm needles (or size needed to obtain given tension)

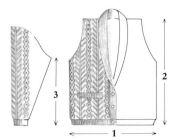

Cable panel

Repeat of 8 sts.

Row 1 (Wrong side) P8.

Row 2 C4b, c4f.

Row 3 P8.

Row 4 K8.

Row 5 P8.

Row 6 C4f, c4b.

Rows 7 and 8 As rows 3 and 4.

These 8 rows form cable panel.

Tree of life panel

Repeat of 12 sts.

Row 1 (Wrong side) K4, p4, k4.

Row 2 P3, sl next st on to cable needle and leave at back, k1, p1 from cable needle, referred to as cr2r, k into front of 2nd st then k first st, sl both sts off needle tog – referred to as tw2, sl next st on to cable needle and leave at front, p1, k1 from cable needle – referred to as cr2l, p3.

Row 3 K3, (p1, k1, p1) twice, k3.

Row 4 P2, cr2r, p1, tw2, p1, cr2l, p2.

Row 5 K2, (p1, k2, p1) twice, k2.

Row 6 P1, cr2r, p2, tw2, p2, cr2l, p1.

Row 7 K1, (p1, k3, p1) twice, k1.

Row 8 Cr2r, p3, tw2, p3, cr2l.

These 8 rows form Tree of life panel.

POCKET LININGS

Using 4½mm needles, cast on 24 sts. Work 12cm in st st, ending with a p row.

Next row (K1, inc in next st, k1) to end. *32 sts.* Leave these sts on a spare needle.

Make another pocket lining to match.

BREAST POCKET LINING

Using 4½mm needles, cast on 16 sts. Work 8cm in st st, ending with a p row.

Next row (K2, inc in next st, k1) to end. *20 sts.* Leave these sts on a spare needle.

LEFT FRONT

Using 3¾mm needles, cast on 41 [45, 50, 56] sts.

Row 1 (Right side) K1 [1, 0, 0] tbl, (p1, k1 tbl) to end.

Row 2 (P1, k1 tbl) to last 1 [1, 0, 0] sts, p1 [1, 0, 0].

Rep these two rows once.

1st and 2nd sizes

***Next row** (Rib 1, inc in next st) 3 times, *rib 4 [5], inc in next st, rib 2, inc in next st, rib 4 [5], inc in next st, (rib 1, inc in next st) twice; rep from * once more, rib 1. *54 [58] sts.* Change to 4½mm needles. Commence patt.

Row 1 (Wrong side) K1, *work row 1 of cable panel, k1 [2], work row 1 of Tree of life panel,

k1 [2]; rep from * once more, work row 1 of cable panel, k1.

Row 2 P1, work row 2 of cable panel, *p1 [2], work row 2 of Tree of life panel, p1 [2], work row 2 of cable panel; rep from * once more, p1***.

3rd and 4th sizes

Next row (Rib 1, inc in next st) 3 times, *rib [4, 5], inc in next st, rib 2, inc in next st, rib [4, 5], inc in next st, (rib 1, inc in next st) twice; rep from * once more, rib [3, 4], inc in next st, rib 2, inc in next st, rib [3, 4]. *[65, 71] sts.* Change to 4½mm needles. Commence patt.

Row 1 (Wrong side) K [0, 1], work row 1 of Tree of life panel, k [0, 1], *work row 1 of cable panel, k [1, 2], work row 1 of Tree of life panel, k [1, 2]; rep from * once more, work row 1 of cable panel, k1.

Row 2 P1, work row 2 of cable panel, *p [1, 2], work row 2 of Tree of life panel, p [1, 2], work row 2 of cable panel; rep from * once more, p [0, 1], work row 2 of Tree of life panel, p [0, 1].

All sizes

These 2 rows establish patt. Cont in patt as set, working appropriate rows of panels, patt 11 rows.

Dec row Patt 9, p2 tog, patt to end. Patt 11 rows straight.

Dec row Patt 20 [22, 20, 22], p2 tog, patt to end.

Patt 5 rows straight.

Place pocket

Next row Patt 11 [14, 19, 23] sts, sl next 32 sts on to stitch holder, patt across 32 sts of pocket lining, patt to end.

Patt 5 rows straight.

Dec row Patt 29 [31, 29, 31], p2 tog, patt to end.

Patt 11 rows straight.

Dec row Patt 40 [44, 40, 44], p2 tog, patt to end. *50 [54, 61, 67] sts.*

Patt 5 rows straight.

Shape front Dec 1 st at end of next row and 6 foll 8th rows. Patt 1 row. Work should measure 42cm from beg.

Designed by Brinion Heaton

Shape armholes Cast off 9 sts at beg of next row. Patt 1 row.

Place breast pocket

Next row Work 2 tog, patt 5 [7, 11, 14], sl next 20 sts on to stitch holder, patt across breast pocket lining, patt to end. Cont dec 1 st at front edge on foll 4th row and 2 [2, 4, 5] foll 8th rows and at the same time dec 1 st at armhole edge on foll 7 [11, 10, 12] alt rows. 23 [23, 29, 32] sts. Cont straight until armhole measures 21 [22, 23, 24]cm, ending at armhole edge.

Shape shoulder Cast off 8 [8, 10, 11] sts at beg of next row and foll alt row. Patt 1 row. Cast off rem 7 [7, 9, 10] sts.

RIGHT FRONT

Using 3¾mm needles, cast on 41 [45, 50, 56] sts. Work 4 rows in rib as given for left front welt.

1st and 2nd sizes
Work as given for left front from *** to ***.

3rd and 4th sizes
Next row Rib [3, 4], inc in next st, rib 2, inc in next st, rib [3, 4], inc in next st, (rib 1, inc in next st) twice, *rib [4, 5], inc in next st, rib 2, inc in next st, rib [4, 5], inc in next st, (rib 1, inc in next st) twice; rep from * once more, rib 1. [65, 71] sts.
Change to 4½mm needles. Commence patt.
Row 1 (Wrong side) K1, work row 1 of cable panel, *k [1, 2], work row 1 of Tree of life panel, k [1, 2], work row 1 of cable panel; rep from * once more, k [0, 1], work row 1 of Tree of life panel, k [0, 1].
Row 2 P [0, 1], work row 2 of Tree of life panel, p [0, 1], work row 2 of cable panel, *p [1, 2], work row 2 of Tree of life panel, p [1, 2], work row 2 of cable panel; rep from * once more, p1.

All sizes
These 2 rows establish patt. Cont in patt as set, working appropriate rows of panels, patt 11 rows.
Dec row Patt to last 11 sts, p2 tog tbl, patt to end. Patt 11 rows straight.
Dec row Patt to last 22 [24, 22, 24] sts, p2 tog tbl, patt to end.
Patt 5 rows straight.
Place pocket
Next row Patt 9 [10, 12, 14], sl next 32 sts on to a stitch holder, patt across 32 sts of pocket lining, patt to end.
Patt 5 rows straight.
Dec row Patt to last 31 [33, 31, 33] sts, p2 tog tbl, patt to end.
Patt 11 rows straight.

Dec row Patt to last 42 [46, 42, 46] sts, p2 tog tbl, patt to end. 50 [54, 61, 67] sts.
Patt 5 rows straight.
Shape front Dec 1 st at beg of next row and 6 foll 8th rows. Patt 2 rows.
Shape armhole Cast off 9 sts at beg of next row.
Next row Patt to last 2 sts, work 2tog.
Complete as given for left front.

BACK

Using 3¾mm needles, cast on 90 [100, 105, 117] sts. Work 4 rows in rib as given for 3rd [3rd, 1st, 1st] sizes on left front welt.
Next row (Rib 1, inc in next st) 3 times, *rib 4 [5, 4, 5], inc in next st, rib 2, inc in next st, rib 4 [5, 4, 5], inc in next st, (rib 1, inc in next st) twice*; rep from * to * once more, **rib 3 [4, 3, 4], inc in next st, rib 2, inc in next st, rib 3 [4, 3, 4], inc in next st, (rib 1, inc in next st) twice**; rep from ** to ** o [0, 1, 1] time more, now rep from * to * twice, rib 1. 118 [128, 138, 150] sts. Change to 4½mm needles. Commence patt.
Row 1 (Wrong side) K1, work row 1 of cable panel, *k1 [2, 1, 2], work row 1 of Tree of life panel, k1 [2, 1, 2], work row 1 of cable panel*; rep from * to * once more, **k0 [1, 0, 1], work row 1 of Tree of life panel, k0 [1, 0, 1], work row 1 of cable panel**; rep from ** to ** o [0, 1, 1] time more, rep from * to * twice, k1.
Row 2 P1, work row 2 of cable panel, *p1 [2, 1, 2], work row 2 of Tree of life panel, p1 [2, 1, 2], work row 2 of cable panel*; rep from * to * once more, **p0 [1, 0, 1], work row 2 of Tree of life panel, p0 [1, 0, 1], work row 2 of cable panel**; rep from ** to ** o [0, 1, 1] time more, now rep from * to * twice, p1.
These 2 rows establish patt. Cont in patt as set, working appropriate rows of panels, patt 11 rows.
Dec row Patt 9, p2 tog, patt to last 11 sts, p2 tog tbl, patt to end.
Patt 11 rows straight.
Dec row Patt 20 [22, 20, 22], p2 tog, patt to last 22 [24, 22, 24] sts, p2 tog tbl, patt to end.
Patt 11 rows straight.
Dec row Patt 29 [31, 29, 31], p2 tog, patt to last 31 [33, 31, 33] sts, p2 tog tbl, patt to end.
Patt 11 rows straight.
Dec row Patt 40 [44, 40, 44], p2 tog, patt to last 42 [46, 42, 46] sts, p2 tog tbl, patt to end. 110 [120, 130, 142] sts.
Cont straight in patt until back matches front to armhole shaping, ending with a wrong side row.
Shape armholes Cast off 9 sts at beg of next 2 rows. Dec 1 st at each end of next row and every foll alt row until 74 [78, 90, 98] sts rem. Cont straight until back matches front to shoulder ending with a wrong side row.
Shape shoulders Cast off 8 [8, 10, 11] sts at beg of next 4 rows and 7 [7, 9, 10] sts at beg of foll 2 rows. Cast off rem 28 [32, 32, 34] sts.

SLEEVES

Using 3¾mm needles, cast on 49 sts. Work 4 rows in rib as given for 1st size on left front welt.
Next row Rib 7, *(inc in next st, rib 1) 3 times, (rib 2, inc in next st) twice, rib 3; rep

from * once more, (inc in next st, rib 1) 3 times, rib 6. 62 sts. Change to 4½mm needles. Commence patt.
Row 1 (Wrong side) P3, k4, (work row 1 of cable panel then row 1 of Tree of life panel) twice, work row 1 of cable panel, k4, p3.
Row 2 Tw2, cr2l, p3, (work row 2 of cable panel then row 2 of Tree of life panel) twice, work row 2 of cable panel, p3, cr3r, tw2.
These 2 rows establish patt. Cont in patt as set, working appropriate rows of panel and inc 1 st at each end of 3rd row and every foll 7th [6th, 5th, 5th] row until there are 86 [90, 94, 96] sts, working extra sts into patt. Cont straight until sleeve measures 42 [43, 43, 44] cm from beg, ending with a wrong side row.
Shape top Cast off 9 sts at beg of next 2 rows. Dec 1 st at each end of next row and every foll alt row until 50 sts rem then on every row until 16 sts rem. Cast off.

BUTTON BANDS AND COLLAR

Button band and collar
Join shoulder seams. Using 3¾mm needles, cast on 11 sts. Work in rib as given for 1st size on left front until band when slightly stretched fits along left front to front shaping, ending with a wrong side row.
Shape collar Cont in rib, inc 1 st at beg of next row and every foll alt row until there are 28 sts then on every foll 4th row until there are 34 [34, 36, 36] sts. Cont straight until collar fits along shaped edge of front to centre back neck. Cast off in rib. Sew in position.
Buttonhole band and collar
Mark button band with pins to indicate buttons, first one to come 2cm up from cast on edge and last one 3cm below beg of collar shaping, rem one spaced equally between.
Work as given for button band, reversing collar shaping and working buttonholes at pin positions as follows:
Buttonhole row Rib 5, cast off 2, rib to end.
Next row Rib to end, casting on 2 sts over those cast off in previous row.
Sew in position then join back seam of collar.

POCKET EDGINGS

With right side facing and using 3¾mm needles, rejoin yarn to the 32 sts left on stitch holder.
Next row K1 tbl, p1, (k1 tbl, p1, k1 tbl, p2 tog) 5 times, (k1 tbl, p1) twice, k1 tbl. 27 sts. Beg 2nd row, work 7 rows in rib as given for 1st size on left front welt. Cast off in rib.
Breast pocket edging
With right side facing and using 3¾mm needles, rejoin yarn to the 20 sts left on stitch holder.
Next row K1 tbl, p1, (k1 tbl, p1, k1 tbl, p2 tog) 3 times, k1 tbl, p1, k1 tbl. 17 sts. Beg 2nd row, work 3 rows in rib as given for 1st size on left front welt. Cast off in rib.

FINISHING

Block each piece as given on p. 140. Catch down pocket linings and sides of pocket edgings. Join side and sleeve seams. Sew in sleeves. Sew on buttons.

WHEAT CABLE ARAN

A delicate Wheat cable used in two different combinations decorates this silky shirt-style sweater. Elaborate patterned welts at the hem and cuffs are interesting characteristics particular to Aran knitting.

MATERIALS

Yarn

Standard 4 ply silk

4 [4, 5, 5] × 100g hanks, fawn

Needles

1 pair size 2¾mm

1 pair size 3¼mm

1 cable needle

Notions

4 buttons 1cm in diameter

MEASUREMENTS

To fit chest 81 [86, 91, 97]cm

32 [34, 36, 38]in

1 Actual chest size 92 [96, 102, 106]cm

36 [38, 40, 42]in

2 Length to back neck 61 [61, 62, 62]cm

24 [24, 24½, 24½]in

3 Sleeve seam 44 [45, 46, 47]cm

17¼ [17¾, 18, 18½]in

Tension

32 sts and 36 rows measure 10cm over pattern on 3¼mm needles (or size needed to obtain given tension)

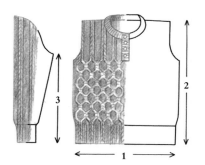

BACK

Using 2¾mm needles, cast on 119 [125, 132, 138] sts.

Row 1 (Wrong side) K2 [1, 2, 1], (p1, k1) 4 [6, 4, 6] times, *p8, k1 (p1, k1) twice; rep from * to last 5 [8, 5, 8] sts, (p1, k1) 2 [4, 2, 4] times, k1 [0, 1, 0].

Row 2 K0 [1, 0, 1], (k1, p1) 5 [6, 5, 6] times, *c4f, c4b, p1, (k1, p1) twice; rep from * to last 5 [8, 5, 8] sts, (k1, p1) 2 [3, 2, 3] times, k1 [2, 1, 2].

Row 3 As row 1.

Row 4 K0 [1, 0, 1], (k1, p1) 5 [6, 5, 6] times, *k8, p1, (k1, p1) twice; rep from * to last 5 [8, 5, 8] sts, (k1, p1) 2 [3, 2, 3] times, k1 [2, 1, 2].

Rep these 4 rows 7 times more, then work rows 1 to 3 once.

Next row K0 [1, 0, 1], (inc in next st, p1) 5 [6, 5, 6] times, *k8, inc in next st, (k1, inc in next st) twice; rep from * to last 18 [21, 18, 21] sts, k8, (p1, inc in next st) 5 [6, 5, 6] times, k0 [1, 0, 1]. *150 [158, 166, 174] sts.*

Change to 3¼mm needles. Commence patt.

Row 1 K15 [19, 15, 19], (p8, k8) to last 7 [11, 7, 11] sts, k7 [11, 7, 11].

Row 2 P15 [19, 15, 19], c4f, c4b, p8) to last 7 [11, 7, 11] sts, p7 [11, 7, 11].

Row 3 As row 1.

Row 4 P15 [19, 15, 19], (k8, p8) to last 7 [11, 7, 11] sts, p7 [11, 7, 11].

Rows 5 to 8 As rows 1 to 4.

Rows 9 and 10 As rows 1 and 2.

Row 11 K15 [19, 15, 19], *p2, ybk, sl4, yfwd, sl same 4 sts back on to left hand needle, ybk, sl4, yfwd – referred to as bind 4, p2, k8; rep from * to last 7 [11, 7, 11] sts, k7 [11, 7, 11].

Row 12 P14 [18, 14, 18], *cr3r, p4, cr3l, p6; rep from * to last 8 [12, 8, 12] sts, p8 [12, 8, 12].

Row 13 K14 [18, 14, 18], (p2, k6) to last 8 [12, 8, 12] sts, k8 [12, 8, 12].

Row 14 P13 [17, 13, 17], (cr3r, p6, cr3l, p4) to last 9 [13, 9, 13] sts, p9 [13, 9, 13].

Row 15 K13 [17, 13, 17], (p2, k8, p2, bind 4) to last 25 [29, 25, 29] sts, p2, k8, p2, k13 [17, 13, 17].

Row 16 P13 [17, 13, 17], k2, (p8, c4f, c4b) to last 23 [27, 23, 27] sts, p8, k2, p13 [17, 13, 17].

Row 17 K13 [17, 13, 17], p2, (k8, p8) to last 23 [27, 23, 27] sts, k8, p2, k13 [17, 13, 17].

Row 18 P13 [17, 13, 17], k2, (p8, k8) to last 23 [27, 23, 27] sts, p8, k2, p13 [17, 13, 17].

Row 19 As row 17.

Rows 20 to 23 As rows 16 to 19.

Row 24 As row 16.

Row 25 As row 15.

Row 26 P13 [17, 13, 17], (cr3l, p6, cr3r, p4) to last 9 [13, 9, 13] sts, p9 [13, 9, 13].

Row 27 As row 13.

Row 28 P14 [18, 14, 18], (cr3l, p4, cr3r, p6) to last 8 [12, 8, 12] sts, p8 [12, 8, 12].

Row 29 As row 11.

Rows 2 to 29 form bodice patt.

Cont in bodice patt until 4 patt reps in all have been worked, ending with row 29. Rows 2 to 5 of bodice form yoke patt**.

Cont in yoke patt, work 4 rows.

Shape armholes Cast off 6 sts at beg of next 2 rows. Dec 1 st at each end of next row and every foll alt row until 124 [124, 132, 140] sts rem. Cont straight until armholes measure 20 [20, 21, 21]cm, ending with a wrong side row.

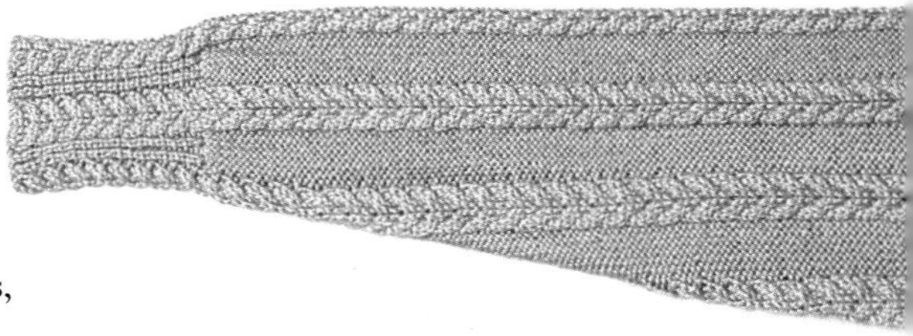

Shape shoulders Cast off 9 [9, 9, 10] sts at beg of next 6 rows and 8 [8, 10, 11] sts at beg of foll 2 rows. Cast off rem 54 [54, 58, 58] sts.

POCKET LINING

Using 3¼mm needles, cast on 20 sts. Beg k row, work 5cm in st st, ending with a p row.

Next row (K2, inc in next st, k2) to end. *24 sts.* Leave these sts on a spare needle.

FRONT

Work as given for back to **. Cont in yoke patt.

Divide for neck opening

Next row Patt 72 [76, 79, 83], cast off next 6 [6, 8, 8] sts, patt to end. Complete right side of front first. Patt 4 rows.

Shape armhole Cast off 6 sts at beg of next row. Dec 1 st at armhole edge on next row and every foll alt row until 59 [59, 62, 66] sts rem. Cont straight until armhole measures 14 [14, 15, 15]cm, ending at neck edge.

Shape neck Cast off 12 sts at beg of next row. Dec 1 st at neck edge on every row until 35 [35, 37, 41] sts rem. Cont straight until front matches back to shoulder, ending at armhole edge.

Shape shoulder Cast off 9 sts at beg of next row and 2 foll alt rows. Work 1 row. Cast off rem 8 [8, 10, 11] sts. With wrong side facing, rejoin yarn to rem sts and patt to end. Patt 3 rows.

Shape armhole Cast off 6 sts at beg of next row. Dec 1 st at armhole edge on foll 4 alt rows. *62 [66, 69, 73] sts.*

Place pocket
Next row Patt 17 [17, 24, 24], sl next 24 sts on to a holder and leave at back, patt across pocket lining, patt to end. Cont to dec at armhole edge on next row and every foll alt row until 59 [59, 62, 66] sts rem. Complete to match right side of front.

SLEEVES

Using 2¾mm needles, cast on 54 sts.
Row 1 (Wrong side) K1, *p4, k1, (p1, k1) twice, p4; rep from * 3 times more, k1.
Row 2 K1, *c4b, p1, (k1, p1) twice, c4f; rep from * 3 times more, k1.
Row 3 As row 1.
Row 4 K1, *k4, p1, (k1, p1) twice, k4; rep from * 3 times more, k1. Rep these 4 rows 7 times more, then work rows 1 to 3 once.
Next row Inc in first st, *k4, inc in next st, (k1, inc in next st) twice, k4; rep from * 3 times more, inc in last st. *68 sts*.

Change to 3¼mm needles. Commence patt.
Row 1 K1, p1, (p4, k8, p4) 4 times, p1, k1.
Row 2 K2, (c4b, p8, c4f) 4 times, k2.
Row 3 As row 1.
Row 4 K2, (k4, p8, k4) 4 times, k2.
These 4 rows form patt. Cont in patt, inc 1 st at each end of 2nd and every foll 4th row until there are 114 [122, 122, 130] sts, working extra sts into patt. Cont straight until sleeve measures 44 [45, 46, 47]cm from beg, ending with wrong side row.
Shape top Cast off 6 sts at beg of next 2 rows. Dec 1 st at each end of next row and every foll alt row until 86 [102, 94, 110] sts rem, then on every row to 40 sts. Cast off 4 sts at beg of next 6 rows. Cast off rem 16 sts.

Designed by
Brinion Heaton

NECKBAND

Join shoulder seams. With right side facing and using 2¾mm needles, pick up and k 30 sts up right side of neck, 44 [44, 48, 48] sts across back neck, 30 sts down left side of neck. *104 [104, 108, 108] sts.*
Row 1 (Wrong side) K1, p2, (k2, p2) to last st, k1.
Row 2 K3, (p2, k2) to last st, k1.
Rep these 2 rows 3 times more then rep row 1 again. Cast off in rib.

BUTTON BANDS

Buttonhole band

With right side facing and using 2¾mm needles, pick up and k 40 sts evenly along right side of neck opening. Beg with 1st row, work 3 rows in rib as given for neckband.
Buttonhole row Rib 6, (cast off 2, rib 8 including st used in casting off) 3 times, cast off 2, rib to end.
Next row Rib to end, casting on 2 sts over those cast off in previous row.
Rib 4 rows. Cast off in rib.

Opposite: Fountain lace Aran, Wheat cable Aran

Button band

Work as given for buttonhole band but picking up sts along left side of neck opening and omitting buttonholes.

POCKET EDGINGS

With right side facing and using 2¾mm needles, rejoin yarn to the 24 sts left on holder. Beg with 2nd row, work 8 rows as given for neckband. Cast off in rib.

FINISHING

Block each piece as given on p. 140. Catch down pocket lining and sides of pocket edging. Overlap buttonhole band over button band and catch down at base of opening. Join side and sleeve seams. Sew in sleeves. Sew on buttons.

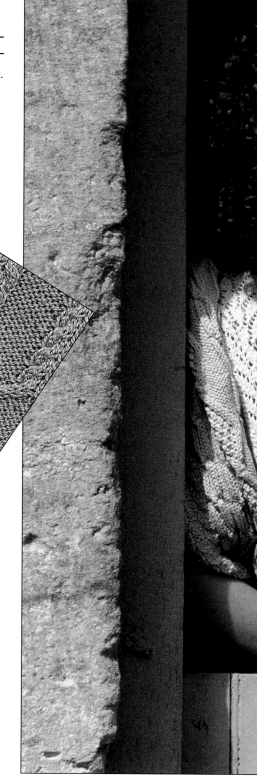

FOUNTAIN LACE ARAN

Alternating panels of Fountain lace and Plait cable are combined in this delicate sweater. A neat collar and buttons at the back neck complete a classic, summery, cotton top.

MATERIALS

Yarn

Standard 4 ply cotton

7 [7, 8, 8] × 50g balls, cream

Needles

1 pair size $2\frac{3}{4}$mm

1 pair size $3\frac{1}{4}$mm

Notions

4 buttons, 1.5cm in diameter

Designed by Brinion Heaton

MEASUREMENTS

To fit chest 81 [86, 91, 97]cm	
32 [34, 36, 38]in	
1 Actual chest size 88 [92, 97, 102]cm	
34½ [36¼, 38, 40]in	
2 Length to back neck 51 [52, 52, 53]cm	
20 [20½, 20½, 21]in	
3 Sleeve seam 9cm, 3½in	

Tension

28 sts and 36 rows measure 10cm over stocking stitch on 3¼mm needles (or size needed to obtain given tension)

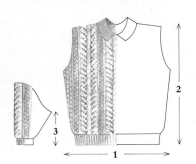

BACK

Using 2¾mm needles, cast on 101 [105, 109, 115] sts.
Row 1 (Right side) K1 tbl, (p1, k1 tbl) to end.
Row 2 P1, (k1 tbl, p1) to end.
Rep these 2 rows until rib measures 6cm, ending with row 1.
Next row Rib 3 [2, 1, 1], (inc in next st, rib 2) to last 5 [4, 3, 3] sts, inc in next st, rib to end. *133 [139, 145, 153] sts.*
Change to 3¼mm needles. Commence patt.
Row 1 (P2, k2) 3 [3, 3, 4] times, p2, *k9, p2 [3, 4, 4], k1, k2 tog, yfwd, k2, k2 tog, k1, yfwd, sl 1, k2 tog, psso, yfwd, k1, yfwd, k2 tog, k2, yfwd, k2 tog tbl, k1, p2 [3, 4, 4]; rep from * twice more, k9, p2, (k2, p2) 3 [3, 3, 4] times.
Row 2 (K2, p2) 3 [3, 3, 4] times, k2, *p9 [3, 4, 4], p19, k2 [3, 4, 4]; rep from * twice more, p9, p2, (k2, k2) 3 [3, 3, 4] times.
Row 3 (K2, p2) 3 [3, 3, 4] times, p2, *c6f, k3, p2 [3, 4, 4], k1, k2 tog, (k3, yfwd, k2 tog, yfwd) twice, k3, k2 tog tbl, k1, p2 [3, 4, 4]; rep from * twice more, c6f, k3, p2, (k2, k2) 3 [3, 3, 4] times.
Row 4 (P2, k2) 3 [3, 3, 4] times, k2, *p9, k2 [3, 4, 4], p19, k2 [3, 4, 4]; rep from * twice more, p9, p2, (k2, p2) 3 [3, 3, 4] times.
Row 5 (P2, k2) 3 [3, 3, 4] times, p2, *k9, p2 [3, 4, 4], k1, k2 tog, (k2, yfwd) twice, k2 tog, k1, k2 tog, (yfwd, k2) twice, k2 tog tbl, k1, p2 [3, 4, 4]; rep from * twice more, k9, p2, (k2, p2) 3 [3, 3, 4] times.
Row 6 (K2, p2) 3 [3, 3, 4] times, k2, *p9, k2 [3, 4, 4], p19, k2 [3, 4, 4]; rep from * twice more, p9, p2, (k2, k2) 3 [3, 3, 4] times.
Row 7 (K2, p2) 3 [3, 3, 4] times, p2, *k3, c6b, p2 [3, 4, 4], k1, k2 tog, k1, yfwd, k3, yfwd, k2 tog, k1, k2 tog, yfwd, k3, yfwd, k1, k2 tog tbl, k1, p2 [3, 4, 4]; rep from * twice more, k3, c6b, p2, (k2, p2) 3 [3, 3, 4] times.
Row 8 (P2, k2) 3 [3, 3, 4] times, k2, *p9, k2 [3, 4, 4], p19, k2 [3, 4, 4]; rep from * twice more, p9, k2, (k2, p2) 3 [3, 3, 4] times.
These 8 rows form patt. Cont in patt until work measures 32 [33, 33, 34]cm from beg, ending with a wrong side row.
Shape armholes Keeping continuity of patt, cast off 6 sts at beg of next 2 rows. Dec 1 st at each end of next row and every foll alt row until 109 [115, 121, 121] sts rem. **Cont straight until armholes measure 9cm, ending with a wrong side row.
Divide for back neck opening
Next row Patt 55 [58, 61, 61] sts and turn; leave rem sts on a spare needle.
Complete right side of neck first. Cont straight until armhole measures 19cm, ending at neck edge.
Shape neck and shoulder
Next row Cast off 12, patt to end.
Next row Cast off 7 [8, 8, 8], patt to last 2 sts, k2 tog.
Next row K2 tog, patt to end.
Rep last 2 rows 3 times more. Cast off rem 7 [6, 9, 9] sts. With right side facing, rejoin yarn to rem sts, cast on 1, patt to end. Complete as given for first side of neck.

FRONT

Work as given for back to **. Cont straight until armholes measure 15cm, ending with a wrong side row.
Shape neck
Next row Patt 45 [48, 51, 51] sts, cast off 19, patt to end.
Complete right side of neck first. Dec 1 st at neck edge on every row until 35 [38, 41, 41] sts rem. Cont straight until front matches back to shoulder, ending at armhole edge.
Shape shoulder Cast off 7 [8, 8, 8] sts at beg of next row and 3 foll alt rows. Work 1 row. Cast off rem 7 [6, 9, 9] sts. With wrong side facing, rejoin yarn to rem sts and patt to end. Complete as given for first side of neck.

SLEEVES

Using 2¾mm needles, cast on 75 sts. Work 2cm in rib as given for back welt, ending with row 1.
Next row Rib 3, (inc in next st, rib 2) to end. *99 sts.*
Change to 3¼mm needles. Commence patt.
Row 1 P4, *k1, k2 tog, yfwd, k2, k2 tog, yfwd, k1, yfwd, sl 1, k2 tog, psso, yfwd, k1, yfwd, k2 tog, k2, yfwd, k2 tog tbl, k1, p4, k9, p4; rep from * once more, k1, k2 tog, yfwd, k2, k2 tog, yfwd, k1, yfwd, sl 1, k2 tog, psso, yfwd, k1, yfwd, k2 tog, k2, yfwd, k2 tog tbl, k1, p4.
Row 2 K4, *p19, k4, p9, k4; rep from * once more, p19, k4.
Row 3 P4, *k1, k2 tog, (k3, yfwd, k2 tog, yfwd) twice, k3, k2 tog tbl, k1, p4, c6f, k3, p4; rep from * once more, k1, k2 tog, (k3, yfwd, k2 tog, yfwd) twice, k3, k2 tog tbl, k1, p4.
Row 4 As row 2.
Row 5 P4, *k1, k2 tog, (k2, yfwd) twice, k2 tog, k1, k2 tog, (yfwd, k2) twice, k2 tog tbl, k1, p4, k9, p4; rep from * once more, k1, k2 tog, (k2, yfwd) twice, k2 tog, k1, k2 tog, (yfwd, k2) twice, k2 tog tbl, k1, p4.

Row 6 As row 2.
Row 7 P4, *k1, k2 tog, k1, yfwd, k3, yfwd, k2 tog, k1, k2 tog, yfwd, k3, yfwd, k1, k2 tog tbl, k1, p4, k3, c6b, p4; rep from * once more, k1, k2 tog, k1, yfwd, k3, yfwd, k2 tog, k1, k2 tog, yfwd, k3, yfwd, k1, k2 tog tbl, k1, p4.
Row 8 As row 2.
These 8 rows form patt. Cont in patt until sleeve measures 9cm from beg, ending with a wrong side row.
Shape top Keeping continuity of patt, cast off 6 sts at beg of next 2 rows. Dec 1 st at each end of next row and every foll alt row until 51 sts rem, ending with a wrong side row. Cast off 3 sts at beg of next 8 rows. Cast off rem 27 sts.

COLLAR

With a crochet hook, work 1 row in dc around back neck opening making 4 buttonhole loops on left side edge. Join shoulder seams. With right side of back facing, using 2¾mm needles, pick up and k 20 sts up left back neck and 38 sts down left front neck to centre.
Row 1 (K1 tbl, p1) to end.
This row forms rib.
Row 2 Rib 34 and turn.
Row 3 Sl 1, rib 9 and turn.
Row 4 Sl 1, rib 15 and turn.
Row 5 Sl 1, rib 21 and turn.
Row 6 Sl 1, rib 27 and turn.
Row 7 Sl 1, rib 33 and turn.
Row 8 Sl 1, rib 39 and turn.
Row 9 Sl 1, rib 45 and turn.
Row 10 Sl 1, rib 51 and turn.
Row 11 Sl 1, rib to end.
Cont in rib across all sts for a further 3cm. Cast off in rib. With right side facing, using 2¾mm needles and beg at centre front, pick up and k 38 sts up right front neck and 20 sts down right back neck. Complete as given for first side.

FINISHING

Block as given on p. 140. Join side and sleeve seams. Sew in sleeves. Sew on buttons.

BLACKBERRY ARAN

Asymmetric patterning, with one front reflecting the opposite sleeve, is a feature of this mandarin-style jacket. The plain texture of the Trellis pattern is heightened by the elaborate patterning of the Blackberry bobbles, Open and Plait cables.

MATERIALS

Yarn

Standard Aran-weight wool

28 × 50g balls, oatmeal

Needles

1 pair size 3¾mm

1 pair size 4½mm

1 pair size 5mm

1 cable needle

Notions

5 buttons, 3cm in diameter

MEASUREMENTS

To fit chest 86–97cm, 34–38in

1 Actual chest size 120cm, 47in

2 Length 75cm, 29½in

3 Sleeve seam 42cm, 16½in

Tension

24 sts and 26 rows measure 10cm over diamond and cable pattern on 4½mm needles (or size needed to obtain given tension)

22 sts and 24 rows measure 10cm over lattice pattern on 5mm needles (or size needed to obtain given tension)

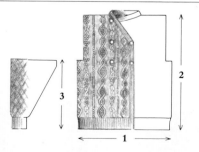

RIGHT FRONT

Using 3¾mm needles, cast on 87 sts.

Row 1 (Right side) K1, (p1, k1) to end.

Row 2 P1, (k1, p1) to end.

Rep these 2 rows until rib measures 7cm, ending with a 2nd row. Change to 4½mm needles. Commence patt.

Row 1 *P6, cr5, p8, mlb, p4, k9, p2*; rep from * to * once, p6, cr5, p6.

Row 2 K6, p2, k1, p2, k6, *k2, p9, k4, p1, k8, p2, k1, p2, k6*; rep from * to * once.

Row 3 *P5, cr3r, p1, cr3l, p7, k1, p4, c6f, k3, p2*; rep from * to * once, p5, cr3r, p1, cr3l, p5.

Row 4 K5, p2, k3, p2, k5, *k2, p9, k4, p1, k7, p2, k3, p2, k5*; rep from * to * once.

Row 5 *P4, cr3r, p1, msb, p1, cr3l, p6, mlb, p4, k9, p2*; rep from * to * once, p4, cr3r, p1, msb, p1, cr3l, p4.

Row 6 K4, p2, k2, p1, k2, p2, k4, *k2, p9, k4, p1, k6, p2, k2, p1, k2, p2, k4*; rep from * to * once.

Row 7 *P3, cr3r, p5, cr3l, p5, k1, p4, k3, c6b, p2*; rep from * to * once, p3, cr3r, p5, cr3l, p3.

Row 8 K3, p2, k7, p2, k3, *k2, p9, k4, p1, k5, p2, k7, p2, k3*; rep from * to * once.

Row 9 *P2, cr3r, p1, msb, p3, msb, p1, cr3l, p4, mlb, p4, k9, p2*; rep from * to * once, p2, cr3r, p1, msb, p3, msb, p1, cr3l, p2.

Row 10 K2, p2, k2, p1, k3, p1, k2, p2, k2, *k2, p9, k4, p1, k4, p2, k2, p1, k3, p1, k2, p2, k2*; rep from * to * once.

Row 11 *P2, k2, p9, k2, p4, k1, p4, c6f, k3, p2*; rep from * to * once, p2, k2, p9, k2, p2.

Row 12 K2, p2, k9, p2, k2, *k2, p9, k4, p1, k4, p2, k9, p2, k2*; rep from * to * once.

Row 13 *P2, k2, p2, msb, p3, msb, p2, k2, p4, mlb, p4, k9, p2*; rep from * to * once, p2, k2, p2, msb, p3, msb, p2, k2, p2.

Row 14 As row 10.

Row 15 *P2, cr3l, p7, cr3r, p4, k1, p4, k3, c6b, p2*; rep from * to * once, p2, cr3l, p7, cr3r, p2.

Row 16 As row 8.

Row 17 *P3, cr3l, p2, msb, p2, cr3r, p5, mlb, p4, k9, p2*; rep from * to * once, p3, cr3l, p2, msb, p2, cr3r, p3.

Row 18 K4, p2, k2, p1, k2, p2, k4, *k6, p1, k8, p1, k6, p2, k2, p1, k2, p2, k4*; rep from * to * once.

Row 19 *P4, cr3l, p3, cr3r, p6, k1, p8, msb, p6*; rep from * to * once, p4, cr3l, p3, cr3r, p4.

Row 20 K5, p2, k3, p2, k5, *k6, p1, k8, p1, k7, p2, k3, p2, k5*; rep from * to * once.

Row 21 *P5, cr3l, p1, cr3r, p7, k1, p7, msb, p1, msb, p5*; rep from * to * once, p5, cr3l, p1, cr3r, p5.

Row 22 K6, p2, k1, p2, k6, *k5, p1, k1, p1, k7, p1, k8, p2, k1, p2, k6*; rep from * to * once.

Row 23 *P6, cr5, p8, k1, p6, (msb, p1) twice, msb, p4*; rep from * to * once, p6, cr5, p6.

Row 24 K6, p2, k1, p2, k6, *k4, (p1, k1) twice, p1, k6, p1, k8, p2, k1, p2, k6*; rep from * to * once.

Row 25 *P5, cr3r, p1, cr3l, p7, k1, p8, k1, p6*; rep from * to * once, p5, cr3r, p1, cr3l, p5.

Row 26 As row 20.

Row 27 *P4, cr3r, p3, cr3l, p6, k1, p8, msb, p6*; rep from * to * once, p4, cr3r, p3, cr3l, p4.

Row 28 K4, p2, k5, p2, k4, *k6, p1, k8, p1, k6, p2, k5, p2, k4*; rep from * to * once.

Row 29 *P4, k2, p2, msb, p2, k2, p6, k1, p7, msb, p1, msb, p5*; rep from * to * once, p4, k2, p2, msb, p2, k2, p4.

Row 30 K4, p2, k2, p1, k2, p2, k4, *k5, p1, k1, p1, k7, p1, k6, p2, k2, p1, k2, p2, k4*; rep from * to * once.

Row 31 *P4, cr3l, p3, cr3r, p6, k1, p6, (msb, p1) twice, msb, p4*; rep from * to * once, p4, cr3l, p3, cr3r, p4.

Row 32 K5, p2, k3, p2, k5, *k4, (p1, k1) twice, p1, k6, p1, k7, p2, k3, p2, k5*; rep from * to * once.

Row 33 *P5, cr3l, p1, cr3r, p7, k1, p8, k1, p6*; rep from * to * once, p5, cr3l, p1, cr3r, p5.

Row 34 As row 2.

These 34 rows form diamond and cable patt. Cont in patt until work measures 42cm from beg, ending with a wrong side row.

Buttonhole row Patt 32, cast off 3, patt to end.

Next row Patt to end, casting on 3 sts over those cast off in previous row. Cont in patt until work measures 46cm from beg, ending with a right side row.

Shape armhole Cast off 13 sts at beg of next row. *74 sts.* Cont straight until armhole measures 12cm, ending with a wrong side row.

Rep the 2 buttonhole rows once. Patt 2 rows.

Shape neck Dec 1 st at beg of next row and at same edge on every row until 44 sts rem.

Buttonhole row Work 2 tog, cast off 3, patt to end.

Next row Patt to end, casting on 3 sts over those cast off in previous row.

Dec 1 st at beg of next row and at same edge on every row until 36 sts rem. Cont straight until armhole measures 27cm, ending at armhole edge.

Shape shoulder Cast off 12 sts at beg of next row and foll alt row. Work 1 row. Cast off rem 12 sts.

LEFT FRONT

Using 3¾mm needles, cast on 90 sts. Work 7cm in k1, p1 rib. Change to 5mm needles. Commence patt.

Designed by Alison Robson

Row 1 (Right side) Sl next st on to cable needle and leave at back, k1, k1 from cable needle, (p6, sl next st on to cable needle, and leave at back, k1, k1 from cable needle) to end.
Row 2 P2, (k6, p2) to end.
Row 3 P1, (sl next st on to cable needle and leave at front, p1, k1 from cable needle – referred to as cr2l, p4, sl next st on to cable needle and leave at back, k1, p1 from cable needle – referred to as cr2r) to last st, p1.
Row 4 K2, (p1, k4, p1, k2) to end.
Row 5 P2, (cr2l, p2, cr2r, p2) to end.
Row 6 K1, (k2, p1, k2, p1, k2) to last st, k1.
Row 7 P1, (p2, cr2l, cr2r, p2) to last st, p1.
Row 8 K2, (k2, p2, k4) to end.
Row 9 P2, (p2, sl next st on to cable needle and leave at front, k1, k1 from cable needle, p4) to end.
Row 10 As row 8.
Row 11 P1, (p2, cr2r, cr2l, p2) to last st, p1.
Row 12 As row 6.
Row 13 P2, (cr2r, p2, cr2l, p2) to end.
Row 14 As row 4.
Row 15 P1, (cr2r, p4, cr2l) to last st, p1.
Row 16 As row 2.
These 16 rows form lattice patt. Cont in patt until work measures 46cm from beg, ending with a wrong side row.
Shape armhole Cast off 12 sts at beg of next row. Cont straight until armhole measures 22cm, ending at front edge.
Shape neck Cast off 25 sts at beg of next row and 5 sts at beg of 4 foll alt rows. Patt 2 rows.
Shape shoulder Cast off 11 sts at beg of next row and foll alt row. Work 1 row. Cast off.

BACK

Using 3¾mm needles, cast on 139 sts. Work 7cm in rib as given for right front welt, ending with a 2nd row and inc 1 st at centre of last row. *140 sts.* Change to 4½mm needles. Commence patt.
Row 1 Rep row 1 of right front patt from * to * 4 times.
Row 2 Rep row 2 of right front patt from * to * 4 times.
Row 3 Rep row 3 of right front patt from * to * 4 times.
Row 4 Rep row 4 of right front patt from * to * 4 times.
These 4 rows establish patt for back. Cont in patt as set until back measures 46cm from beg, ending with a wrong side row.
Shape armholes Cast off 13 sts at beg of next 2 rows. *114 sts.* Cont straight until back matches front to shoulder shaping, ending with a wrong side row.
Shape shoulders Cast off 12 sts at beg of next 6 rows. Cast off rem 42 sts.

RIGHT SLEEVE

Using 3¾mm needles, cast on 49 sts. Work 7cm rib as given for right front welt, ending with a 1st row.
Next row (Rib 1, pick up loop lying between needles and p tbl) to last st, inc in last st, *98 sts.*
Change to 5mm needles. Cont in lattice patt as given for left front, inc 1st at each end of 9th row and every foll 6th row until there are 120 sts, working extra sts into patt. Cont straight until sleeve measures 42cm from beg. Mark each end of last row. Work a further 5cm, ending with a wrong side row. Cast off.

LEFT SLEEVE

Using 3¾mm needles, cast on 49 sts. Work 7cm rib as given for right front welt, ending with a 1st row.
Next row (Work 3 times into next st) 3 times, (work 3 times into next st, rib 1) 21 times, (work 3 times into next st) 3 times, work twice in last st. *104 sts.*
Change to 4½mm needles. Commence patt.
Row 1 K2, p8, mlb, p4, k9, p2, now rep row 1 of right front patt from * to * twice, p6, k2.
Row 2 P2, k6, now rep row 2 of right front patt from * to * twice, k2, p9, k4, p1, k8, p2.
Row 3 Cr3l, p7, k1, p4, c6f, k3, p2, now rep 3rd row of right front patt from * to * twice, p5, cr3r.
Row 4 K1, p2, k5, now rep row 4 of right front patt from * to * twice, k2, p9, k4, p1, k7, p2, k1.
These 4 rows establish patt for left sleeve. Cont in patt as set, inc 1 st at each end of 5th row and every foll 6th row until there are 130 sts, working extra sts into diamond patt. Complete as given for right sleeve.

BUTTON BANDS

Button band
Using 3¾mm needles, cast on 9 sts. Work in rib as given for right front welt until band when slightly stretched fits along left front to beg of neck shaping**. Cast off in rib. Sew band in position.
Buttonhole band
Join shoulder seams. Work as given for button band to ** making 2 buttonholes in line with 1st and 2nd buttonholes on right front as follows:
Buttonhole row Rib 3, cast off 3, rib to end.
Next row Rib to end, casting on 3 sts over those cast off in previous row.
Cont in rib until band fits along right front neck, across back and along left front neck and button band. Cast off in rib. Sew band in position.

FINISHING

Block each piece as given on p. 140. Sew in sleeves, sewing rows above markers to cast off sts at armholes. Join side and sleeve seams. Sew on buttons.

BOBBLE FAN
ARAN

Deep armholes and a loose fit make this boat-neck sweater comfortable to wear. Plain cotton yarn shows off the intricate stitch patterns which include Bobble fans, Open cables and Twisted cables.

MATERIALS

Yarn

Standard double knitting cotton

24×50g balls, jade

Needles

1 pair size 3mm

1 pair size $3\frac{3}{4}$mm

1 cable needle

MEASUREMENTS

To fit chest 86-91cm, 34-36in

1 Actual chest size 100cm, $39\frac{1}{2}$in

2 Length to shoulder 62cm, $24\frac{1}{2}$in

3 Sleeve seam 50cm, $19\frac{3}{4}$in

Tension

24 sts and 26 rows measure 10cm over pattern on $3\frac{3}{4}$mm needles (or size needed to obtain given tension)

Designed by Alison Robson

Diamond panel

Worked over 19 sts.
Row 1 (Wrong side) K7, p2, k1, p2, k7.
Row 2 P7, cr5, p7.
Row 3 As row 1.
Row 4 P6, cr3r, p1, cr3l, p6.
Row 5 K6, p2, k3, p2, k6.
Row 6 P5, cr3r, p1, msb, p1, cr3l, p5.
Row 7 K5, p2, k2, p1, k2, p2, k5.
Row 8 P4, cr3r, p5, cr3l, p4.
Row 9 K4, p2, k7, p2, k4.
Row 10 P3, cr3r, p1, msb, p3, msb, p1, cr3l, p3.
Row 11 K3, p2, k2, p1, k3, p1, k2, p2, k3.
Row 12 P3, k2, p9, k2, p3.
Row 13 K3, p2, k9, p2, k3.
Row 14 P3, k2, p2, msb, p3, msb, p2, k2, p3.
Row 15 As row 11.

Row 16 P3, cr3l, p7, cr3r, p3.
Row 17 As row 9.
Row 18 P4, cr3l, p2, msb, p2, cr3r, p4.
Row 19 As row 7.
Row 20 P5, cr3l, p3, cr3r, p5.
Row 21 As row 5.
Row 22 P6, cr3l, p1, cr3r, p6.
Row 23 As row 1.
Rows 24 to 27 As rows 2 to 5.
Row 28 P5, cr3r, p3, cr3l, p5.
Row 29 K5, p2, k5, p2, k5.
Row 30 P5, k2, p2, msb, p2, k2, p5.
Rows 31 to 34 As rows 19 to 22.
These 34 rows form diamond panel pattern.

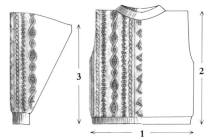

Bobble fan panel

Worked over 17 sts.
Row 1 (Wrong side) P1, k15, p1.
Row 2 K1, p7, mlb, p7, k1.
Row 3 P1, k7, p1 tbl, k7, p1.
Row 4 K1, p4, mlb, p2, k1 tbl, p2, mlb, p4, k1.
Row 5 P1, k4, (p1 tbl, k2) 3 times, k2, p1.
Row 6 K1, p2, mlb, p1, sl next st on to cable needle and leave at front, p1, k1 tbl from cable needle – referred to as cr2l, p1, k1 tbl, sl next st on to cable needle and leave at back, k1 tbl, p1 from cable needle – referred to as cr2r, p1, mlb, p2, k1.
Row 7 P1, k2, p1 tbl, k2, (p1 tbl, k1) 3 times, k1, p1 tbl, k2, p1.
Row 8 K1, p1, (p1, cr2l) twice, k1 tbl, (cr2r, p1) twice, p1, k1.

Row 9 P1, k3, sl next st on to cable needle and leave at back, k1, p1 tbl from cable needle – referred to as tw2l, k1, p3 tbl, k1, sl next st on to cable needle and leave at front, p1 tbl, k1 from cable needle – referred to as tw2r, k3, p1.
Row 10 K1, p4, cr2l, pick up loop lying between needles and p tbl – referred to as m1, sl1, k2 tog, psso, m1, cr2r, p4, k1.
Row 11 P1, k5, tw2l, p1 tbl, tw2r, k5, p1.
Row 12 K1, p6, m1, sl1, k2 tog, psso, m1, p6, k1.
Row 13 As row 3.
Row 14 K1, p15, k1.
Row 15 As row 1.
Row 16 As row 14.
These 16 rows form bobble panel pattern.

BACK

Using 3mm needles, cast on 111 sts.
Row 1 (Right side) K1, (p1, k1) to end.
Row 2 P1, (k1, p1) to end.
Rep these 2 rows until rib measures 3cm, ending with a 2nd row.
Next row Rib 6 (inc in next st, rib 8) to last 6 sts, inc in next st, rib to end. *123 sts.* Change to 3¾mm needles. Commence patt.
Row 1 (Wrong side) P2, *k3, p6, k5, p1, k1, work row 1 of diamond panel, k1, p1, k5, p6, k3*; work row 1 of bobble panel, now rep from * to * once, p2.
Row 2 K2, *p3, k6, p5, msb, p1, work row 2 of diamond panel, p1, msb, p5, k6, p3*; work row 2 of bobble panel, now rep from * to * once, k2.
Row 3 P2, *k3, p6, k5, p1, k1, work row 3 of diamond panel, k1, p1, k5, p6, k3*; work row 3 of bobble panel, now rep from * to * once, p2.
Row 4 K2, *p3, c6f, p4, msb, k1, msb, work row 4 of diamond panel, msb, k1, msb, p4, c6f, p3*; work row 4 of bobble panel, now rep from * to * once, k2.
Row 5 P2, *k3, p6, k4, p3, work 5th row of diamond panel, p3, k4, p6, k3*; work row 5 of bobble panel, now rep from * to * once, p2.
Row 6 K2, *p3, k6, p5, k1, p1, work row 6 of diamond panel, p1, k1, p5, k6, p3*; work row 6 of bobble panel, now rep from * to * once, k2.
These 6 rows establish patt. Cont in patt as set, working appropriate rows of panels until work measures 32cm from beg, ending with a wrong side row.
Shape armholes Cast off 2 sts at beg of next 2 rows. Dec 1 st at each end of 5th row and every foll 6th row until 99 sts rem. Cont straight until armholes measure 30cm, ending with a wrong side row.
Shape neck and shoulders
Next row Patt 36 sts, cast off 27, patt to end. Complete left side of neck first.
Next row Patt to end.
**Next row Cast off 5, patt to end.
Next row Cast off 7, patt to end.
Rep last 2 rows once.
Next row Cast off 5, patt to end.
Cast off rem 7 sts**. With wrong side facing, rejoin yarn to rem sts and complete as given for first side from ** to **.

FRONT

Work as given for back until armholes measure 27cm, ending with a wrong side row.

Shape neck
Next row Patt 46 sts, cast off 7, patt to end. Complete right side of neck first.
Next row Patt to end.
Next row Cast off 4, patt to end.
Rep these last 2 rows 4 times.
Shape shoulder
Next row Cast off 7, patt to end.
Next row Cast off 5, patt to end.
Next row Cast off 7, patt to end.
Patt 1 row. Cast off rem 7 sts. With wrong side facing, rejoin yarn to rem sts.
Next row Cast off 4, patt to end.
Next row Patt to end.
Rep last 2 rows 3 times.
Next row Cast off 4, patt to end.
Shape shoulder
Complete as given for first side.

SLEEVES

Using 3mm needles, cast on 51 sts. Work 5cm rib as for back welt, ending with a 2nd row.
Next row (Inc in next st, rib 1) to last st, inc in last st. *77 sts.* Change to 3¾mm needles. Commence patt.
Row 1 (Wrong side) K2, p2, k1, p2, k8, p1, k5, p6, k3, work row 1 of bobble panel, k3, p6, k5, p1, k8, p2, k1, p2, k2.
Row 2 P2, cr5, p8, msb, p5, k6, p3, work row 2 of bobble panel, p3, k6, p5, msb, p8, cr5, p2.
Row 3 K2, p2, k1, p2, k8, p1, k5, p6, k3, work row 3 of bobble panel, k3, p6, k5, p1, k8, p2, k1, p2, k2.
Row 4 P1, cr3r, p1, cr3l, p6, msb, k1, msb, p4, c6f, p3, work row 4 of bobble panel, p3, c6f, p4, msb, k1, msb, p6, cr3r, p1, cr3l, p1.
Row 5 K1, p2, k3, p2, k6, p3, k4, p6, k3, work row 5 of bobble panel, k3, p6, k4, p3, k6, p2, k3, p2, k1.
Row 6 Cr3r, p1, msb, p1, cr3l, p6, k1, p5, k6, p3, work 6th row of bobble panel, p3, k6, p5, k1, p6, cr3r, p1, msb, p1, cr3l.
These 6 rows establish patt. Cont in patt as set, working appropriate rows of panels, inc 1 st at each end of next row and every foll 3rd row until there are 151 sts, working extra sts into patt. Patt 1 row.
Shape top Cast off 8 sts at beg of next 12 rows. Cast off rem 55 sts.

BACK NECK EDGING

With right side facing and using 3mm needles, pick up and k 75 sts evenly along neck. Beg with a 2nd row, work 12 rows in rib as given for back welt, dec 1 st at each end of every foll alt row. Rib a further 12 rows, inc 1 st at each end of every foll alt row. Cast off in rib.

FRONT NECK EDGING

With right side facing and using 3mm needles, pick up and k 83 sts evenly along neck. Complete as given for back neck edging.

FINISHING

Block each piece as given on p. 140. Join shoulder and neck edging seams. Fold neck edging in half to wrong side and slip stitch. Sew in sleeves. Join side and sleeve seams.

CLASSIC COTTON ARAN

This traditional crew-neck features a variety of stitch patterns, including a central Honeycomb panel, Aran diamonds with Moss stitch and Knotted chain cable. It can be knitted equally well in Aran weight wool or double knitting cotton.

MATERIALS

Yarn

Standard double knitting cotton

16 [17, 18] × 50g balls, pale green

Needles

1 pair size 3¾mm

1 pair size 4½mm

2 cable needles

MEASUREMENTS

To fit chest 86 [91, 97]cm

34 [36, 38]in

1 Actual chest size 98 [104, 110]cm

38½ [41, 43¼]in

2 Length to back neck 60 [62, 64]cm

23¾ [24½, 25¼]in

3 Sleeve seam 44 [46, 48]cm

17¼ [18, 19]in

Tension

19 sts and 27 rows measure 10cm over basket pattern on 4½mm needles (or size needed to obtain given tension)

23 sts measure 10cm over diamond and cable pattern on 4½mm needles (or size needed to obtain given tension)

30 sts measure 10cm over honeycomb pattern on 4½mm needles (or size needed to obtain given tension)

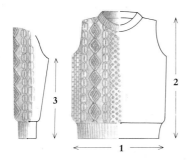

BACK

Using 3¾mm needles, cast on 88 [92, 96] sts. Work 7cm in k1 tbl, p1 rib.

Next row Rib 3 [2, 1], (inc in next st, rib 2) to last 4 [3, 2] sts, inc in next st, rib to end. *116 [122, 128] sts.*

Change to 4½mm needles. Commence patt.

Row 1 (Wrong side), Po [3, 3], (k3, p3) twice, ko [0, 1], *(k2, p2) twice, k7 [7, 8], p4, k7 [7, 8], (p2, k2) twice*, p24; rep from * to * once, ko [0, 1], (p3, k3) twice, po [3, 3].

Row 2 Ko [3, 3], (p3, k3) twice, po [0, 1], *p2, sl next 2 sts on to first cable needle and leave at back, sl next 2 sts on to 2nd cable needle and leave at front, k2, p2 from cable needle at front, k2 from cable needle at back – referred to as c6, p7 [7, 8], c4f, p7 [7, 8], c6, p2*, (c4b, c4f) 3 times; rep from * to * once, po [0, 1], (k3, p3) twice, ko [3, 3].

Row 3 As row 1.

Row 4 Po [3, 3], (k3, p3) twice, po [0, 1], *(p2, k2) twice, p6 [6, 7], cr3r, cr3l, p6 [6, 7], (k2, p2) twice*, p24; rep from * to * once, po [0, 1], (p3, k3) twice, po [3, 3].

Row 5 Ko [3, 3], (p3, k3) twice, ko [0, 1], *(k2, p2) twice, k6 [6, 7], p2, k1, p3, k6 [6, 7], (p2, k2) twice*, p24; rep from * to * once, ko [0, 1], (k3, p3) twice, ko [3, 3].

Row 6 Po [3, 3], (k3, p3) twice, po [0, 1], *(p2, k2) twice, p5 [5, 6], cr3r, k1, p1, cr3l, p5 [5, 6], (k2, p2) twice*, (c4f, c4b) 3 times; rep from * to * once, po [0, 1], (p3, k3) twice, po [3, 3].

These 6 rows establish basket patt at each side.

Row 7 Po [3, 3], (k3, p3) twice, ko [0, 1], *(k2, p2) twice, k5 [5, 6], p2, (k1, p1) twice, p2, k5 [5, 6], (p2, k2) twice*, p24; rep from * to * once, ko [0, 1], (p3, k3) twice, po [3, 3].

Row 8 Ko [3, 3], (p3, k3) twice, po [0, 1], *(p2, k2) twice, p4 [4, 5], cr3r, (k1, p1) twice, cr3l, p4 [4, 5], (k2, p2) twice*, k24; rep from * to * once, po [0, 1], (k3, p3) twice, ko [3, 3].

These 8 rows establish honeycomb patt at centre.

Row 9 Po [3, 3], (k3, p3) twice, ko [0, 1], *(k2, p2) twice, k4 [4, 5], p2, (k1, p1) 3 times, p2, k4 [4, 5], (p2, k2) twice*, p24; rep from * to * once, ko [0, 1], (p3, k3) twice, po [3, 3].

Row 10 Po [3, 3], (k3, p3) twice, po [0, 1], *(p2, k2) twice, p3 [3, 4], cr3r, (k1, p1) 3 times, cr3l, p3 [3, 4], (k2, p2) twice*, (c4b, c4f) 3 times; rep from * to * once, po [0, 1], (p3, k3) twice, po [3, 3].

Row 11 Ko [3, 3], (p3, k3) twice, ko [0, 1], *(k2, p2) twice, k3 [3, 4], p2, (k1, p1) 4 times, p2, k3 [3, 4], (p2, k2) twice*, p24; rep from * to * once, ko [0, 1], (k3, p3) twice, ko [3, 3].

Row 12 Po [3, 3], (k3, p3) twice, po [0, 1], *(p2, k2) twice, p2 [2, 3], cr3r, (k1, p1) 4 times, cr3l, p2 [2, 3], (k2, p2) twice*, k24; rep from * to * once, po [0, 1], (p3, k3) twice, po [3, 3].

These 12 rows establish cable patt at each side of diamond patt.

Row 13 Po [3, 3], (k3, p3) twice, ko [0, 1], *(k2, p2) twice, k2 [2, 3], p2, (k1, p1) 5 times, p2, k2 [2, 3], (p2, k2) twice*, p24; rep from * to * once, ko [0, 1], (p3, k3) twice, po [3, 3].

Row 14 Ko [3, 3], (p3, k3) twice, po [0, 1], *p2, c6, p2 [2, 3], cr3l, (p1, k1) 4 times, cr3r, p2 [2, 3], c6, p2*, (c4f, c4b) 3 times; rep from * to * once, po [0, 1], (k3, p3) twice, ko [3, 3].

Row 15 Po [3, 3], (k3, p3) twice, ko [0, 1], *(k2, p2) twice, k3 [3, 4], p2, (k1, p1) 4 times, p2, k3 [3, 4], (p2, k2) twice*, p24; rep from * to * once, ko [0, 1], (p3, k3) twice, po [3, 3].

Row 16 Po [3, 3], (k3, p3) twice, po [0, 1], *(p2, k2) twice, p3 [3, 4], cr3l, (p1, k1) 3 times, cr3r, p3 [3, 4], (k2, p2) twice*, k24; rep from * to * once, po [0, 1], (p3, k3) twice, po [3, 3].

Row 17 Ko [3, 3], (p3, k3) twice, ko [0, 1], *(k2, p2) twice, k4 [4, 5], p2, (k1, p1) 3 times, p2, k4 [4, 5], (p2, k2) twice*, p24; rep from * to * once, ko [0, 1], (k3, p3) twice, ko [3, 3].

Row 18 Po [3, 3], (k3, p3) twice, po [0, 1], *(p2, k2) twice, p4 [4, 5], cr3l, (p1, k1) twice, cr3r, p4 [4, 5], (k2, p2) twice*, (c4b, c4f) 3 times; rep from * to * once, po [0, 1], (p3, k3) twice, po [3, 3].

Row 19 As row 7.

Row 20 Ko [3, 3], (p3, k3) twice, po [0, 1] *(p2, k2) twice, p5 [5, 6], cr3l, p1, k1, cr3r, p5 [5, 6], (k2, p2) twice*, k24; rep from * to * once, po [0, 1], (k3, p3) twice, ko [3, 3].

Row 21 Po [3, 3], (k3, p3) twice, ko [0, 1], *(k2, p2) twice, k6 [6, 7], p2, k1, p3, k6 [6, 7], (p2, k2) twice*, p24; rep from * to * once, ko [0, 1], (p3, k3) twice, po [3, 3].

Row 22 Po [3, 3], (k3, p3) twice, po [0, 1], *(p2, k2) twice, p6 [6, 7], cr3l, cr3r, p6 [6, 7], (k2, p2) twice*, (c4f, c4b) 3 times; rep from * to * once, po [0, 1], (p3, k3) twice, po [3, 3].

Row 23 Ko [3, 3], (p3, k3) twice, ko [0, 1], *(k2, p2) twice, k7 [7, 8], p4, k7 [7, 8], (p2, k2) twice*, p24; rep from * to * once, ko [0, 1], (k3, p3) twice, ko [3, 3].

Row 24 Po [3, 3], (k3, p3) twice, po [0, 1], *(p2, k2) twice, p7 [7, 8], c4f, p7 [7, 8], (k2, p2) twice*, k24; rep from * to * once, po [0, 1], (p3, k3) twice, po [3, 3].

These 24 rows form patt. Cont in patt until work measures 39 [40, 41]cm from beg, ending with a wrong side row.

Shape armholes Cast off 4 sts at beg of next 2 rows. Dec 1 st at each end of next row and every foll alt row until 92 [94, 98] sts rem. Cont straight until armholes measure 19 [20, 21]cm, ending with a wrong side row.

Shape shoulders Cast off 6 [7, 7] sts at beg of next 6 rows and 8 [6, 8] sts at beg of foll 2 rows. Cast off rem 40 sts.

FRONT

Work as given for back until armholes measure 11 [12, 13]cm, ending with a wrong side row.

Shape neck

Next row Patt 34 [35, 37] sts and turn; leave rem sts on a spare needle. Complete left side of neck first. Dec 1 st at neck edge on next 8 rows. 26 [27, 29] sts.

Cont straight until front matches back to shoulder, ending at armhole edge.

Shape shoulder Cast off 6 [7, 7] sts at beg of next row and foll 2 alt rows. Patt 1 row. Cast off rem 8 [6, 8] sts. With right side facing, rejoin yarn to rem sts, cast off first 24 sts, patt to end. Complete as given for left side of neck.

SLEEVES

Using 3¾mm needles, cast on 42 [44, 46] sts. Work 7cm k1 tbl, p1 rib.

Next row Rib 1 [2, 3], (inc in next st, rib 2) to last 2 [3, 4] sts, inc in next st, rib to end. 56 [58, 60] sts.

Change to 4½mm needles. Commence patt.

Row 1 (Wrong side) Po [1, 2], (k2, p2) twice, k2, now rep row 1 as given for 3rd size on back from * to * once, k2, (p2, k2) twice, po [1, 2].

Row 2 Ko [1, 2], p2, c6, p2, now rep 2nd row as given for 3rd size on back from * to * once, p2, c6, p2, ko [1, 2].

Row 3 Po [1, 2], (k2, p2) twice, k2, now rep 3rd row as given for 3rd size on back from * to * once, k2, (p2, k2) twice, po [1, 2].

Row 4 Po [1, 2], (p2, k2) twice, p2, now rep 4th row as given for 3rd size on back from * to * once, p2, (k2, p2) twice, po [1, 2].

Row 5 Ko [1, 2], (k2, p2) twice, k2, now rep 5th row as given for 3rd size on back from * to * once, k2, (p2, k2) twice, ko [1, 2].

Row 6 Po [1, 2], (p2, k2) twice, p2, now rep 6th row as given for 3rd size on back from * to * once, p2, (k2, p2) twice, po [1, 2].

These 6 rows establish patt for sleeve. Cont in patt as set, working appropriate rows of diamond and cable patt and working additional cable at each side of centre panel. Inc 1 st at each end of next row and every foll 5th row until there are 86 [90, 94] sts, working extra sts into basket patt. Cont straight until sleeve measures 44 [46, 48]cm from beg, ending with wrong side row.

Shape top Cast off 4 sts at beg of next 2 rows. Dec 1 st at each end of next row and every foll alt row until 58 [58, 62] sts rem, then on every row to 40 sts. Cast off.

NECKBAND

Join right shoulder seam. With right side facing and using 3¾mm needles, pick up and k 21 sts down left side of neck, 16 sts across centre front, 21 sts up right side of neck, 36 sts across back neck. 94 sts. Work 6cm in k1 tbl, p1 rib. Cast off in rib.

FINISHING

Block as given on p. 140. Join left shoulder and neckband seam. Fold neckband in half to wrong side and slip stitch. Join side and sleeve seams. Sew in sleeves.

Designed by
Brinion Heaton

SHETLAND LACE

Shetland lace knitting
survives as a demonstration of the skill
of earlier generations of knitters, who could
produce intricate openwork shawls
as fine as a spider's web.

Even though the coloured Fair Isle work of the Shetland Islands is better known (see p. 54), the lace knitting from Shetland should not be overlooked. Highly prized "wedding ring" shawls, made from 1 ply wool, demonstrate the amazing skills of the Islanders and are famous the world over. Shetland spinners could produce 6,000 yards of yarn from about two ounces of fleece, and this would be knitted up into one shawl so fine that it could easily be pulled through a wedding ring, although it would measure perhaps 6ft square. The shawls would be worn first as a bridal veil, and then used for the christenings; black shawls would be made for mourning.

Lace knitting was well established in Europe by the 14th century, particularly in Russia and Spain, and it seems likely that Shetland lace was derived from the Spanish patterns which originally reached the islands by trading routes. Lace knitting seems to have started around 1830, as a result of the effort of various individuals to provide employment for the knitters when the market for plain knitting faced a decline as machines took over.

Although the rise of lace knitting as a cottage industry was relatively rapid, it lasted as a commercial success for only about 60 years. In 1837 in an attempt to popularize Shetland lace, Queen Victoria and the Duchess of Kent were presented with fine lace stockings from Shetland, and shortly after this a Mr Edward Standen, a hosiery dealer from Oxford, introduced the lace to the London market. Lace underwear, stockings and children's dresses became much in demand, and every lady of fashion had items of Shetland lace in her wardrobe. In 1851 the fine craftsmanship of the Shetland knitters was acknowledged when a lace wedding veil, commissioned by Mr Standen, was shown at the Great Exhibition at Crystal Palace.

One of the reasons for the success of Shetland lace must have been the quality of the wool. The native Shetland sheep is a small, hardy breed, and it has been on the Islands since the Stone Age. The wool has a long staple, and is very fine and soft. It becomes loose naturally in the summer as the new fleece grows, and it can be "rooed" or plucked away from the sheep by hand. As it does not need to be sheared from the animal it has no cut ends. Only the best part of the fleece, from the animal's neck, was used for the fine hand-spun lace yarn. The lace knitted from this was light and delicate, but it was warm.

The Shetland women themselves wore plain Shetland "haps" or shawls made of the thicker jumper wool, which were often knitted in the natural undyed shades with striped borders, similar to the one shown on p. 128. These "haps" were part of traditional crofting women's dress and would be worn around the shoulders, crossed over the chest and with the ends tied at the back of the waist. This way the women would have the benefit of the warmth of the shawl tied closely around them, and still have both hands free for the work of bringing in the peat, or knitting.

It would be pleasant to say that the skill and hard work of the Shetland women was always well rewarded, but unfortunately this is not so. For many years the knitters of Shetland were bound into a "truck system", whereby they had to exchange their knitting for goods at a hosiery store. There they could only get dry goods, tea and drapery, but

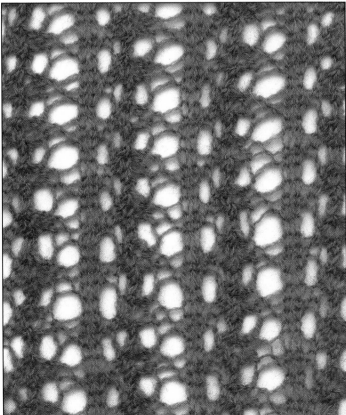

not food, and when the Royal Commissioners on the truck system visited Shetland in 1872, a local pastor is recorded as finding some knitters "starving in finery" because of this appalling system. Knitters alive today remember knitting into the middle of the night to complete their work, and then having to walk several hours to Lerwick to barter their knitting at the drapers, and "if you insisted on taking the money they only gave you ninepence out of every shilling that was due".

As the Victorian age came to an end, so did the demand for Shetland lace. Machine-made lace, manufactured in Nottingham, began to be mass-produced at very low prices, and hand-knitting could not compete. During the Second World War, when factories were turned over to the production of munitions, there was a brief revival in the hand-knitting market and the striped lace jumper and plain cardigan in this book are reminiscent of the styles that were very popular in the Forties. Today, lace knitting in 1 ply is very rare, but one or two younger women are learning the craft. Old pieces are highly prized family heirlooms, or museum pieces, and remind us of the time when a skilled spinner and knitter might take the entire winter to produce a single lace shawl.

Above left: Shetland sheep
Above: Crofts in the Shetland Isles
Far left: Tormentil used in dyeing
Left: The lace pattern featured on the Eyelet cardy, p. 120

This pattern was traditionally used for fine lace scarves; here it has been adapted to a 4 ply weight sweater in either wool or cotton with matching scarf. A delicate pointed edging finishes off the lower edge and cuff.

MATERIALS

The sweater and scarf shown here are knitted in Shetland 2 ply jumper weight wool, which is the equivalent of standard 4 ply wool. The sweater shown overleaf is knitted in mercerised 4 ply cotton. Yarn quantities given are sufficient for making the sweater and the scarf.

Yarn

Shetland 2 ply jumper weight wool

A 3 [3] × 2oz hanks, purple mix

B 2 [2] × 2oz hanks, navy

C 1 [1] × 2oz hanks, brown

D 1 [1] × 2oz hanks, red

E 1 [1] × 2oz hanks, red mix

F 1 [1] × 2oz hanks, blue mix

Mercerised 4 ply cotton

A 4 [4] × 50g balls, stone

B 3 [3] × 50g balls, dark sage

C 2 [2] × 50g balls, natural

D 1 [2] × 50g balls, brick

E 1 [2] × 50g balls, light sage

F 2 [2] × 50g balls, sand

Needles

1 pair size 3¾mm

1 pair size 2¼mm

Crochet hook

Notions

2 stitch holders

MEASUREMENTS

Sweater

To fit chest 76 [81, 86]cm

30 [32, 34]in

1 Actual chest size 82 [90, 98]cm

32¼ [35½, 38½]in

2 Length to back neck 56 [58, 60]cm

22 [22¾, 23½]in

3 Sleeve seam 48cm, 19in

Scarf

4 Width 25cm, 10in

5 Length, including fringe 160cm, 53in

Tension

24 sts and 25 rows measure 10cm over pattern on 3¾mm needles (or size needed to obtain given tension)

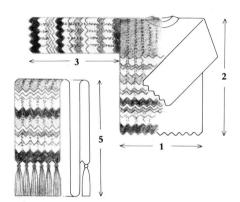

SCARF

Using 3¾mm needles and yarn B, cast on 61 sts.
Commence patt.
Row 1 (Right side) K1, (yfwd, k3, k3 tog, k3, yfwd, k1) to end.
Row 2 Knit.
These 2 rows form patt. Cont in patt and colour sequence as follows:
8 rows in B, 2 rows in E, 4 rows in A, 6 rows in F, (2 rows in A, 2 rows in D) 3 times, 2 rows in A, 6 rows in B, 4 rows in A, (2 rows in F, 2 rows in E) 3 times, 2 rows in F, 6 rows in C, 4 rows in A, 8 rows in F, 4 rows in B, 2 rows in F, 2 rows in B, 2 rows in A, 8 rows in D, 4 rows in E, 2 rows in D, 2 rows in E, 6 rows in B, 4 rows in E, 4 rows in C, (2 rows in A, 2 rows in D) twice, 2 rows in A, 8 rows in F, 6 rows in C, 4 rows in B, 2 rows in F, 2 rows in A, 12 rows in B. Leave these sts on a spare needle. Work another piece in same way, but do not sl stitches on to a spare needle.
With right sides of the two pieces together, cast off sts, taking 1 st from each needle and working them tog.
Finishing
Block as given on p. 140. To make fringe, cut yarn B into 32cm lengths. Using 13 strands together and crochet hook, make fringe into every point at each end of scarf.

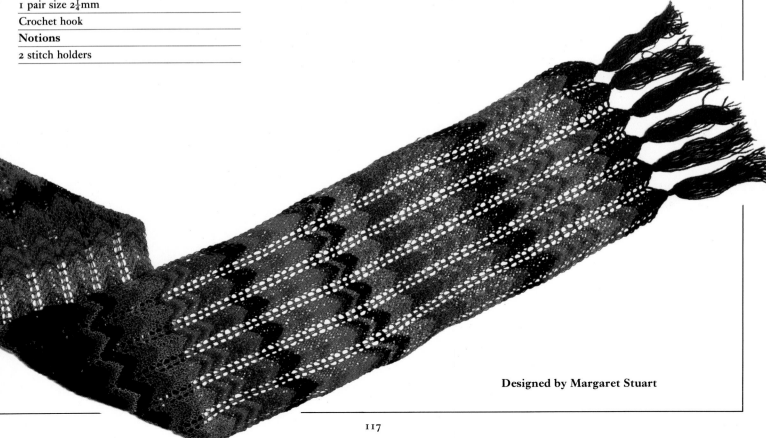

Designed by Margaret Stuart

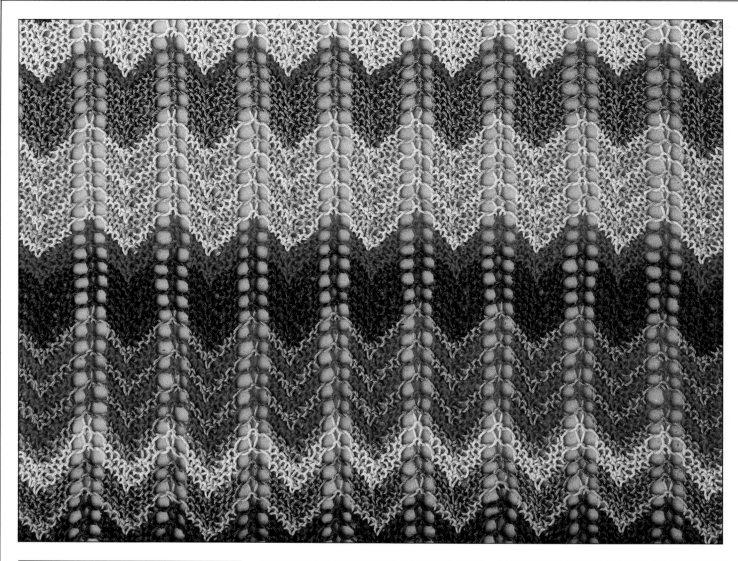

BACK

Using 3¾mm needles and yarn B, cast on 101 [111, 121] sts. **Commence patt.
Row 1 (Right side) K1, (yfwd, k3, k3 tog, k3, yfwd, k1) to end.
Row 2 Knit.
These 2 rows form patt. Cont in patt and coloured sequence as follows:
8 rows in B, 2 rows in F, 4 rows in E, 4 rows in C, (2 rows in A, 2 rows in D) 3 times, 2 rows in A, 8 rows in B, 4 rows in D, (2 rows in C, 2 rows in F) 3 times, 2 rows in C, 8 rows in E, 2 rows in D, 8 rows in C, 2 rows in B, 2 rows in C, 2 rows in B, 2 rows in D, 8 rows in A, 2 rows in F, 2 rows in A, 2 rows in F**.
Cont in A only until work measures 56 [58, 60]cm from beg, ending with a wrong side row.
Shape neck
Next row Patt 37 [41, 45] and turn; leave rem sts on a spare needle. Complete right side of neck first.
Dec 1 st at neck edge on next 4 rows then on every foll alt row until 29 [33, 37] sts rem. Patt 1 row. Cast off. With right side facing, sl centre 27 [29, 31] sts on to stitch holder, rejoin yarn to rem sts and patt to end.
Complete as given for first side of neck.

FRONT

Work as given for back until work measures 52 [54, 56]cm from beg, ending with a wrong side row.
Shape neck
Next row Patt 41 [45, 49] and turn; leave rem sts on a spare needle.
Complete left side of neck first.
Dec 1 st at neck edge on next 6 rows then on every foll alt row until 29 [33, 37] sts rem. Cont straight until front matches back to shoulder, ending with a wrong side row. Cast off.
With right side facing, sl centre 19 [21, 23] sts on to stitch holder, rejoin yarn to rem sts and patt to end. Complete as given for first side of neck.

SLEEVES

Using 3¾mm needles and yarn B, cast on 91 [101, 101] sts. Work as given for back from ** to **.
Work 8 rows in C, 2 rows in F, 2 rows in D, 8 rows in A. Cast off.

NECKBAND

Join right shoulder seam. With right side facing, using 2¼mm needles and yarn A, pick up and k 23 sts down left front neck, k across 19 [21, 23] centre front sts, pick up and k 23 sts up right front neck, 14 sts down right back neck, k across 27 [29, 31] centre back sts, pick up and k 14 sts up left back neck. *120 [124, 128] sts.*
Work 13 rows in k1, p1 rib. Cast off in rib.

FINISHING

Block each piece as given on p. 140. Join left shoulder and neckband seam. Mark positions of armholes 19 [20, 20]cm down from shoulders on back and front. Sew in sleeves between markers. Join side and sleeve seams.

Above: Detail of the cotton New shell sweater.
Right: The cotton New shell sweater and the Eyelet cardy.

EYELET CARDY
SHETLAND LACE

A traditional Shetland Eyelet pattern worked in 2 ply lace wool makes a gossamer-fine openwork cardigan suitable for summer or evening wear.

MATERIALS

Yarn

Shetland 2 ply lace weight wool

5 × 1oz hanks, green

Needles

1 pair size 2¾mm

1 pair size 3mm

1 set of double-pointed needles size 2¾mm

1 set of double-pointed needles size 3mm

Notions

6 buttons, 1.5cm in diameter

2 stitch holders

MEASUREMENTS

To fit chest 81–97cm, 32–38in

1 Actual chest size 106cm, 41¾in

2 Length to back neck 58cm, 23in

3 Sleeve seam 51cm, 20in

Tension

22 sts and 28 rows measure 10cm over pattern on 3mm needles (or size needed to obtain given tension)

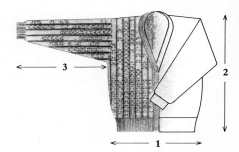

POCKET LININGS

Using 3mm needles, cast on 21 sts. Beg k row, work 24 rows in st st. Leave these sts on a spare needle. Make another pocket lining to match.

BACK and FRONTS

This cardigan is knitted in one piece to the armholes. Using 2¾mm needles, cast on 171 sts.

Row 1 K1, (p1, k1) to end.

Row 2 P1, (k1, p1) to end.

Rep last 2 rows 14 times then row 1 again.

Next row Rib 4, (inc in next st, rib 2) to last 2 sts, rib 2. *226 sts.* Change to 3mm needles. Commence patt.

Row 1 (Right side) K2, (yfwd, k1, k3 tog, k1, yfwd, k2) to end.

Row 2 Purl.

Row 3 K3, (yfwd, k3 tog, yfwd, k4) to last 6 sts, yfwd, k3 tog, yfwd, k3.

Row 4 Purl.

These 4 rows form patt. Cont in patt until work measures 15cm from beg, ending with a p row.

Place pockets

Next row Patt 8, sl next 21 sts on to a stitch holder, patt across sts of first pocket lining, patt to last 29 sts, sl next 21 sts on to a stitch holder, patt to end. Cont in patt until work measures 38cm from beg, ending with row 4.

Divide for armholes

Next row K2 tog, patt 47, k2 tog and turn; leave rem sts on a spare needle.

Complete right front first. Patt 1 row. Dec 1 st at beg of next row and every foll alt row until 22 sts rem. Patt 1 row. Cast off.

With right side facing, sl next 19 sts on to a

safety pin, rejoin yarn to rem sts, k2 tog, patt 82, k2 tog and turn, leave rem sts on a spare needle. Complete back first. Cont straight until back matches front to shoulder, ending with a wrong side row. Cast off.

With right side facing, sl next 19 sts on to a safety pin, rejoin yarn to rem sts, k2 tog, patt to last 2 sts, k2 tog. Patt 1 row. Dec 1 st at end of next row and every foll alt row until 22 sts rem. Patt 1 row. Cast off.

SLEEVES

Join shoulder seams. With right side facing and using set of double-pointed needles size 3mm, pick up and k 79 sts evenly around armhole edge, then patt across 19 sts on safety pin. Work in rounds as follows:

Round 1 Knit.
Round 2 (K3, yfwd, k3 tog, yfwd, k1) to end.
Round 3 Knit.
Round 4 (K2, yfwd, k1, k3 tog, k1, yfwd) to end.
Next round Patt 86, k2 tog, k1, k2 tog, patt to end.
Keeping cont of patt, work 7 rounds.
Next round Patt 85, k2 tog, k1, k2 tog, patt to end.
Keeping cont of patt, work 7 rounds.
Cont dec in this way on next round and 4 foll 8th rounds.
Next round Patt 80
(k2 tog, k1) twice.
Sl last 2 sts of last round
on to next needle.

Next round Sl 2, patt to end.
Work 6 rounds.
Next round K2 tog, patt to last 3 sts, k2 tog, k1.
Work 7 rounds.
Next round K2 tog, patt to last 3 sts, k2 tog, k1.
Rep last 8 rounds until 72 sts rem.
Work 7 rounds.
Next round (K2 tog, k1) to end. *48 sts.*
Change to double-pointed needles size 2¾mm.
Work 32 rounds in k1, p1 rib. Cast off in rib.

FRONT BAND

Mark right front with pins to indicate buttonholes. First one to come 1cm up from lower edge and last one 7cm down from beg of front shaping, rem 4 evenly spaced between. Using 2¾mm needles, cast on 11 sts.
Row 1 K1, (p1, k1) to end.
This row forms moss st. Cont in moss st until band when slightly stretched fits along right front, across back neck and down left front, making buttonholes at pin positions as follows:

Next row (K1, p1) twice, yrn, p2 tog, k1, (p1, k1) twice.
Cast off.

POCKET EDGINGS

With right side facing and using 2¾mm needles, rejoin yarn to the 21 sts left on stitch holder. Work 8 rows in moss st. Cast off.

FINISHING

Block as given on p. 140. Sew on front band and buttons. Catch down pocket linings and sides of pocket edgings.

Traditional design by Margaret Stuart

OLD SHELL SHETLAND LACE

This delicate openwork sweater is made from 2 ply Shetland lace wool. The shaded stripes of greys and pinks combined with the famous Old Shell pattern makes a timeless and classic sweater.

MATERIALS

Yarn

Shetland 2 ply lace weight wool

A 4 [5, 6] × 1oz hanks, light grey

B 1 [1, 1] × 1oz hank, dark grey

C 1 [1, 1] × 1oz hank, dark pink

D 1 [1, 1] × 1oz hank, mid grey

E 1 [1, 1] × 1oz hank, pale pink

Needles

1 circular needle size 2¼mm, 60cm long

1 circular needle size 3mm, 80cm long

1 set of double-pointed needles size 2¼mm

1 set of double-pointed needles size 3mm

1 pair size 2¼mm

Notions

4 buttons, 1cm in diameter

1 stitch holder

MEASUREMENTS

To fit chest 76-81 [86-91, 97-102]cm

30-32 [34-36, 38-40]in

1 Actual chest size 90 [101, 112]cm

35½ [39¾, 44]in

2 Length to back neck 58 [61, 63]cm

22¾ [24, 24¾]in

3 Sleeve seam 53cm, 20¾in

Tension

32 sts and 38 rows measure 10cm over pattern

on 3mm needles (or size needed to obtain

given tension)

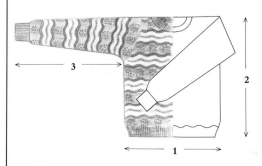

BACK and FRONT

This sweater is knitted in one piece to the armholes.

Using circular needle size 2¼mm and yarn A, cast on 264 [288, 324] sts. Work in rounds of k1, p1 rib for 5cm.

Next round *Rib 11 [8, 9], pick up loop lying between sts and work tbl; rep from * to end. *288 [324, 360] sts.*

Change to circular needle size 3mm. Commence patt.

Rounds 1 and 2 Knit.

Round 3 *(K2 tog) 3 times, (yfwd, k1) 6 times, (k2 tog) 3 times; rep from * to end.

Round 4 Knit.

These 4 rounds form chevron patt. Cont in chevron patt and colour sequence as follows:

Rounds 5 to 18 In yarn A.

Round 19 In yarn B.

Rounds 20 and 21 In yarn C.

Round 22 In yarn B.

Rounds 23 and 24 In yarn D.

Rounds 25 and 26 In yarn A.

Rounds 27 and 28 In yarn E.

Round 29 In yarn D.

Round 30 In yarn C.

Round 31 In yarn E.

Round 32 In yarn C.

Round 33 In yarn D.

Rounds 34 and 35 In yarn E.

Rounds 36 and 37 In yarn A.

Rounds 38 and 39 In yarn D.

Round 40 In yarn B.

Rounds 41 and 42 In yarn C.

Round 43 In yarn B.

Round 44 In yarn A.

These 44 rounds form colour sequence. Cont in chevron patt and colour sequence until work measures 38cm from beg, ending with round 36.

Divide for back and front

Next round *Patt 9 and sl these sts on to a safety pin, patt 126 [144, 162], patt 9 and sl these sts on to a safety pin; rep from * once more.

Complete back first. Keeping continuity of colour sequence work backwards and forwards as follows:

Next row Purl.

**Row 1 Cast off 2, k7, including st used in casting off, *(k2 tog) 3 times, (yfwd, k1) 6 times, (k2 tog) 3 times; rep from * to last 9 sts, k9.

Row 2 Cast off 2, p to end.

Row 3 Cast off 2, k to end.

Row 4 As row 2.

These 4 rows establish continuity of chevron patt. Keeping continuity of chevron patt and colour sequence, cast off 2 sts at beg of next 10 rows. Dec 1 st at each end of next row and 2 foll alt rows. *92 [110, 128] sts**.*

Cont straight until armholes measure 15 [16,

18]cm, ending with a wrong side row.

Divide for back neck opening

Next row Patt 42 [51, 60] sts and turn; leave rem sts on a spare needle. Complete right side of back neck first.

Cont straight until armhole measures 20 [23, 25]cm, ending at armhole edge. Leave these sts on a spare needle.

With right side of back facing, sl centre 8 sts on to a safety pin, rejoin appropriate yarn to rem sts and patt to end. Complete to match first side of neck.

With wrong side of front facing, rejoin appropriate yarn to rem sts, p to end. Work as given for back from ** to **. Cont straight until armholes measure 13 [15, 15]cm, ending with a wrong side row.

Shape neck

Next row Patt 36 [45, 54] and turn; leave rem sts on a spare needle.

Complete left side of front neck first. Cast off 2 [2, 3] sts at beg of next row and 2 sts at beg of every foll alt row until 20 [29, 33] sts rem. Cont straight until front matches back to shoulder, ending at armhole edge.

Graft left shoulder With right sides of back and front facing, cast off 20 [29, 33] sts, taking 1 st from each needle and working them tog. Leave rem 22 [22, 27] sts on back neck on a spare needle.

With right side of front facing, sl centre 20 sts on to stitch holder, rejoin appropriate yarn to rem sts and patt to end. Patt 1 row. Complete as given for first side of front neck.

NECKBAND

With right side facing, using circular needle size 2¼ mm and yarn A, k 22 [22, 27] sts from left back neck, pick up and k 32 [34, 38] sts down left front neck, k 20 centre front sts, pick up and k 32 [34, 38] sts up right front neck and k 22 [22, 27] sts from right back neck. *128 [132, 150] sts.* Work backwards and forwards in k1, p1 rib for 9 [11, 13] rows. Cast off in rib.

BUTTON BANDS

Button band
With right side facing using 2¼mm needles and yarn A and beg at base of opening, pick up and k 26 [32, 32] sts along left edge to top of neckband.
Row 1 (Wrong side) (K1, p1) to end.
Row 2 (P1, k1) to end.
These 2 rows form moss st. Work a further 9 rows in moss st. Cast off.

Buttonhole band
With right side facing and using 2¼mm needles, rejoin yarn A to 8 sts on to a safety pin at base of opening. Work 4 [6, 6] rows in moss st patt as given for buttonband.
Next row Moss st 3, cast off 2, moss st to end.
Next row Moss st to end, casting on 2 sts over those cast off in previous row.
Work 8 [10, 10] rows in moss st. Rep last 10 [12, 12] rows twice more then the buttonhole rows again. Work 4 [6, 6] rows in moss st. Cast off. Sew buttonhole band in position. Catch down button band on wrong side of base opening. Sew on buttons.

SLEEVES

With right side facing, using double-pointed needles size 3mm and yarn A, k 9 sts from left hand side safety pin, pick up and k 108 [126, 144] sts evenly around armhole edge, k 9 from rem safety pin. *126 [144, 162] sts.*
Cont in rounds in chevron patt and colour sequence as given for back and front. Work 44 rounds.
Next round K1, k2 tog, patt to last 3 sts, k2 tog, k1.
Patt 7 [4, 4] rounds straight. Rep last 8 [5, 5] rounds until 90 [90, 108] sts rem. Cont straight until sleeve measures 49cm. Change to double-pointed needles size 2¼mm.
Next round *K1, (k2 tog) 4 times; rep from * to end. *50 [50, 60] sts.* Work in rounds of k1, p1 rib for 7cm. Cast off in rib.

FINISHING

Block as given on p. 140.

Traditional design by Margaret Stuart

Above: Woollen Fern spencer
Opposite: Old shell sweater
Below: Buttoning detail from Old shell sweater

FERN SPENCER
SHETLAND LACE

The traditional use for a spencer would have been as an undergarment. Shown here in Botany wool or cotton, it makes a pretty summer top.

MATERIALS

Yarn

4 ply Botany wool

7 × 25g hanks, cornflower blue

Alternative yarn

4 ply mercerised cotton

5 × 50g balls, natural

Needles

1 pair size 3¼mm

1 circular needle size 3¼mm, 60cm long

MEASUREMENTS

To fit chest 81-86cm, 32-34in

1 Actual chest size 92cm, 36¼in

2 Length to back neck 55cm, 21½in

3 Sleeve seam 45cm, 17in

Tension

21 sts and 34 rows measure 10cm over garter stitch on 3¼mm needles (or size needed to obtain given tension)

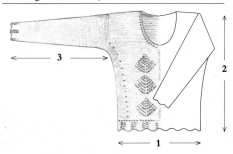

Panel pattern

Repeat of 25 sts

Row 1 Knit.

Row 2 and every foll alt row Knit.

Row 3 K10, k2 tog, yfwd, k1, yfwd, k2 tog, k10.

Row 5 K9, k2 tog, yfwd, k3, yfwd, k2 tog, k9.

Row 7 K8 (k2 tog, yfwd) twice, k1, (yfwd, k2 tog) twice, k8.

Row 9 K7 (k2 tog, yfwd) twice, k3, (yfwd, k2 tog) twice, k7.

Row 11 K6, (k2 tog, yfwd) 3 times, k1, (yfwd, k2 tog) 3 times, k6.

Row 13 K5 (k2 tog, yfwd) 3 times, k3, (yfwd, k2 tog) 3 times, k5.

Row 15 K4 (k2 tog, yfwd) 4 times, k1, (yfwd, k2 tog) 4 times, k4.

Row 17 K3 (k2 tog, yfwd) 4 times, k3, (yfwd, k2 tog) 4 times, k3.

Row 19 K2, (k2 tog, yfwd) 5 times, k1, (yfwd, k2 tog) 5 times, k2.

Row 21 As row 17.

Row 23 As row 15.

Row 25 As row 13.

Row 27 As row 11.

Row 29 As row 9.

Row 31 As row 7.

Row 33 As row 5.

Row 35 K11, yfwd, k3 tog, yfwd, k11.

Row 36 Knit.

These 36 rows form panel pattern.

BACK and FRONT

This sweater is worked in one piece to the armholes. Using 3¼mm needles, cast on 143 sts. Knit 1 row.

Row 1 K2, (yfwd, k3, k3 tog, k3, yfwd, k1) to last st, k1.

Row 2 Knit.

These 2 rows form welt patt. Rep these 2 rows 9 times.

Next row K15 (k2 tog, k26) 4 times, k2 tog, k14. *138 sts.*

Knit 1 row.

Next row K1, (yfwd, k2 tog) to last st, yfwd, k1. *139 sts.*

Knit 1 row. Cont in patt as follows:

Row 1 Knit.

Row 2 and every foll alt row Knit.

Row 3 Work row 3 of panel patt, k1, yfwd, k16, yfwd, k to last 42 sts, yfwd, k16, yfwd, k to last 42 sts, yfwd, k16, yfwd, k1, work row 3 of panel patt.

Row 5 Work row 5 of panel patt, k to last 25 sts, work row 5 of panel patt.

Row 7 Work row 7 of panel patt, k to last 25 sts, work row 7 of panel patt.

Row 9 Work row 9 of panel patt, k to last 25 sts, work row 9 of panel patt.

Row 11 Work row 11 of panel patt, k2, yfwd, k16, yfwd, k to last 43 sts, yfwd, k16, yfwd,

k2, work row 11 of panel patt.

Cont in this way, working appropriate rows of panel patt and inc sts as set on every foll 8th row until there are 195 sts. Work 1 row.

Divide for armholes

Next row K2, k2 tog, yfwd, k1, k2 tog, k34 and turn; leave rem sts on a spare needle. Complete right side of neck first.

Row 1 K to last 4 sts, yfwd, k2 tog, k2.

Row 2 K2, k2 tog, yfwd, k to end.

Rows 3 and 4 As rows 1 and 2.

Row 5 As row 1.

Row 6 K2, k2 tog, yfwd, k1, k2 tog, k to end.

Rep these 6 rows 7 times then rows 1 and 2 again. Cast off rem 32 sts.

With right side facing, sl next 15 sts on to a safety pin, rejoin yarn to rem sts, k83 and turn; leave rem sts on a spare needle. Knit 49 rows.

Shape shoulders Cast off 28 sts at beg of next 2 rows. *27 sts.*

Next row K1 (yfwd, k2 tog) to end.

K3 rows. Cast off.

With right side facing, sl next 15 sts on to a safety pin, rejoin yarn to rem sts, k to last 7 sts, k2 tog, k1, yfwd, k2 tog, k2.

Row 1 K2, k2 tog, yfwd, k to end.

Row 2 K to last 4 sts, yfwd, k2 tog, k2.

Rows 3 and 4 As rows 1 and 2.

Row 5 As row 1.

Row 6 K to last 7 sts, k2 tog, k1, yfwd, k2 tog, k2.

Rep these 6 rows 7 times then row 1 again. Cast off rem 32 sts.

SLEEVES

Join shoulder and neck edge border seams. With right side facing and using circular needle size 3¼mm, k 7 sts from safety pin, pick up and k 52 sts evenly around armhole edge then k rem 8 sts on safety pin. *67 sts.* Work backwards and forwards. K 57 rows.

Next row K2 tog, k to last 3 sts, k2 tog, k1.

K 7 rows straight. Rep last 8 rows 7 times.

Next row K2 tog, k to last 3 sts, k2 tog, k1.

K 3 rows straight. Rep last 4 rows 3 times. *43 sts.* Work 12 rows in welt patt as given for main part. Cast off.

FINISHING

Block as given on p. 140. Join centre front and sleeve seams.

Traditional design by Margaret Stuart

The Shetland Isles have been famous for their shawls for centuries, and the "jumper wool" shawls often had borders using all the shades of the natural undyed wool. This shawl is knitted in the traditional way, from separate sections which are grafted together. The border features the famous Old shell pattern, and a pointed lace edging.

MATERIALS

Yarn

This shawl is knitted in Shetland 2 ply jumper wool, which is the equivalent of standard 4 ply wool

A 3 × 2oz hanks, black

B 1 × 2oz hank, charcoal

C 1 × 2oz hank, dark grey

D 1 × 2oz hank, mid grey

E 1 × 2oz hank, pale grey

F 1 × 2oz hank, cream

Needles

1 long pair size 5mm

MEASUREMENTS

1 Approximately 135cm, 53in square

Tension

14 sts and 28 rows measure 10cm over garter stitch on 5mm needles (or size needed to obtain given tension)

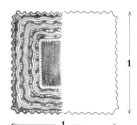

Special note

The shawl is knitted in sections as follows:
Part 1 The scalloped lace edging that goes around two sides.
Part 2 The striped border for two sides with Old Shell pattern, and with Openwork stitch at centre of rows (ie dividing the two sides) and one end of rows.
Parts 3 and 4 As parts 1 and 2, to make the

edging and border for the other two sides.
Part 5 Centre panel, which is worked from the inside edge of half of one of the border pieces (ie one side of the shawl), knitting in the other half of the same border piece, and half of the other border piece.

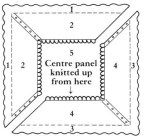

- - - - - Stitches picked up and knitted

〰〰〰 Stitches held on needles

°°°° Openwork stitch

SCALLOPED LACE EDGING

This is part 1 on the diagram.
Using 5mm needles and yarn A cast on 6 sts.
Row 1 K4, yfwd, k2.
Row 2 K2, yfwd, k5.
Row 3 K6, yfwd, k2.
Row 4 K2, yfwd, k7.
Row 5 K8, yfwd, k2.
Row 6 K2, yfwd, k9. *12 sts.*
Row 7 K7, k2 tog, yfwd, k2 tog, k1.
Row 8 K1, k2 tog, yfwd, k2 tog, k6.
Row 9 K5, k2 tog, yfwd, k2 tog, k1.
Row 10 K1, k2 tog, yfwd, k2 tog, k4.
Row 11 K3, k2 tog, yfwd, k2 tog, k1.
Row 12 K1, k2 tog, yfwd, k2 tog, k2. *6 sts.*
Rows 13 to 18 Knit.
Rep these 18 rows 28 times more, then work rows 1 to 17.
Next row Cast off these 6 sts, but do not turn and break off yarn.

STRIPED BORDER

This is part 2 on the diagram.
Pick up and k 270 sts along straight edge of work.
Next row (Wrong side) *K2, yfwd, k2 tog, k5, (k2 tog, k7) 14 times; rep from * once more. *242 sts.*
Commence patt. Change to yarn B.
Row 1 (K119, yfwd, k2 tog) twice.
Row 2 (K2, yfwd, k2 tog, k117) twice.
Row 3 **K6, *(k2 tog) 3 times, (yfwd, k1) 5 times, yfwd, (k2 tog) 3 times, k1, rep from * 5 times more, k5, yfwd, k2 tog**; rep from ** to ** once more.
Row 4 As row 2.
Rows 5 to 8 Rep rows 1 and 2 twice.
These 8 rows form patt. Cont in patt and yarn sequence as follows:-
6 rows in C, (2 rows in D, 2 rows in F) twice, 2 rows in D, 6 rows in A, 6 rows in C, 4 rows

in D, (2 rows in B, 2 rows in E) twice, 2 rows in B.
Shape border
Change to yarn A.
Row 1 **K5, (k2 tog) 3 times, (yfwd, k1) 4 times, yfwd, (k2 tog) 4 times, *k1, (k2 tog) 3 times, (yfwd, k1) 5 times, yfwd, (k2 tog) 3 times; rep from * 3 times more, k1, (k2 tog) 4 times, (yfwd, k1) 4 times, yfwd, (k2 tog) 3 times, k5, yfwd, k2 tog**; rep from ** to ** once more.
Row 2 (K2, yfwd, k2 tog, k113) twice.
Row 3 (K115, yfwd, k2 tog) twice.
Row 4 As row 2.
Rows 5 and 6 As rows 3 and 4.
Change to yarn B and rep rows 3 and 4 once.
Row 9 **K4, (k2 tog) 3 times, (yfwd, k1) 3 times, yfwd, (k2 tog) 4 times, *k1, (k2 tog) 3 times, (yfwd, k1) 5 times, yfwd, (k2 tog) 3 times; rep from * 3 times more, k1, (k2 tog) 4 times, (yfwd, k1) 3 times, yfwd, (k2 tog) 3 times, k4, yfwd, k2 tog**; rep from ** to ** once more.
Row 10 (K2, yfwd, k2 tog, k107) twice.
Row 11 (K109, yfwd, k2 tog) twice.
Row 12 As row 10.
Change to yarn C and rep rows 11 and 12 twice. Change to yarn D.
Row 17 **K3, (k2 tog) 3 times, (yfwd, k1) twice, yfwd, (k2 tog) twice, k3 tog, *k1, (k2 tog) 3 times, (yfwd, k1) 5 times, yfwd, (k2 tog) 3 times; rep from * 3 times more, k1, k3 tog,

(k2 tog) twice, (yfwd, k1) twice, yfwd, (k2 tog)
3 times, k3, yfwd, k2 tog**; rep from ** to **
once more.
Row 18 (K2, yfwd, k2 tog, k99) twice.
Change to yarn F.
Row 19 (K101, yfwd, k2 tog) twice.
Row 20 As row 18.
Change to yarn D and rep rows 19 and 20 once.
Change to yarn F and rep rows 19 and 20 once.
Change to yarn D.
Row 25 **K3, (k2 tog) 3 times, yfwd, k1,
yfwd, (k2 tog) twice, *k1, (k2 tog) 3 times,
(yfwd, k1) 5 times, yfwd, (k2 tog) 3 times; rep
from * 3 times more, k1, (k2 tog) twice, yfwd,
k1, yfwd, (k2 tog) 3 times, k3, yfwd, k2 tog**;
rep from ** to ** once more.
Row 26 (K2, yfwd, k2 tog, k93) twice.
Change to yarn B.
Row 27 (K95, yfwd, k2 tog) twice.
Row 28 As row 26.
Rep rows 27 and 28 twice. Change to yarn C.
Row 33 **K3, (k2 tog) twice, yfwd, (k2 tog)
twice, *k1, (k2 tog) 3 times, (yfwd, k1) 5 times,
yfwd, (k2 tog) 3 times; rep from * 3 times
more, k1, (k2 tog) twice, yfwd, (k2 tog) twice,
k3, yfwd, k2 tog**; rep from ** to ** once
more.
Row 34 (K2, yfwd, k2 tog, k87) twice.
Row 35 (K89, yfwd, k2 tog) twice.
Row 36 As row 34.
Change to yarn D and rep rows 35 and 36 once
then row 35 again.

Next row (K2, yfwd,
k2 tog, k42, k2 tog, k43)
twice. *180 sts.* Change to yarn A.
Next row K2, (yfwd, k2 tog) to end.
K 1 row. Break off yarn and leave sts on a spare
needle.
To make parts 3 and 4 on the diagram, work
another scalloped lace edging and striped
border as given above. Do not break off yarn.

CENTRE PANEL

This is part 5 on the diagram.
Next 2 rows Taking 1 st from sts on spare
needle and next st on left hand needle, k2 tog,
k88, k2 tog and turn, k90 and turn.
Rep last 2 rows until 180 rows have been
worked. With right side of centre panel and
rem border together, cast off 90 sts taking 1 st
from each needle and working them tog.

FINISHING

Join corner seams, matching stripes. Block as
given on p. 140.

Traditional design by Margaret Stuart

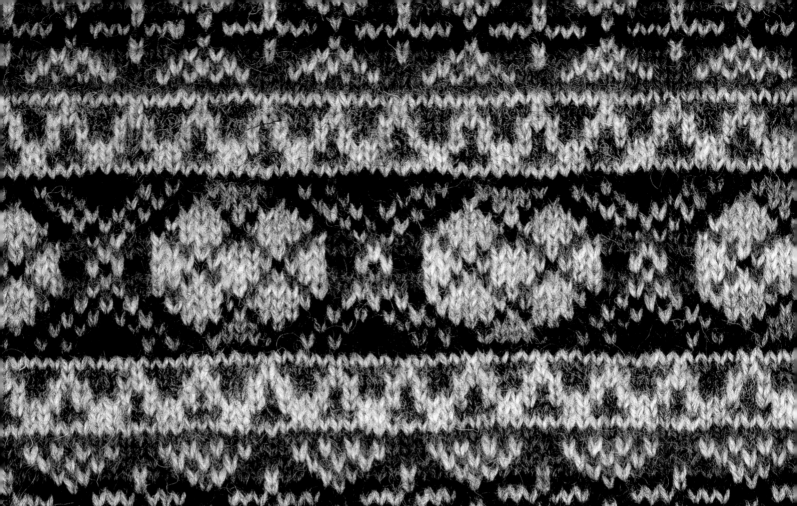

BASIC
TECHNIQUES

The information on the following pages
will tell you all you need to know
to make the patterns in the book.
The instructions are written and illustrated for
right-handed knitters. If you are left-handed,
reverse any instructions for left and right,
or prop the book up in front of a mirror
and follow the diagrams in reverse.

EQUIPMENT

Basically all you need to start knitting are needles and some yarn. However there are a few additional accessories that are useful from time to time. For example, when knitting in the round you need a circular needle or a set of four double-pointed needles. These are available in a full range of thicknesses. When making cables you need a special cable needle. These are short, double-pointed needles. Some are straight, some have a small kink in the middle to prevent the stitches from slipping off the needle. Cable needles are available in two thicknesses, choose the most appropriate size for the yarn you are using. Stitch holders, which are like large safety pins, are handy for keeping unworked stitches on until they are needed at a later stage in the pattern. A spare needle, a length of yarn or a safety pin may usually be used instead, depending on the number of stitches to be held.

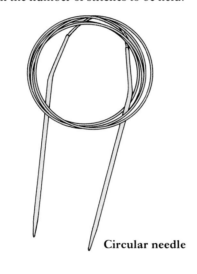

Circular needle

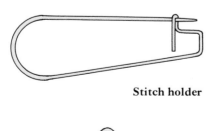

Stitch holder

Cable needles

CASTING ON

When you begin work on a pattern, placing the first row of stitches on the needles is known as "casting on". All further rows are worked into these initial loops. Casting on can be done in a number of ways, using one or two needles, two of the most common methods are given here.

The different methods produce slightly different edges – a strong edge is produced by the cable cast on method, a fairly elastic edge is produced by the thumb cast on method. Practise both methods and then choose the one with which you can produce the neatest edge, with the stitches evenly spaced and not too tight.

A slip loop is the first stitch to be made, and is the foundation for all the subsequent stitches.

MAKING A SLIP LOOP

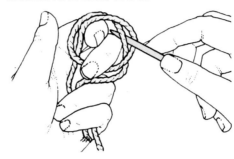

1 Wrap the yarn twice around two fingers, so that the second wrapping lies below the first.

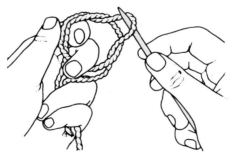

2 With a knitting needle, pull a loop of the second wrapping through the twisted yarn on the fingers.

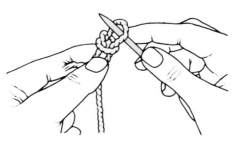

3 To tighten the slip loop, pull the yarn ends.

CABLE CAST ON

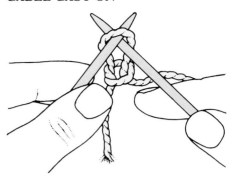

1 With the slip loop on your left-hand needle, insert your right-hand needle through the loop from front to back.

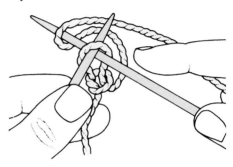

2 Bring the yarn under and over your right-hand needle.

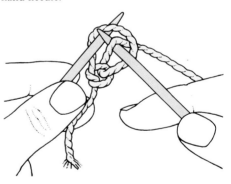

3 Draw up the yarn through the slip loop to make a stitch.

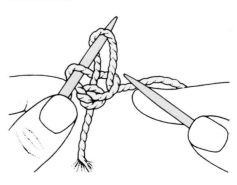

4 Place the stitch on the left-hand needle. Continue to make more stitches inserting the right-hand needle between the last two stitches worked.

THUMB CAST ON

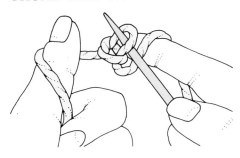

1 Make a slip loop at a distance from the yarn end that equals 2cm for each stitch to be cast on. Hold needle with slip loop in the right hand and wrap the working yarn over the right forefinger. Wrap the loose end of yarn around the left thumb from front to back.

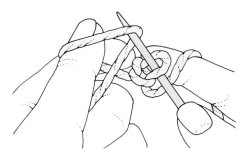

2 Put the needle through the yarn on the thumb.

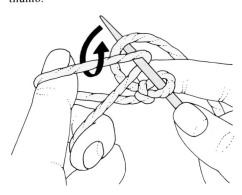

3 With the right forefinger, pass the working end of the yarn over the needle. Draw the yarn through the loop on the thumb to make the new stitch.

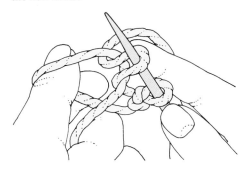

4 Release the yarn from the thumb and pull the loose end to secure the stitch. Repeat these steps.

HOLDING NEEDLES AND YARN

The way in which you hold your knitting will affect the tension and evenness of the fabric. Threading the working end of the yarn through the fingers not only makes knitting faster, but also produces a firm even result.

Holding yarn in the right hand

With the working yarn in your right hand, use the right forefinger to wrap the yarn over the needles.

Holding yarn in the left hand

With the working yarn in your left hand, use the left forefinger to position the yarn while you move the right needle to encircle the yarn to form a new loop.

CASTING OFF

When you end a piece of knitting, such as a sleeve, or part of a piece of knitting, such as up to the neck, you must secure all the stitches by "casting off". This is preferably done on a knit row but you can employ the same technique on a purl row. The stitches, whether knit or purl,

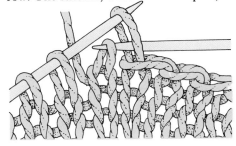

1 Knit the first two stitches and insert the tip of your left-hand needle through the first stitch.

The working end of the yarn may be threaded through the fingers of the left or the right hand.

When working with two colours, as in Fair Isle knitting, combine the two methods, controlling one colour with each hand.

Threading the yarn

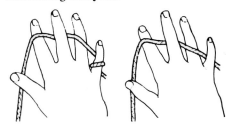

Place the working yarn through the fingers of your right hand in either of the ways shown above.

Threading the yarn

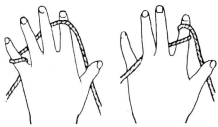

Place the working yarn through the fingers of your left hand in either of the ways shown above.

should be made loosely.

When casting off in rib you must follow the pattern and cast off in both knit and purl. Whether casting off in knit or purl the basic technique remains the same. Instead of knitting all the stitches, knit and purl alternately for single rib, knit two, purl two for double rib.

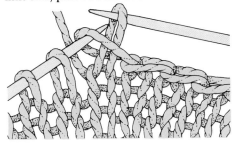

2 Lift the first stitch over the second stitch and discard it. Knit the next stitch and continue to lift the first stitch over the second stitch to the end of the row. Be careful not to knit too tightly. For the last stitch, cut your yarn, slip the end through the stitch and pull the yarn tight to fasten off securely.

BASIC STITCHES

Knit stitch and purl stitch are the two basic knitting stitches. When every row is knitted back and forth on two needles, garter stitch is formed. When one row is knitted and the next purled, stocking stitch is formed. When working in the round, knitting every row produces stocking stitch. A combination of knit and purl stitches, usually one or two knit stitches and then one or two purl stitches, in the same row, is known as ribbing. Ribbing is used on sleeve and body edges to form a neat, stretchable finish. It is usually worked on smaller needles than the body of the garment.

KNIT STITCH (K)

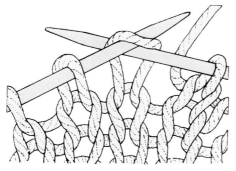

1 With the yarn at the back, insert your right-hand needle from front to back into the first stitch on your left-hand needle.

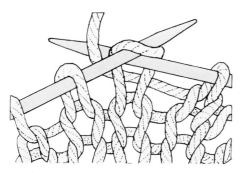

2 Bring your working yarn under and over the point of your right-hand needle.

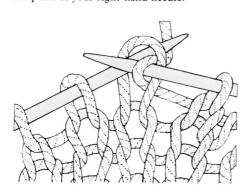

3 Draw a loop through and slide the first stitch off your left-hand needle while the new stitch is retained on your right-hand needle. Continue in this way to the end of the row.

4 To knit the next row, turn the work around so that the back is facing you and the worked stitches are held on the needle in your left hand. Proceed to make stitches as given above, with the initially empty needle held in your right hand.

PURL STITCH (P)

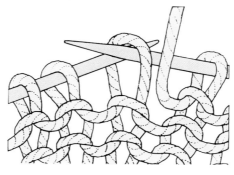

1 With the yarn at the front, insert your right-hand needle from back to front into the first stitch on your left-hand needle.

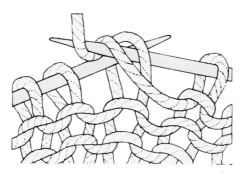

2 Bring your working yarn over and around the point of your right-hand needle.

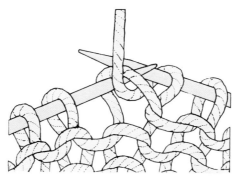

3 Draw a loop through and slide the first stitch off your left-hand needle while the new stitch is retained on your right-hand needle. Continue in this way to the end of the row.

4 To purl the next row, turn the work around so that the back is facing you and the worked stitches are held on the needle in your left hand. Proceed to make stitches as given above, with the initially empty needle held in your right hand.

SINGLE RIB

When changing from a knit stitch to a purl stitch bring the yarn to the front. When changing from a purl stitch to a knit stitch bring the yarn to the back. Cast on an odd number of stitches.

Row 1 *Knit 1, purl 1; repeat from * to the last stitch, knit 1.
Row 2 *Purl 1, knit 1; repeat from * to the last stitch, purl 1.
Repeat rows 1 and 2 until the rib is the required length.

DOUBLE RIB

When changing from a knit stitch to a purl stitch bring the yarn to the front. When changing from a purl stitch to a knit stitch bring the yarn to the back. Cast on a multiple of 4 stitches, plus 2.

Row 1 *Knit 2, purl 2; repeat from * to the last 2 sts, knit 2.
Row 2 *Purl 2, knit 2; repeat from * to the last 2 sts, purl 2.
Repeat rows 1 and 2 until the rib is the required length.

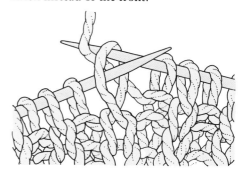

Single rib   Double rib

TWISTED RIB

This is worked in almost the same way as ordinary rib, except that the right-hand needle is put into the *back* of the knit stitch instead of the front.

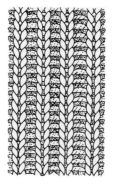

1 Knit into the back of the first and every knit stitch.

2 Purl in the ordinary way.

3 Work back across the following rows in the same way, beginning every row with a knit stitch, unless instructed otherwise in the pattern.

TENSION

At the beginning of every pattern is a tension measurement, such as *22 sts and 30 rows measure 10cm over stocking stitch on 4mm needles.*

Basically this tension measurement tells you how large the stitches are on the garment, so that you can match the size and thus produce a garment of the correct size. However since one stitch is too small to be measured accurately, the tension measurement states how many stitches (and rows) there are over ten centimetres. Unless you match the tension exactly, your garment will not be the correct size.

Four factors affect the tension measurement: needle size, stitch pattern, yarn, and you, the knitter. The combination of these four things determines the size of the stitch.

Needle size
Larger needles produce larger stitches and smaller needles produce smaller stitches. The needle size given in the tension measurement should only be used as a guide – you have to match the *tension* exactly, not the *needle size*.

Stitch pattern
Different stitch patterns produce different tensions, even when the needle size, yarn and knitter are the same. Therefore you must check your tension each time you embark on a new pattern, using the stitch pattern specified.

Yarn
Patterns worked in finer yarns have more stitches and rows to the centimetre than those worked in thicker yarns. It is very important to check your tension when substituting a different yarn, or when patterns give yarn types, rather than brand names.

The knitter
Even when using identical yarn, needles and stitch pattern, two knitters may not produce knitting at the same tension, because individual knitters knit at different tensions. The tension measurement given in the pattern is that produced by the designer of the garment. It is imperative that this tension is matched, however it should *not* be done by deliberately knitting more tightly or more loosely, but by changing to a larger or smaller needle size. If larger or smaller needles are used in the pattern for other parts of the garment, such as the rib, these must be adjusted accordingly.

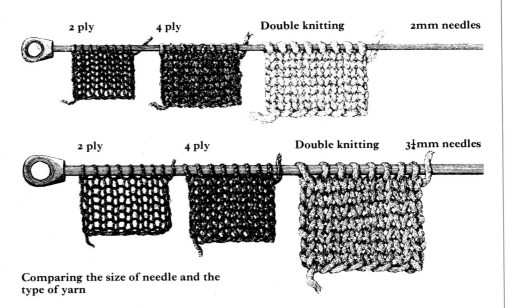

Comparing the size of needle and the type of yarn

MAKING A TENSION SAMPLE

1 Using the same yarn, needles and stitch pattern called for in the pattern instructions, knit a sample slightly larger than 10cm square.

2 Block the sample as the finished garment would be blocked.

3 Place the sample the right way up on a flat surface, being careful not to stretch it.

4 To measure the number of stitches, place a rigid ruler horizontally across the bottom of a row of stitches. Use pins to mark the beginning and end of a 10cm measurement. Count the number of stitches between the pins, including any half stitches. This gives you the figure for the stitch tension of the sample.

5 To measure the number of rows, place a rigid ruler vertically along one side of a column of stitches. Using pins, mark out a 10cm measurement. Count the number of rows between the pins to give the figure for the row tension of the sample.

6 If you produce fewer stitches and rows than given in the tension measurement then your knitting is too loose and you should make another tension sample using smaller needles.

7 If you produce more stitches and rows than given in the tension measurement then your knitting is too tight and you should make another tension sample using larger needles.

8 Repeat the process on different sized needles until you match the number of stitches and rows given in the tension measurement. As a general guide, changing the needles one size larger or one size smaller makes a difference of one stitch every five centimetres.

9 Changing your needle size is normally sufficient to adjust the dimensions. However, occasionally it is impossible to match both stitch and row tension. In such cases use a needle size so that you have the correct *stitch* tension, and work more or fewer rows to adjust the length.

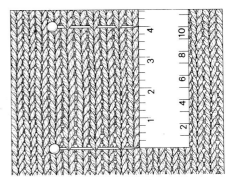

Measuring the number of stitches

Measuring the number of rows

CORRECTING MISTAKES

Occasionally you may drop a stitch – especially if you leave off working in the middle of a row – or make a mistake. The techniques given on this page show how to rectify such problems.

Picking up a dropped knit stitch

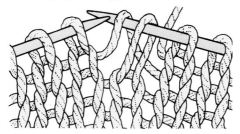

1 Pick up both the stitch and strand on your right-hand needle, inserting the needle from front to back.

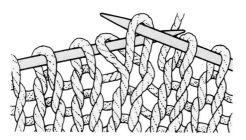

2 Insert your left-hand needle through the stitch only, from back to front. With your right-hand needle only, pull the strand through the stitch to make the extra stitch. (Drop the stitch from your left-hand needle.)

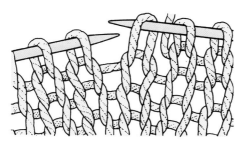

3 Transfer the re-formed stitch back to your left-hand needle, so that it untwists and faces the correct way. It is now ready for knitting again.

LADDERS

If a dropped stitch is left, it can unravel downwards and form a "ladder". In such a case it is easiest to use a crochet hook to pick up the stitches in pattern. If you make a mistake in your knitting, you may have to "unpick" a stitch, in which case a ladder may result. Pick up one dropped stitch at a time, securing any others with a safety pin to prevent further unravelling. Whichever row is being worked, turn the fabric so that the knit side is facing you.

Picking up a dropped purl stitch

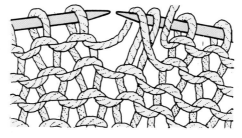

1 Pick up both the stitch and strand on your right-hand needle, inserting the needle from back to front.

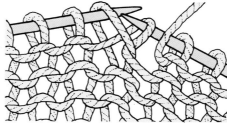

2 Insert your left-hand needle through the stitch only, from front to back. With your right-hand needle only, pull the strand through the stitch to make the extra stitch. (Drop the stitch from your left-hand needle.)

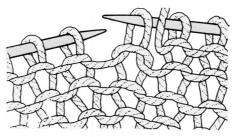

3 Transfer the re-formed stitch back to your left-hand needle, so that it untwists and faces the correct way. It is now ready for purling again.

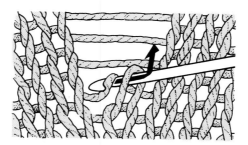

Insert a crochet hook through the front of the dropped stitch. Hook up one strand and pull it through the stitch to form a new stitch one row up. Continue in this way to the top of the ladder, and then slip the last stitch from the crochet hook on to the needle.

PICKING UP STITCHES

Occasionally you will come across instructions telling you to pick up a certain number of stitches. Sometimes you have to do this along a straight edge, such as for a button band, at other times you have to pick up around a curve, such as for a neckband.

The number of stitches you pick up does not necessarily correspond with the number of rows in the edge along which you are picking up stitches.

For a stronger, neater finish, pick up stitches from the last line of knitting before the cast-off edge or side selvedge.

Always pick up stitches with the right side of the work facing you.

To space stitches neatly on a curved edge, divide the edge into small sections by placing pins at regular intervals along it. Divide the number of stitches needed by the number of sections, then pick up this number from each section.

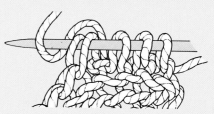

1 Place your needle through the work one stitch in from the edge and bring the yarn round as if knitting the stitch.

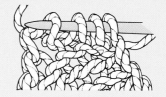

2 Pull the yarn through the stitch from the main work, to make a stitch.

UNPICKING MISTAKES

Knit row   Purl row

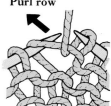

Holding the stitch on your right-hand needle insert your left-hand needle into the row below and undo the stitch. Repeat undoing until the error has been reached.

INCREASING and DECREASING

In order to shape knitting, you have to add (increase) or take away (decrease) stitches. Increasing and decreasing techniques are also used for certain stitch patterns, such as bobbles and lace fabrics.

Stitches can be added at the outer edges of the piece you are knitting, such as sleeve edges, or they can be added evenly across the row to give slight fullness, such as across a front or back in the last row of ribbing. There are several ways of increasing, the method shown below is the most common.

There are two ways to lose stitches for shaping and these are to knit or purl two stitches together (k2 tog or p2 tog) at the beginning, end or any given point in a row, or to use the slip stitch method (sl 1). Knitting stitches together is the simpler method, but slipping stitches produces a more decorative effect on a garment. Decreases are always visible and have a definite angled slant. It is important to pair decreases so that the direction of slant for the decreases is balanced.

INCREASING IN A KNIT ROW

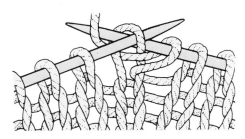

Knit into the front of the stitch in the usual way. Without discarding the stitch on your left-hand needle, knit into the back of it, making two stitches.

INCREASING IN A PURL ROW

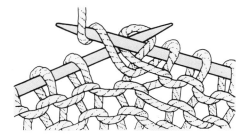

Purl into the front of the stitch in the usual way. Without discarding the stitch on your left-hand needle, purl into the back of it, making two stitches.

INCREASING AT ENDS OF ROWS

When increasing at the beginning or end of knit or purl rows, use the same technique as illustrated above, but work twice into the first or last stitch in the row.

SLIP STITCH DECREASE

Abbreviated as sl 1, k1, psso (slip one, knit one, pass slip stitch over), the decrease forms a slant to the left on the

In a knit row

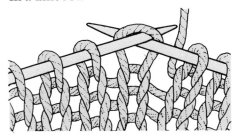

1 Insert your right-hand needle "knitwise" and lift off the first stitch from your left-hand needle.

2 Leave the stitch on the needle and knit the next stitch on your left-hand needle in the usual way.

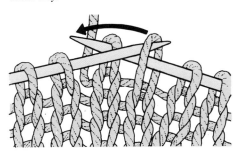

3 Using the point of your left-hand needle, bring the slipped stitch off your right-hand needle, over the knitted stitch.

KNITTING STITCHES TOGETHER

Abbreviated as k2 tog or p2 tog, the decrease forms a slant to the right if the

In a knit row (k2 tog)

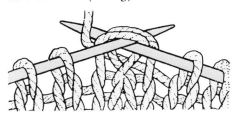

Insert your right-hand needle through the front of the first two stitches on your left-hand needle. Knit them together as a single stitch.

front of the knitting. A slant to the right is formed on the front if it is made on the purl row – sl 1, p1, psso (slip one, purl one, pass slip stitch over).

In a purl row

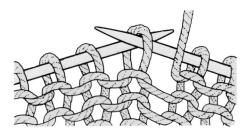

1 Insert your right-hand needle "purlwise" and lift off the first stitch from your left-hand needle.

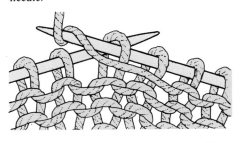

2 Leave the stitch on the needle and purl into the next stitch on your left-hand needle in the usual way.

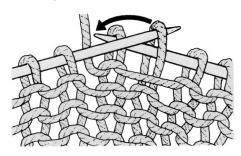

3 Using the point of your left-hand needle, bring the slipped stitch off your right-hand needle, over the purled stitch.

stitches are knitted together through the front, and a slant to the left if knitted together through the back.

In a purl row (p2 tog)

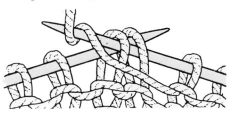

Insert your right-hand needle through the front of the first two stitches on your left-hand needle. Purl them together as a single stitch.

SPECIAL TECHNIQUES

Although the patterns provided in this book are traditional, there may be some techniques you have not come across before. These include knitting in the round with circular or double-pointed needles, making cables, following colour pattern charts and working with two colours of yarn in a row. None of these is difficult, but, in case you are not familiar with them, they are all explained here in full.

KNITTING IN THE ROUND

Some of the traditional Fair Isle garments and the fisher ganseys have been knitted in the round, in one piece, on double-pointed or circular needles. If you are not used to working in the round you may find the prospect a little daunting. However, it is no more difficult than knitting back and forth on two needles and, once you have tried it, you will appreciate the advantages. By knitting in the round there is much less – if any – sewing to do at the finishing stage. Also, the front of the work always faces you, so it's easier to follow pattern charts, whether they are colour or stitch pattern charts. Whereas when working back and forth on two needles you have to knit and purl alternate rows in order to produce stocking stitch, when working in the round, knitting every row produces stocking stitch.

Circular needles are used from the beginning when knitting a garment, but a set of double-pointed needles are more useful when picking up stitches, such as for knitting necklines or sleeves.

When knitting in the round, you should use a length of contrasting thread to mark "seam" lines every half round, so you know where to divide for the front and the back. Alternatively, seam lines on ganseys may be indicated by a column of purl stitches.

Using a circular needle

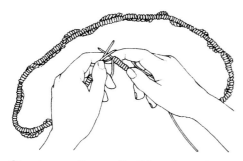

Circular needles are flexible nylon tubes which have two pointed metal ends which are traditionally sized. They are available in different lengths. To knit in the round, cast on stitches in the usual way and then

knit into the first stitch to make a continuous round. You must be certain that your cast on row is not twisted when commencing your first round or your knitting will be twisted.

Remember, the outside of the work will always face you, so that when knitting stocking stitch, you simply knit every row. If you wish to knit straight, and not in the round, simply use the two ends of the needle in the same way as ordinary needles, and work backwards and forwards.

Using four or more needles

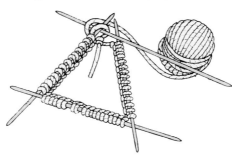

Sets of double-pointed needles are available in the traditional sizes. They are usually sold in sets of four, but as many as six needles can be used if the area is large.

When knitting with double-pointed needles, the stitches are divided among all but one of the needles. This needle is used to knit off, so that each needle in turn holds stitches and then is used to knit off.

To knit, divide your stitches among the needles and knit a round. To close the circle, knit the first stitch with the working yarn from the last stitch. Keep your last and first needle as close together as possible. Make sure your first knitted stitch (you should mark this) is close to the last needle so that no gap forms in the knitting.

Continue to work around in this way, using your empty needles to knit off and keeping the stitches evenly divided. Hold the two working needles as usual, and drop the others to the back of the work when not in use.

If you find it difficult to avoid gaps when changing from one needle to another, you can rotate this changeover point around the work by moving two or three stitches onto your right hand needle each time you change from one needle to the next. If you do this, it is even more important to mark your side stitches and centre back and front.

CABLES

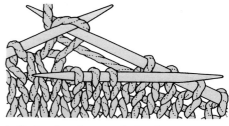

A distinctive characteristic of many of the Aran sweaters is the use of cables. These are created when stitches are moved out of position so that plaited, rope-like twists are formed in the knitting. Although there are countless cable variations, they are all, essentially, made in the same way, using special, small, double-pointed needles.

To twist stitches out of their normal order, a given number of stitches are taken to either the front or the back of the work and held on a cable needle. A certain number of stitches are then worked from the main needle, then the stitches held on the cable needle are worked.

Stitches held at the front twist a cable from right to left when knitted off; stitches held at the back twist the cable from left to right when knitted off.

STITCH PATTERN CHARTS

As well as for colour work, charts are often used for stitch patterns, particularly simple patterns containing only knit and purl stitches, such as those used on Fisher ganseys.

In these charts, one symbol represents a knit stitch and another a purl stitch, and when knitting in the round, with the right side facing, the chart is read *every row from right to left*.

For flat knitting, working backwards and forwards, read the first row (and all odd numbered rows) from *right to left*, and the second (and all even numbered rows) from *left to right*. However, since the chart represents the right side of the work, all wrong side rows must be "translated", with the knit stitches being worked as purl, and the purl stitches as knit.

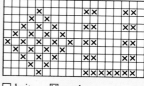

☐ knit   ☒ purl

FAIR ISLE KNITTING

In order to knit authentic Fair Isle successfully, you need to know about three knitting techniques: working in the round, working from colour pattern charts, and using two colours of yarn in a row. Information about working in the round is given on the left, the other techniques are explained on this page.

Colour pattern charts

Colour patterns are often given in the form of a chart, where each square on the chart represents one stitch, and each line on the chart represents one row. The different colours are indicated either by symbols, or by colours corresponding to those used for the knitting – as in the pattern instructions given in this book.

A chart is worked from bottom to top, and the rows are often numbered with odd numbers on the right hand side of the chart, and even numbers on the left. The same chart can be used for flat and circular knitting, though it will be read differently.

In circular knitting, every row on the chart, or specified number of repeats of that row, represents a round of knitting. Since you will always have the right side of the work facing you, every stitch will be a knit stitch, and you must read *every row from right to left*. Make sure that you mark the beginning of each round with a stitch marker.

For flat knitting, working backwards and forwards in stocking stitch, you must read the first row (and every following odd numbered row) from *right to left*, and work in knit. These are right side rows. Read the second row (and every following even numbered row) from *left to right* and work in purl. These are wrong side rows.

Where the design consists of a repeating motif, the chart shows where to start and end the repeat for different sizes, or different parts of the garment, and details of which parts of the chart to follow are given clearly in the pattern instructions.

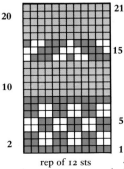

rep of 12 sts

A typical colour pattern chart

Using two colours of yarn in a row

When using two colours of yarn in a row, the yarn that is not being used has to be carried across the back of the knitting ready for use when called for by the chart. The way this is done can greatly influence the tension of the knitting so it must be done correctly. There are two different ways of carrying the yarn not in use across the back of the knitting: stranding and weaving. Stranding yarn basically means just leaving the yarn not being used in a strand across the back of the work; weaving involves knitting so that the yarn not being used is woven into the knitting.

The advantage of stranding is that the fabric produced by this method is softer and less dense than when weaving in yarns. It is also the traditional method used by the Shetland knitters, so it is the method recommended for use with patterns in this book.

Stranding yarn in a knit row

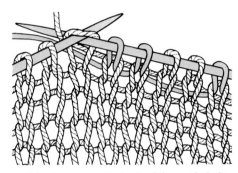

With both yarns at the back of the work, knit the required number of stitches with yarn A (in this case two), and then drop it to the back. Pick up yarn B and knit the required number of stitches and then drop it to the back. Both yarns should be stranded loosely along the back of the work.

Joining in new yarn

Try to avoid joining a new ball of yarn in the middle of a round or a row. To judge whether the remaining length of yarn is long enough to complete the round or row, use this rough guideline; in stocking stitch each round or row takes about three times the width of the knitting. In cabled or textured knitting, the length of yarn needed is about five times the width.

When working Fair Isle in the round, always join the new colour at the beginning of a round. Break off the old yarn and leave a few inches of spare yarn. Join the new colour and the finished colour with a single knot, making sure the knot is close to the last stitch on your right-hand needle. Begin the next round and weave the spare yarn into the first

It is very important that the strands at the back of the work are not pulled too tightly; they must be loose enough to allow the natural "give" of knitted fabric. To ensure this, every time you change colour, gently but firmly pull back the last ten or so stitches on the right-hand needle so that your knitting is slightly stretched.

Since authentic Fair Isle patterns rarely have more than five stitches before a colour change, you will not be left with long loops at the back of the fabric.

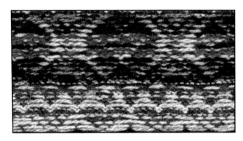

Stranding yarn in a purl row

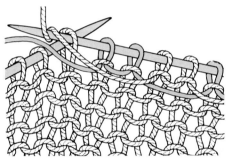

With both yarns at the front of the work, purl the required number of stitches with yarn A (in this case two), and then drop it. Pick up yarn B and purl the required number of stitches, then drop it. Both yarns should be stranded loosely along the front (side facing you).

ten stitches of the round, before carefully trimming away the excess. This can be done by weaving in as you knit, or it may be done later, at the finishing stage, with a darning needle.

The same method can be used for joining new yarn at the edge of Fair Isle knitting, when working backwards and forwards. If you weave in the excess wool with a darning needle, it is sometimes easier to control exactly where your ends are worked in. When you have several colours joining in a short distance, you can run the end up or down the knitting for a row or two before darning it across the back of the work: this avoids too much bulk in any one row. Some knitters prefer to work their ends in as they progress, so avoiding a long job of finishing at the end.

FINISHING

When you have finished all the knitting, there are still one or two things that remain to be done before your garment is ready to be worn. If the garment is made from several separate pieces, they should all be blocked, and then sewn together; if it has been made in one piece it can be blocked as a complete garment. Different types of garments need to be treated differently, some guidelines to follow are given below.

BLOCKING

Basically this just involves pinning each garment piece (or the finished garment if it is made in one piece) out on a flat surface, to the correct measurements. This pulls all the stitches into place and makes it easier to sew the pieces together. If you omit this stage, your garment will not have a professional finish. You can block the garment either damp or dry.

The blocking surface can be a blanket, folded in half, or foam, covered with light-weight cotton fabric such as sheeting or gingham. Using gingham makes the process easier, since it provides straight lines and right angles to work with.

Lay the piece of knitting wrong side up on the blocking surface and gently coax it into the right shape and size. Pin the knitting to the surface, spacing the pins two or three centimetres apart.

Gansey

The traditional ganseys knitted in the round in the real guernsey wool would not originally have been blocked at all, but if you wish you may pin them out as given above, and spray them with cold clean water using a plant spray. Leave to dry naturally before removing the pins.

For the contemporary woollen ganseys made from several separate pieces, each piece should be pinned out and then dampened and left to dry as given above before sewing together.

For cotton ganseys, pin out each piece and then lightly press using a damp cloth, or a steam iron. Set your iron at the appropriate heat setting and press the knitting very gently with up and down movements. Avoid moving the iron across the fabric.

Fair Isle

In the Shetland Islands all the knitwear is "dressed", or stretched out while still damp, and left to dry naturally. Dampen woollen garment or garment pieces very thoroughly by spraying with cold clean water and then pin out to the correct shape on your blocking surface. Smooth the knitting out to its full extent, adjusting the pins as necessary. This is to ensure that any puckered look that stranding might produce is eliminated. Leave to dry naturally before removing the pins.

For the cotton Fair Isle garments follow the instructions given for cotton ganseys, above.

Aran

In general the heavier the texture and the garment, the less need there is for blocking. However, the lighter weight woollen Aran styles will benefit from being pinned out dry, and then sprayed with water. Leave to dry naturally before removing the pins.

The cotton and silk styles may be gently pressed with a steam iron as given for the cotton ganseys.

Shetland lace

It is particularly important to block the lace garments out to their full extent, in order to get the correct shape, and to obtain the openwork effect. Block lace knitting while damp, very gently easing it so that it is stretched to its full extent, but remember that Shetland wool, particularly the lace wool, is very delicate. Where a feature of the garment is a pointed edge, place a pin at the bottom of each point.

SEWING TOGETHER

Sewing together is a most important part of making knitted garments. None of the techniques are particularly difficult, and time and care spent on them will achieve professional looking results. Described below are the various stitches you will need, and their uses.

Mattress stitch

This is the most versatile stitch. It provides a strong, invisible seam, the only real disadvantage being that it is bulky on the underside. However, it is well-suited to raglan-sleeve seams, side seams, and seams that join two pieces of patterned knitting. This is because it is sewn with the right side facing, so you can match the pattern as you go. You will need a tapestry needle and some yarn.

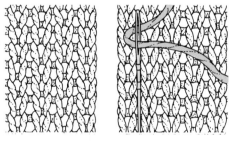

1 Place the two seam edges side by side, right side up. Thread the needle and stitch through two stitchbars, one stitch in from the edge on one side.

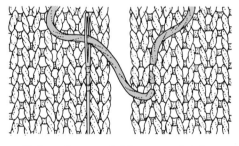

2 Pick up the two stitchbars one stitch in on the other side.

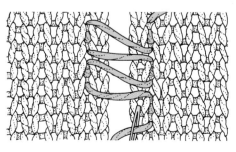

3 Without pulling the stitches taut, pick up the next two stitchbars on the first side. Then pick up the next two stitchbars on the other side, and so on.

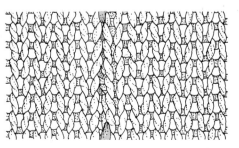

4 When the thread is zigzagged across the two seam edges about five times pull it taut – the seam will be pulled together. Continue picking up the next two stitchbars on each side in turn, pulling the thread taut after about every five stitches until the seam is complete.

Grafting

This is another seam that, if well done, is both invisible and firm. It is often used for shoulder seams or at any time when a flat seam is required. You will need a tapestry needle which you thread with the yarn remaining from the last stitch. Be sure to leave enough yarn on the work to cover the intended seam length, times three.

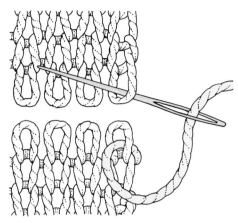

1 Lay the two seam edges side by side, right side up. Bring the needle back through the loop of the first stitch, then take the needle through the first loop on the other side.

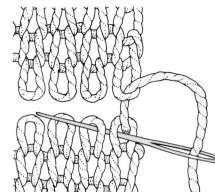

2 Stitch the needle back down through the first loop on the first side, and through the second loop on the same side.

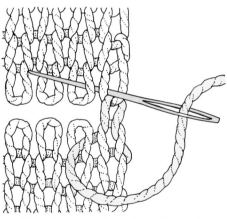

3 Take the needle through the first and second loops on the other side.

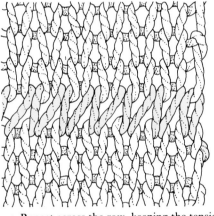

4 Repeat across the row, keeping the tension as close as you can to the tension of the two pieces you are joining.

Edge to edge seam

This produces an almost invisible seam, forms no ridge, and is the best seam to use when a hard edge must be avoided.

1 Place the pieces to be joined edge to edge with the heads of the knit stitches locking together. Match the pattern pieces carefully row for row and stitch for stitch.

It is useful for joining patterned knitting, but it is not as strong as a mattress stitch seam. You will need a tapestry needle and yarn to match the knitting.

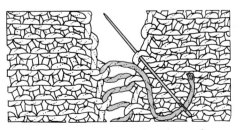

2 Using the same yarn and sewing at the same tension as the knitting, sew into the head of each stitch alternately.

Backstitch

Backstitch provides a quick, satisfactory seam for many purposes, as well as being a technique that most people already know. However, it is difficult to get as neat a finish as with either mattress stitch or by grafting and it is not suitable for garments made from heavier weight yarns. When you sew through both pieces of knitting check that the corresponding stitches are in line with each other. You will need a tapestry needle and yarn to match the knitting.

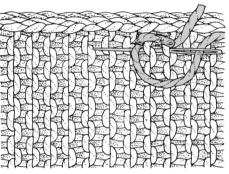

1 Lay the two pieces you are joining with right sides together. With the needle threaded, sew three small stitches one on top of the other at the beginning of the seam.

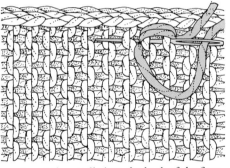

2 Insert the needle into the back of the first stitch and take it out one stitch along.

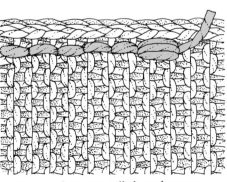

3 Repeat the process all along the seam, keeping the tension constant and the stitches as tight as you can without puckering or distorting the knitting.

CONVERSION CHARTS
WEIGHTS

ounces	1	2	3	4	5	6	7	8	9	10	11	12	13	14	15	16	17	18	19	20
grams	28	57	85	113	142	170	198	227	255	283	312	340	369	397	425	454	482	510	539	567

Please note that these conversions are approximate to the nearest gram.

grams	25	50	75	100	125	150	175	200	225	250	275	300	325	350	375	400	425	450	475	500
ounces	1	1¾	2¾	3½	4½	5¼	6¼	7	8	8¾	9¾	10½	11½	12¼	13¼	14	15	15¾	16¾	17¾

Please note that these conversions are approximate to the nearest ¼ ounce.

MEASUREMENTS

centimetres	1	2	3	4	5	6	7	8	9	10	11	12	13	14	15	16	17	18	19	20
inches	½	¾	1¼	1½	2	2¼	2¾	3¼	3½	4	4¼	4¾	5	5½	6	6¼	6¾	7	7½	7¾
centimetres	21	22	23	24	25	26	27	28	29	30	31	32	33	34	35	36	37	38	39	40
inches	8¼	8¾	9	9½	9¾	10¼	10¾	11	11½	11¾	12¼	12½	13	13½	13¾	14¼	14½	15	15¼	15¾

Please note that these conversions are approximate to the nearest ¼ inch.

KNITTING NEEDLES

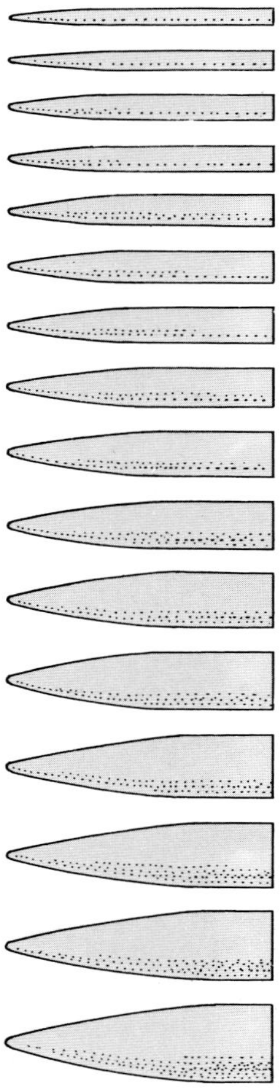

Metric	English	US
2	14	0
2¼	13	1
2¾	12	2
3	11	3
3¼	10	4
3¾	9	5
4	8	6
4½	7	7
5	6	8
5½	5	9
6	4	10
6½	3	—
7	2	10½
7½	1	11
8	0	13
9	00	15

(mm)

WASHING KNITWEAR

After spending a lot of time and trouble hand knitting a sweater it pays to wash it with care and respect. Some yarns are produced that may be safely machine washed, but the great majority of yarns should be washed by hand, using pure soap flakes, or a special wool detergent. Wash and rinse thoroughly, in warm water, not hot water.

Before washing a brightly-coloured garment, check that it is colourfast by dipping a small piece of it into the soapy water. Press it out in a white cloth. If it leaves a stain, wash in cold water.

Never leave knitted garments to soak, especially if they are deep-dyed or multi-coloured.

1 Always squeeze the suds into the garment gently and do not rub or felting will occur. Don't leave the garment to soak, but rinse and remove quickly. Make certain the rinse water is clear before removing the garment. Add fabric softener to the last rinse if you wish.

2 Place the garment in a thick towel, white if possible, and roll both up. Place extra towels on top of the garment for extra absorption before rolling up. Press the roll with your hands or "hammer" it with your fists to remove as much water as possible. Repeat this with another towel if the garment is still very wet. Alternatively, put the garment in a pillowcase and give it a fast, short spin in a washing machine. If the yarn is a fine quality wool, the length of the spin must be only a few seconds or the garment may become matted.

3 For Arans and ganseys, finish drying the garment by laying it out flat on another clean towel, away from direct heat. Make sure the knitting is correctly shaped. Fair Isles and Shetland lace will benefit from being re-blocked each time you wash them, see p. 140. Store the garment in a drawer; never hang it up as it can be easily pulled out of shape.

YARN INFORMATION

Since the sweaters in this book have been made from standard, readily available yarns (4 ply, double knitting, etc), specific information as to the brand names of yarns has not been included in the individual patterns. However if you do wish to use exactly the same yarns as shown, full details of the yarns used are given below. Write to the yarn manufacturers for the address of your nearest stockist. If you have difficulty in obtaining yarns please write to Madeline Weston at The Scottish Merchant.

GANSEY
Flamborough p. 14
Wilkinson's 5 ply guernsey wool, shade 18
Child's gansey p. 18
Poppleton's 5 ply guernsey wool, shade 500
Woven checks p. 20
Lang "Pony" 4 ply wool, shade 8882
Polperro p. 22
Jamieson & Smith "Brora Soft Spun" 2 ply Shetland wool, shade BSS17
Newbiggin p. 26
Jamieson & Smith "Brora Soft Spun" 2 ply Shetland wool, shade BSS17
Cotton gansey p. 28
Rowan DK cotton, shade 251
Jacob's ladder p. 30
Fil d'Écosse cotton cannelé, shade 4
Fife banded gansey p. 32
Rowan DK wool, shade 616
Sanquhar p. 36
R.W. Pyrah Aran weight natural British Jacob wool
Eriskay p. 38
Natural – Poppleton's 5 ply guernsey wool, shade 500
Grey – Wilkinson's 5 ply guernsey wool, shade 1
Ladder and cable p. 45
Sunbeam pure new wool DK, shade 5925
Chevron and cable p. 48
Sunbeam pure new wool DK, shade 3102
Caister p. 50
Wilkinson's 5 ply guernsey wool, shade 1

FAIR ISLE
Cross and flower p. 56
Rowan DK wool: yarn A shade 61, yarn B shade 99, yarn C shade 616, yarn D shade 65, yarn E shade 118, yarn F shade 71
Cross and square p. 59
Main colour combination
Jamieson & Smith 2 ply jumper weight Shetland wool: yarn A shade 36, yarn B shade FC14, yarn D shade 4, yarn F shade FC43; Jamiesons Spinning 2 ply jumper weight Shetland wool: yarn C shade 577, yarn E shade 763, yarn G shade 577/108
Alternative colour combination
Rowan 4 ply wool: yarn A shade 54, yarn B shade 125, yarn C shade 90, yarn D shade 12
Child's set p. 62
Jamieson & Smith 2 ply jumper weight Shetland wool: yarn A shade 135, yarn C shade 1, yarn D shade 28; Jamiesons Spinning 2 ply jumper weight Shetland wool: yarn B shade 578
Diamond p. 64
Main colour combination
Jamieson & Smith 2 ply jumper weight

Shetland wool: yarn A shade 33, yarn B shade 72, yarn C shade 28, yarn D shade 1a
Alternative colour combination
Fil d'Écosse cotton cannelé: yarn A shade 138, yarn B shade 17, yarn C shade 21, yarn D shade 9
Katie's Fair Isle p. 68
Main colour combination
Jamieson & Smith 2 ply jumper weight Shetland wool: yarn A shade 135, yarn B shade 28, yarn C shade 4, yarn D shade 1a, yarn F shade 5; Jamiesons Spinning 2 ply jumper weight Shetland wool: yarn E shade 578
Alternative colour combination
Fil d'Écosse cotton cannelé: yarn A shade 15, yarn B shade 1, yarn C shade 20, yarn D shade 8, yarn E shade 18, yarn F shade 12
Three cross p. 71
Rowan lightweight DK wool: yarn A shade 502, yarn B shade 122, yarn C shade 10, yarn D shade 67, yarn E shade 85, yarn F shade 407
O.X.O. p. 73
Main colour combination
Jamieson & Smith 2 ply jumper weight Shetland wool: yarn A shade 5, yarn B shade 54, yarn C shade 27, yarn D shade 203, yarn E shade 202, yarn F shade 4
Alternative colour combination
Rowan 4 ply Botany wool: yarn A shade 54, yarn B shade 52, yarn C shade 103, yarn D shade 69, yarn E shade 64, yarn F shade 65
Adult's set p. 76
The same yarns as Katie's Fair Isle, main colour combination, as given above

ARAN
Cable and moss p. 84
Rowan Aran wool, shade 111
Medallion p. 88
Rowan Aran wool, shade 113
Chevron p. 90
Rowan Aran wool, shade Natural
Plait cable p. 92
Lang "Pony" 4 ply wool, shade 8821
Tree of life p. 94
Rowan Aran wool, shade 69
Wheat cable p. 98
Lhasafin 4 ply silk, shade 305
Fountain lace p. 102
Mayflower cotton 8, shade 501
Blackberry p. 104
Lister's Aran yarn, shade 193
Bobble fan p. 107
Yarnworks DK cotton, shade 110
Classic cotton p. 110
Rowan DK cotton, shade 270

SHETLAND LACE
New shell p. 116
Wool sweater
Jamieson & Smith 2 ply jumper weight Shetland wool: yarn A shade FC14, yarn B shade 36, yarn C shade 4; Jamiesons Spinning 2 ply jumper weight Shetland wool: yarn D shade 577, yarn E shade 577/108, yarn F shade 763
Cotton sweater
Fil d'Écosse cotton cannelé: yarn A shade 20, yarn B shade 138, yarn C shade 9, yarn D shade 17, yarn E shade 21, yarn F shade 11
Eyelet cardy p. 120
Jamieson & Smith 2 ply lace weight Shetland

wool, shade L25
Old shell sweater p. 122
Jamieson & Smith 2 ply lace weight Shetland wool: yarn A shade L203, yarn B shade L54, yarn C shade L70, yarn D shade L27, yarn E shade L101
Fern spencer p. 126
Blue – Rowan 4 ply Botany wool, shade 501; Natural – Fil d'Écosse cotton cannelé, shade 8
Old shell shawl p. 128
Jamieson & Smith 2 ply jumper weight Shetland wool: yarn A shade 77, yarn B shade 81, yarn C shade 54, yarn D shade 27, yarn E shade 203, yarn F shade 1a

ADDRESSES
The first two companies will supply direct to individuals. Please write for a price list, enclosing a stamped addressed envelope. In addition, knitting packs for the Shetland wool garments may be obtained from Margaret Stuart.

Jamieson & Smith (Shetland Wool Brokers) Ltd
90 North Road, Lerwick, Shetland ZE1 0PQ

Jamiesons Spinning Shetland Ltd
Jamiesons Knitwear, 93-95 Commercial Street, Lerwick, Shetland ZE1 0BD

Margaret Stuart
Shetlands from Shetland, Burnside, Walls, Shetland ZE2 9PG

Madeline Weston
The Scottish Merchant, 16 New Row, Covent Garden, London WC2N 4LA

Lister Handknitting
Whiteoak Mills, Westgate, Wakefield, West Yorkshire WF2 9SF

Richard Poppleton & Sons Ltd
Albert Mills, Horbury, Wakefield, West Yorkshire WF4 5NJ

R.W. Pyrah Ltd
Rookes Mill, Norwood Green, Nr Halifax, West Yorkshire HX8 8RA

Rowan Yarns
Green Lane Mill, Washpit, Holmfirth, West Yorkshire HD7 1RW. Telephone 0484 686714

Sunbeam Knitting Wools
Crawshaw Mills, Pudsey, West Yorkshire LS28 7BS

Wilkinson Knitwear
6 The Row, Tregavarras, Gorran, St Austell, Cornwall PL26 6LN

Yarnworks Ltd
4th floor, Waring and Gillow Building, Western Avenue, London W3 0TA

Lhasafin silk is obtainable from
Brinion Heaton
Homefield Close, Saltford, Bristol BS18 3EF

Lang yarns are available from
J. Henry Smith Ltd
Park Road, Calverton, Nottingham NG14 6LL

Fil d'Écosse cotton is available from
Yeoman Yarns Ltd
31 High Street, Kibworth, Leicestershire LE8 0NP

Mayflower cotton 8 is available from
Scheepjeswol (UK) Ltd
7 Colemeadow Road, Redditch, Worcestershire B98 9NZ

ACKNOWLEDGMENTS

PHOTOGRAPHIC CREDITS
Sandra Lousada assisted by **Susanna Price**
Model shots
Paul Fletcher Flat shots
Vincent Oliver Details
p. 12 Scarborough Tourism Department
p. 54 HIDB Photo Library
p. 55 Bobby Tulloch
p. 82 Michael St Maur Sheil/Susan Griggs
Agency
p. 114 Bobby Tulloch
p. 115 Bobby Tulloch

STYLIST
Fanny Rush

HAIR AND MAKE-UP
Barbara Jones

ILLUSTRATORS
John Hutchinson Charts and line drawings
Robert Kettell Wood cuts

TYPESETTING
Chambers Wallace

REPRODUCTION
Repro Color Llovet SA Barcelona

PATTERN CONTRIBUTORS
Rae Compton, Gayle Crowther, Valerie
Dunlop, Brinion Heaton, Sarah Keogh,
Margaret MacInnes, Audur Norris, Alison
Robson, Jenny Sandler, Debbie Scott, Brenda
Sparkes, Margaret Stuart, Sue Turton.

KNITTERS
FISHER GANSEYS
Mrs Isabel Compton, Mrs Frances Cowling,
Mrs Pat Harvey, Mrs Nancy James, Miss
Margaret Pacy, Mrs Vivienne Robinson,
Mrs Joyce Scattergood.
FAIR ISLE AND SHETLAND LACE
Mrs Joyce Buss, Mrs Barbara Fraser,
Mrs Marigold Garrick, Mrs Ina Irvine,
Mrs Mary Jamieson, Mrs Ruby Jamieson,
Mrs Joan Johnson, Mrs Marilyn O'Neil,
Mrs Ruby Shipley, Mrs Isabella Thomason,
Mrs Zena Thomson, Miss Ina Williamson.
ARAN
Mrs Gladys Baldwin, Mrs Ruby Clements,
Mrs Janet Jenkins, Mrs Lottie Kiteley,
Mrs Jean Preston, Mrs Joyce Travill,
Mrs Betty Van.

I would like to say how much I have enjoyed
working on this book; this has largely been
due to the enthusiasm of the contributors, and
the staff at the publishers, all of whom I
would like to thank unreservedly. In particular, I would like to thank Margaret Stuart and
Rae Compton, both experts in their fields;
Rosella Downie for writing down many of the
Fair Isle and Shetland patterns that have
never been written out before; Elspeth
Sinclair for information about Sanquhar;
Audur Norris, Sarah Keogh, Rakhshinda
Khursheed and Jane Addey for technical
advice and the numerous working of tension
swatches! My special thanks also go to
Melanie Miller who has been indefatigable in
the long process that has seen the sweater
patterns transformed into the printed page
and, most of all, made the work a pleasure.
I would also like to thank Michele Walker and
Sandra Lousada, whose visual interpretation
has been so entirely right and in sympathy
with the work.

Madeline Weston

Dorling Kindersley would like to thank Anne
Smith and Tina Egleton for their careful
checking of the patterns, Debbie Alder for
typing them; Pie Dorling, Joanna Godfrey
Wood and Sarah Ponder for editorial and
design assistance; John Hutchinson, Tony
Wallace and Vic Chambers for their patience;
Susan Griggs Agency; and the following
companies for the loan of clothes, jewellery
and other items:

p. 3 shirt from Flip, Long Acre, Covent Garden;
pp. 4-5 shirts from Flip, hat from The Hat Shop,
Neal Street, Covent Garden, trousers from
Marvelette, Antiquarius, Kings Road, scarf from
Liberty, Regent Street; p. 7 shirt from Farlows of
St James's; pp. 10-11 his shirt from Flip, her
trousers from Marvelette, scarf from Liberty;
pp. 14-17 her dungarees from American Classics,
Kings Road; pp. 20-21 skirt from Monsoon, The
Piazza, Covent Garden; pp. 24-25 binoculars from
Nautical Antiques, Antiquarius, trousers from
Marvelette, scarf from Liberty; pp. 28-31 skirt from
Monsoon, hat from The Hat Shop, trousers from
Marvelette, boots from Natural Shoe Shop, Kings
Road; pp. 32-35 hat from The Hat Shop, shirts
from Flip; pp. 38-39, 42-43 his shirt from Flip, her
skirt from Monsoon, scarf from Liberty; pp. 46-47
skirt from Monsoon, scarf from Liberty, shirt from
Flip; pp. 52-53 boots and shirts from Farlows of
St James's, trousers from Flip; pp. 58-59 her
trousers and shirt from Flip, his shirt from Farlows
of St James's; pp. 60-61 shirt from Flip; pp. 64-65
shirt on the left from Flip, shirt on the right from
Farlows of St James's; pp. 68-69 his trousers from
Hackets, Parsons Green, New Kings Road, denim
shirts from American Classics; pp. 70-71 shirts from
American Classics, coat from Hackets; pp. 72-73
trousers from Hackets, shirt from Farlows of St
James's; pp. 74-75 boots and shirts from Farlows of
St James's, trousers from Flip; pp. 78-79 coat from
Hackets; pp. 80-81 his trousers from Moss Bros,
Bedford Street, Covent Garden, shirt from Workshop Clothing, Lawrence Street, Chelsea, her
trousers from Flip, scarf from Liberty; pp. 86-89
scarves from Monsoon, shirts from Workshop
Clothing, his trousers from Moss Bros; pp. 92-93
dress from Monsoon; pp. 96-97 shirt from Workshop, scarf from Liberty; pp. 98-101 scarf from
Monsoon, trousers from Flip; pp. 106-107 trousers
from Flip, scarf from Liberty; pp. 108-109 scarf
from Monsoon, trousers on the left from Flip,
trousers on the right from Burberry's, Regent
Street; pp. 112-113 paisley shawls from Paul Jones,
Antiquarius, patchwork quilt from The Patchwork
Dog and Calico Cat, Chalk Farm Road, Camden,
bloomers from Persiflage, Antiquarius; pp. 118-119
dresses and shoes from Pineapple Studios, Langley
Street, Covent Garden; pp. 124-125 bloomers from
Persiflage.